"A savvy and generous-hearted book, rich and gritty and wise. There have been many well-intentioned but formulaic takes on what it is to be a child of divorce, but this unique and fearless novel, beautifully written by poet Caryn Mirriam-Goldberg, is fresh and unpredictable, pulsing with its young protagonist's wit, determination, and courage as she journeys through painful and frightening times, transporting herself by sheer force of will from a shattered world to a world made whole through self-determination and the saving grace of art."

—Patricia Traxler, author of *Blood* and *Forbidden Words*

"*The Divorce Girl* is as smart and funny as its teenage protagonist, whose struggles to make sense of the chaos into which her family descends will keep you riveted. Caryn Mirriam-Goldberg delivers a story that is poignant yet sharp, timeless yet fresh. Her characters come alive on the page, real as our own parents and siblings and assortment of other zany relatives. This is a book that will make you care about them all."

—Katie Towler, author of the Snow Island Trilogy

"When her family explodes, Deborah shuts down. Her world shrinks to what she sees through her camera's viewfinder. As she focuses on images she creates, her life emerges, filled with possibilities beyond bruises, beyond self-destruction. Art creates for her a life she could not imagine in any other way. *The Divorce Girl* is a visionary novel, a powerful story of pain and healing."

—Peggy Shumaker, Alaska State Writer Laureate, and author of *Just Breathe Normally*

"Full of great characters and charm!"

—Laura Moriarity, author of *The Center of Everything*

"At the beginning of *The Divorce Girl*, 15-year-old Deborah confidently asserts, 'I knew all about divorce.' Beset by challenges, adventures, and difficulties, but always finding transcendence, Mirriam-Goldberg's pitch-perfect narrator grows on the reader while she grows toward the light of her womanhood and her art. Caryn Mirriam-Goldberg, long a celebrated Kansas poet and nonfiction writer, gives us a winning fictional debut."

> — Thomas Fox Averill, Writer-in-residence, Washburn University, is the author of *rode*, awarded Outstanding Western Novel of 2011

"Written in first person, the reader may feel as if he or she has stumbled onto Deborah's diary or journal. The narrator's voice is authentic and revealing. Mirriam-Goldberg tells the story well. With the language of a poet and the acumen of one who understands family dysfunction from the inside out, the author delivers a fascinating story of loss and grief, of endurance and healing."

> —Cheryl Unruh, author of *Flyover People*

The Divorce Girl

Caryn Mirriam-Goldberg

Ice Cube Press
North Liberty, Iowa

The Divorce Girl—A Story of Art and Soul

ISBN 9781888160666

1 3 5 7 9 8 6 4 2

Library of Congress Control Number: 2011943260

Ice Cube Press, LLC (Est. 1993)
205 N. Front Street
North Liberty, Ia 52317
www.icecubepress.com
Steve@icecubepress.com

The paper used in this publication meets the minimum requirements of the American National Standard for Information Sciences—Permanence of Paper for Printed Library Materials, ANSI Z39.48-1992

Manufactured in the United States of America with recycled paper

Cover photo used with permission of Stephen Locke

Stephen Locke is a director of photography and professional storm chaser. He produces motion and still photography for business and private collections. Based in Kansas City, his Tempest Gallery is a showcase of storm imagery shot throughout the Great Plains. Stephen is also well known for his time-lapse cinematography. Clients include Andrews McMeel Publishing, Accord Publishing, CBS, the Mayo Clinic, the Weather Channel, Discovery, Severe Studios, and TornadoVideos.net. He is currently working on a collaborative book on storms in poetry and photography with Caryn Mirriam-Goldberg. www.TempestGallery.com

for Barry, Lauren, & Jen
my siblings who also found their way

Part I

Chapter One

The moment I saw Dad's car instead of Mom's in the driveway I knew it was too late. I had been trying to photograph the falling leaves ever since the school bus had dropped me off at the bottom of our horseshoe-shaped street. But when I spotted his car through the viewfinder, I let the camera fall to my chest and walked quickly, my books heavy in my arms as the future rushed toward me.

As soon I crossed the threshold, I saw Dad just where I expected him—on the living room sofa, waiting. One half of me obediently walked over and sat down beside him, ready to hear whatever bad news had brought him home from work in the middle of the afternoon. The other half of me lifted my new 35 millimeter camera and stepped back to frame the shot, focusing on the heavy drapes behind us, the crisp lines of the plastic-covered cushions, while blurring our faces. When he said, "I have some bad news to tell you," one part of me nodded as the other snapped the shutter. Yet both parts of me knew that this room, this house, this family, were already turning into something different, just as the black screen of a Polaroid picture loses its blankness for an image.

"Deborah, your mother and I are getting divorced."

Even though I knew it was coming, I still jumped a little inside. Then I calmed myself by imagining him moving out, like other dads, into a North Jersey apartment. He would come every Saturday to take my little brother, sister, and me bowling or ice-skating. There would be less yelling in the house, and I'd probably end up seeing Dad more.

"I thought that might happen," I said. That's when the other me, not so calm about the future, felt suddenly nauseous. I blinked, thinking how strange it was that I was scared.

We stood up, oddly formal with each other, as we spun inside our heads a picture of what life would look like a year from now. There would be alimony checks and phone calls. There'd be bowling alleys in the evenings, Pop-Tarts for breakfast, Sunday afternoon matinees with popcorn for lunch. We'd visit Dad at his messy little apartment and joke about his inability to cook spaghetti. I'd seen it happen with the neighbors and in the movies on television. I was fifteen years old, and I knew all about divorce.

My parents met while Mom, her main occupation tennis, was still attending high school in the Flatbush section of Brooklyn. Dad was working in the city for Taxi Central, the family cab company, and moonlighting at a Chock Full O'Nuts coffee shop three evenings a week. A mutual friend told Dad, who wore thick glasses and was already overweight, about this tennis whiz who liked guys with ambition, even if they were funny looking. He went to watch her on the court outside her high school, a little nervous since he had never dated before. Although she was pretty, in a petite kind of way, she wasn't the kind of girl who got asked out on many dates, so maybe he had a chance with her. There was something odd about her face, one side a little lower than the other. But he liked how high she could leap and how hard she could hit. With some coaching from his friend, he introduced himself and congratulated her on her win. From there, they started going out for bowling, movies, and Chinese.

That's all I really know. Sometime that fall they decided to get married. Mom wore an off-the-shoulder white gown that made her look like a porcelain doll and carried a bouquet of white roses, baby's breath, and yellow carnations. The wedding was held in the living room of Dad's parents' house and put into motion by his mother, who preferred that we call her "Mimi" rather than Grandma. It might seem a bit strange that the groom's mother was the one who conjured up the caterer, the photographer, and the invitations, but Mom's mother, Nana Rochelle, was already dying in slow motion from lung cancer and she was no match for Mimi's will nor her money. Neither were the men: Mimi's husband, Saul, hardly spoke and spent most of his time fishing or going to flower shows in enormous convention centers, while Pop, Nana's husband, liked to tell jokes about nudist colonies in between playing his own mean game of tennis at the Y. The rest of the family politely acquiesced, many of them out of habit.

I was born in 1960 in a Jewish hospital in East Flatbush, just after midnight. Since I've always hated tight spaces, I imagine myself shooting out of the womb like a red fish, terrified and wailing for my lost skin to return. Surely they washed and weighed and poked and bundled me in pink, then gave my mother the little pill that would dry up her milk and me the glass bottle of formula. Surely I collapsed and slept for many hours, like all babies, exhausted and despondent, in a chorus of glass baby trays arranged before a large picture window through which my nervous father and my grandparents were watching me.

"There she is," one would say, pointing me out as if I were one of so many boats on the horizon, sailing briefly into view before floating away.

Surely my mother, hidden away in a hospital room, barely nineteen, emptied and drugged, sobbed herself to sleep as the trembling walls of the future pressed in on her from all sides. A future where her tennis racket would be replaced by me. But when they put me in her arms the next day, she probably stared into my eyes to tell me it's all right, kiddo, you're just alive.

Then there was the musty house, squeezed into one of the noisier sections of East Flatbush, where the back yards were eight by eight feet, impoverished trees grew along the curbs at regular intervals, and a pizzeria thrived on every corner. We lived just two blocks from Mimi (who fortunately had so many volunteer obligations that she had no time to criticize Mom's parenting) and Grandpa Saul, who kept the company books when he wasn't fishing off bridges or watching westerns on TV with a hot cup of tea and milk in his hands. Several times a week he was on his hands and knees in the postage-stamp-sized back yard, tending the roses.

Sometime after I was a year old, we moved into a bigger apartment. It was jammed with borrowed furniture that other relatives couldn't stand any more, the cushions deemed new again by my mother after she covered them in soft, shiny plastic that stuck to my thighs whenever I wore shorts. By the time we finally graduated to a narrow house of our own, one in a long row of similar houses differentiated only by the stained glass seagull or moon in the living room window, my brother Roger had arrived. He was everything my mother had ever wanted in a baby: a sleeping, green-eyed boy with blond ringlets who, even when awake, demanded little from anyone. He didn't talk, though, and that's where I came in. He would point toward whatever it was he wanted—a loaf of bread, or the refrigerator for chocolate milk—and I would translate for him.

When we left the city for our new Levitt house in New Jersey, I was in the fifth grade. I helped my pregnant mother leaf through the catalogue and pick out our bathroom tile, Formica countertops, carpeting, and even the color of the house, although I was disappointed that the options didn't include cobalt blue or tangerine. I chose the pale blue house, but six-year-old Roger preferred pale yellow, which my mother agreed would look cleaner on overcast days.

Our house wasn't one of the thousands of split levels that were sprouting up all over Jersey at that time—it had only two floors, a big garage, and a walk-in attic full of fiberglass batting. Yet the house was surrounded by air, something almost mystical to me after living in the city. Best of all, it was new and smelled like daisies would smell, if they had a scent.

Our house sat in the middle of a block called "Seaton Lane," amidst a maze of other curved lanes with rhyming names like "Keyton Lane," "Treeton Lane" and even "Zeeton Lane." Each house stood on half an acre of lawn. Each backyard had in its center a trim, manufactured mound that could be landscaped with flowers and sprawling juniper bushes or, as our next-door neighbors did, crowned with a small statue of the Virgin Mary surrounded by a garland of fake poinsettias. Our neighbors to the other side, Black Jews who ran a chain of dry cleaning shops and ate lots of bacon, built on their mound an eight-foot-tall Jewish star with bright red Christmas lights that they lit up for summer evening barbeques. Mom liked to joke that whenever that Jewish star came on, the agonizingly sweet smell of ribs (something we never ate—we avoided pork, although we didn't keep kosher) was not far behind.

I missed that intoxicating scent on many occasions that summer, which was largely spent waiting around at hospitals and doctors' offices. Something was wrong with Joshua, the new baby born in the spring, so Roger and I found ourselves stuck in waiting rooms, trying to behave well for whichever relative was smiling and handing us a new box of crayons. I remember walking with my parents through endless rooms of monitors and meters as a doctor wrote out yet another prescription for formula.

After a few months, the baby seemed better. My parents chanced a night out, going over to eat coffeecake with the neighbors and leaving me in charge. It was my first time babysitting. Roger was in bed, and my one assignment was to call my parents if the baby, who was sleeping in a worn bassinet in the foyer, woke up. I was excited to be old enough for this responsibility.

"Watch him very carefully, he's delicate as hell," Mom said. "Call me if he wakes up, even just a little bit." I nodded.

The baby didn't wake. I went to his side and watched him sleeping on his belly. The house was clean, the walls freshly papered with damask gold that felt like velvet, and I was wonderfully elated. I got my Instamatic camera out of my pocketbook and snapped a few pictures. Joshua looked tiny through the viewfinder, as if he wasn't real or even our baby at all. Then I sat down on the matching gold couch with a glass of orange soda, a Ding Dong cake, and a book about a girl lost in the wilderness, pleased as I watched the baby's miniature back rise and fall.

I slipped out early the next morning to play with Carly, the daughter of one of my mother's oldest friends. In the family room of her identical Levitt house, we were acting out the scenes from the song "Leaving on a Jet Plane," laughing wildly at the line "so many times I played around," because we knew it meant sex. We were making Barbie and Ken have sex and yelping so loudly with disgust and laughter that we didn't hear the phone ring. Then, right in the middle of our playing the record for the tenth time, Carly's mother walked in and lifted the needle off the 45.

"Deborah, the baby died. You need to stay here or play with other friends until dinner time."

I received these words like a news flash about a place I had never heard of, or the tally of how many casualties had occurred in Vietnam that day. It simply didn't register, either for me or for Carly. Carly's mother turned, ran upstairs, and locked herself in her room for a long time, which didn't help make her announcement any more real.

We shrugged in a way that erased what we had just heard and started drawing naked men and women with Rachel, another friend who had just arrived. Rachel and Carly drew funny saltshaker penises on the men, while I drew realistic penises with little sacks of balls drooping behind them. They looked just like the drawings in *Your Body is a Wonderful Gift*, a booklet that my mother made me read aloud to her even though it bored her and humiliated me.

"Yours are so disgusting."

"Yeah, yours are gross."

I tried to defend my man with the penis. "But I'm drawing what you're drawing."

"No," said Rachel, "ours are funny, but you draw too well. Yours are sick."

We ate grilled cheese sandwiches and miniature cheese puffs from a bag for lunch. Then we played outside for a few hours, yet it still wasn't time yet for me to go home. Carly and I had never spent more than a few hours together because we didn't like each other that much. After playing every board game, pretend game, tag game, and hula hoop game we could muster, we must have started fighting, because I marched out her front door and slammed it behind me.

I walked along Seaton Lane until I could see my house with cars parked all around, in the drive, on the street. A big party place. I felt sad I couldn't be there, but I was hopeful that silver trays of Wise potato chips and little dishes of M&M's awaited me, just like they did on those mornings after my parents had hosted a party.

I went over to visit Linda Finkel, who was the most popular girl at school and barely tolerated me. Her mother, a tiny woman who wore the longest fake eyelashes and the brightest blue eye shadow on the block, pulled the door open and pursed her lips into a smile.

"Is Linda home?"

"Just a minute. I'll check." She went to a room I couldn't see, and I heard Linda hiss, "No, I hate her."

Her mother returned and said, "Linda's very busy right now. Maybe you can play another day." She didn't even look embarrassed.

I don't know why I said the next thing I said. Maybe it was to make Linda feel guilty, maybe to make her mother droop, or maybe to make my own life seem more real to me.

"My baby brother died today."

Linda's mother burst into sobs, the blue mascara rushing down her cheeks in torrents. I could hardly believe that a few words could do that to an adult.

Finally, I went up to my own house, to the front door. Even if it was only four o'clock, I figured that everyone else was there already, so why not me? Suddenly, I wondered if it was my fault that the baby died, since I'd been the one watching him last night. On a trip to Lancaster County, Dad had told me not to take pictures of the Amish because it was against their religion, although he wasn't sure why. Did my pictures of Joshua steal his life from him? While I was still deciding whether or not to run back to Carly's house, the door opened and I was swept into the arms of my grandmothers, one on each side pressing me into her lean or ample body.

Mimi and Nana had been as distant as continents from each other for years, but now they were smothering me in Yiddish, the language that levels everything. Mimi took off one of her silver bangle bracelets and put it on my wrist, even though the bracelet was far too big. Nana sobbed into her apron between loud coughs. Other relatives filled our living room and dining room, drinking coffee out of our good china and talking in a way that they had never done before: quietly.

My Uncle Leo, a bowling champion I'd seen only once before at a family wedding, came up to me and patted my bottom. "Growing up, you'll help your mother, I know." He handed me a gift wrapped in Peter Max flower power paper. "From your Aunt Talia," he said, referring to his wife, a fashion model who made a living with her hands, which famously appeared in dishwashing commercials and diamond ring ads. I ripped the paper off slowly, so he wouldn't think I was greedy, and there it was: a Polaroid camera with a flash attachment, several packs of film, and a little booklet called *Taking the Perfect Family Portrait*. I had been begging my parents for a Polaroid for a year. The way Polaroids turned out photos right on the spot was the most magical thing I had ever heard of.

Then I remembered that this gift was because my brother died, so I tried to stop my smile. "Just a little something," Uncle Leo said, signaling to Grandpa, who was circling the room with a bottle of vodka, to refill his glass.

Nana followed right after Grandpa and ushered me into the kitchen, seating me at the table with my brother, who kept his head down and avoided eye contact. Suddenly he looked very large to me, but maybe it was just the contrast with the baby—the dead baby, I corrected myself. Nana served us chicken soup and jello on the good china as a heavy rain began. It pounded the house and then suddenly stopped. The sun slid back out of the clouds and an eerie view of storm and sunlight was framed in the sliding glass door, with our bare little back yard hill at center stage.

Barefoot, I walked out onto the patio. In the air, happy and clear, was something I had never seen before: a rainbow. I ran back inside to fetch the relatives. My grandmothers looked up and burst out crying, toddling toward each other and sobbing in Yiddish. A rainbow right over our house was surely a sign ("what God gave us," one of the grandmas explained, "for taking the baby away").

I ran next to the door of my parents' bedroom and knocked. "Wake up, there's a rainbow, a rainbow!" I yelled. But they did not come out.

So I got my new camera and loaded the film, worrying that my hands were moving too slowly to catch the rainbow. The rainbow, however, didn't seem to have any place else to go. While the other relatives gathered in the strange light, pointing with one hand, holding cups of coffee or vodka in the other, I backed up to get a bigger view. That's when I noticed there were other rainbows, too—one above and one below, like pastel shadows.

After each shot, I watched the black square of paper in my hand turn to color. Crescents of rainbow showed up with the corners of Mimi's face, the back of Pop's head, one of my brother's hands. Everything appeared out of its usual proportion, to make room for the rainbow.

There was another baby less than a year later, a girl this time, who was named Melissa but always called Missy. My Bat Mitzvah came and went, its most memorable moment a mass of kids running through the house, pretending to be drunk on a bottle of vodka that Dad had given us—without telling us, of course, that he had replaced the vodka with water.

There were also lots of fights and the sounds of crying from my parents' room. Broken dishes on the kitchen floor late at night. My mother hysterically weeping in the bathroom and not opening the door, no matter how hard I knocked. My father, one Sunday morning, following my mother into the bedroom, yelling loud enough for everyone to hear, "You killed the baby!"

Now a divorce.

Chapter Two

The day after my father told me about the divorce, my mother told my brother. "Tit for tat," she explained, as we sat at the kitchen counter with Geraldine, her nervous, giraffe-like older sister. Aunt Geraldine often laughed uncontrollably while covering her mouth at the same time, shielding the sane world from her crazy laugh. Geraldine was what my mother called "willowy," although I thought it was just a nice way of saying tall and skinny. We were eating big slabs of kosher salami dipped in mustard from the deli and guzzling cream soda. For some reason, they were treating me like a girlfriend who was merely posing as a daughter.

"I mean, if he tells our oldest daughter, I tell our only son." They nodded and sliced more salami. The kitchen, for which my mother had chose an avocado refrigerator, stove, and dishwasher with complementary yellow speckled countertops, was usually clean. At times, however, the light falling through the window on all that green made the room look sick, or perhaps just very tired. I thought of taking a picture, but I knew the picture would look washed out, no matter which angle I used.

"Bev, you mark my words, you're gonna be better off once this is over," said Geraldine. "How many hours a week do you suppose he works, or *says* he works? Sixty? Eighty? You've seen him lately only on Sundays, and even then he's always yelling for you to do something."

Mom sighed, and then broke into a giggle as she mimicked my father. "'Beverly, get me my ice water! Beverly, I need another pillow! Beverly, with all the money I'm making you, can't you bring me a decent bowl of ice cream?'"

She stopped abruptly, remembering the big diet. Mimi had suggested for years that Dad watch his weight, as he grew from a little pudgy to the size of a refrigerator. With his small bones, he seemed all out of proportion, skinny legs and long neck jutting from a huge wall of fat. Then he joined Fat Fighters, a weight loss program in the city, in response to a bet from Lou, one of his cab drivers, and in fear of dying from a heart attack like his father. Lou had boldly challenged the man who had built a taxi fleet from five cars to over sixty to aim that same willpower toward his own health.

Dad took Lou's bet, and in no time he was yelling at Mom to weigh each slice of the liver she broiled for him, and asking her to buy more of the canned asparagus that smells like dirty feet. We never imagined that the weight would pour off him so fast. Here he was, six months later, leaving the taxi garage in the middle of the afternoon to shop for new polyester leisure suits and leather ankle boots with zippers. "I'm a new man," he had said last night, "and I need a new life."

My mother wrapped up the salami without asking if I wanted more, assuming my stomach somehow got full at the same speed as hers. I knew it was her only meal of the day—not because the fridge wasn't packed with macaroni salad, pudding cups, and various hunks of leftover brisket, but because she had stopped eating weeks ago. "Nerves," she told me, whenever I coaxed her to eat half of my corned beef sandwich. For as long as I could remember, those "bad nerves" had kept her away from the fridge.

"Bev, you got any cake?"

"Nah."

Instead of serving dessert, Mom stuck her skinny hands into her pocketbook and fished out a lime-beaded cigarette case. She had started smoking again right after the baby died. She pointed the case at Geraldine, who waved it away. "Nah, I had half a pack driving down here, thinking of what he's doing to you. I gotta cut back."

I studied Mom's loose blue polyester pants and orange Nehru shirt. She looked like someone dressed badly for bowling, and the hip-hugger flare of her pants didn't help. She caught my stare and looked away. My own tweed gaucho pants and matching vest were her gifts, tokens of a mother who cared more about dressing us than herself. She and I were "skinny-bolinkies," according to Nana, and we were going to die soon unless we gained more weight.

"And who should know better than me?" Nana had asked, raising her right eyebrow. She had been dying ever since I was born. It was a miracle she was still alive, according to Mom.

Mom glanced back at me and took a drag off her cigarette, trying to decide whether I was a kid or an adult. I leaned back, picked up the beaded case as if I were going to shake out a cigarette, too, and said, "He's a real bastard." Matter-of-factly, as if I were saying, "It's fall carnival night at school," or "I'd like my sour cream on the side."

Mom blew her smoke out quickly and opened her mouth as if about to say, "You're too young to talk like that." But the doorbell rang, so instead she muttered, "Don't be fresh."

The visitor was the other Bev, Mom's long-time friend. "Go do your homework," Mom said, and I went upstairs to my bedroom, a stolen cigarette up my sleeve.

Everything in my bedroom, including the French provincial furniture, was pale green. Why take perfectly good brown furniture and paint it that greenish white with dark green trim? I was still angry with Mom for picking out the set for me when she knew I really wanted the blond bedroom furniture from the Sears catalogue.

Leaning against my windowsill, I smoked my second-ever cigarette and watched the red-leafed maple swaying in the back yard. Halfway through my second inhalation, I started wondering if smoking one and a half cigarettes might explain why I still hadn't gotten my first period.

Mom called up the stairs that it was time to leave, so I grabbed my camera and galloped back down to the kitchen. I had begged Mom weeks ago to let me take a photography class, "Shooting the World for Teens," taught by the owner—she called herself Miz Liz—of Karmic Clothes, a little boutique at the shopping center. Mom agreed, even though the class cost a bundle.

When we arrived at the boutique, Mom walked in with me, holding Roger's hand. A sign over the cash register read, "Stealing is bad karma. Look out for your future lives." Roger noticed the sign and looked up at Mom, but she ignored him. "You sure this is a real class? I don't have money to throw down the toilet."

Before I could answer, Liz came out of the back room clutching a list of names. She was short with fire-red hair, her green-rimmed eyeglasses adorned with white polka dots. She looked older than my mom, or maybe just more tired, but she smiled when she saw us. "Let me guess—you're Deborah Shapiro."

I nodded, scanning the walls of jeans on hangers, some of them placed so high that they must just have been for show.

"You're cool. Go to the back room," she said, raising her eyebrows and lowering her voice, "where you'll meet the others." She laughed, then caught sight of my mother's face. Mom hated flamboyant people.

"Anyway," she said to Mom, "we'll just be getting started today—covering what photography is really about, and all that stuff about F-stops, apertures, focus. Pick her up in an hour, okay, hon?" Mom also hated being called "hon."

Liz turned around quickly and spoke to the clerk at the register. "You get the baby for the next hour," she told him.

"You have a baby?" I asked.

"Nah, I meant the store. It's my only offspring."

In the back room, kids sat around in a circle of folding chairs, beanbags, and a green plastic bench. Liz directed me to a stool, although it made me feel even taller than usual. I recognized one of the girls on the folding chairs as Eshe, the most popular—and wildest—girl at my high school. She had had two abortions already. When a speaker at a school assembly tried to warn us away from sex by flashing slides of half-aborted babies, Eshe had leapt onto the stage and slammed his projector to the ground, screaming, "Get out of here, you motherfucker!" She was suspended for two days, but everyone admired her even more. I also recognized Abby, a short girl I knew from temple but had never really talked to, and a guy about my height with a long dark ponytail down his back. He looked up and half smiled. A short, overweight boy next to him was playing with a calculator. He glanced at me, and then turned back to his numbers.

Liz plopped a plate of chocolate éclairs onto the table in the center of the room. "Whoa boy! Get a look at those doggies! When I'm gonna shoot, I gotta eat first, and nothing helps my artist's eye like an éclair."

When no one made a move toward the pastries, she added, "Hey, I'm not going to narc you out to your diet doctor. Have one." She reached in and carefully lifted the largest éclair. The boy with the calculator looked both directions, took one, and then everyone else joined in.

"Let me tell you where we are in the universe before we talk photography," Liz said. "This shop, left to me by my ex-husband, is right next to Dino's Head Shop. They buy mobiles and shit from India for pennies, and sell it to kids like you for dollars.

"On the other side of us is D & D Bagels, which stands for 'Douchbag and Dumbshit.' Those Hassids think they're better than everyone else, but you know what they need?" A few of us shook our heads, and she answered, "Blowjobs!"

Eshe laughed, and so did the longhaired guy. The rest of us concentrated intently at our éclairs, blushing at the suggestive shape of the pastries. Last week, someone at school had told me what a blowjob was, so I knew Liz was trying to shock us. I wondered if Mom had driven home already.

"Me? I've been all over, and that's why I can teach this class. You've got to see the world before you can really see it. I joined the Peace Corps years ago, went to Tanzania to teach English, but ended up showing women how to make potholders so they could stop burning their hands. You'd be amazed at what a potholder can do.

"Then I went to Paris for a few years, fell in love with Frank and ended up riding the rails around Asia with him, buying and selling cheap clothing. He wouldn't stop using drugs, so I dumped him, moved to Australia and met Rick, who owned this store. Next thing I know I'm divorced and living in Jersey, just like I've never been anywhere."

"And what does this have to do with photography, man?" Eshe asked. "I mean, it's not like I don't dig your life story, but let's get on with it." She had a deep voice and long, wavy black hair. I desperately wanted hair as thick and a voice as low as hers.

I thought Liz would be insulted, but she seemed delighted. "That's what it means to be an artist—you don't take shit from anyone." She gave Eshe a high five. "Okay, tell me your names quick and why you're here."

"I'm Mark," said the tall, ponytailed guy. "I like seeing how what's in front of me changes into something else in a picture." Liz nodded like a satisfied doctor.

"I'm Abby, and I'm basically bored with my life. My parents said I should take this class, mostly so they wouldn't have to worry about me so much." Abby had deep dimples, the kind I always wished for, and freckles on her cheeks.

"Taz," the guy with the calculator blurted out. "I call myself Taz, and I want to travel the world with my camera. No one is going to stop me, either."

"Eshe, and I'm here to learn how to take fucking pictures so I can sell them to the paper and make some extra bucks." Liz seemed satisfied with this, too.

I was last. "My name is Deborah, and I like taking pictures," I said, then added quickly, "I mean, of trees." I had a dozen photo albums full of tree pictures. Usually I looked straight up at the trees to show the light filling the branches, like some of the Georgia O'Keeffe paintings I had seen. "I try to get pictures looking at trees from angles that make them more interesting."

This last part was a lie. No matter what the angle, I had always found trees interesting, starting with the pine tree in the back yard of our Brooklyn house where I loved to hide as a child. Now I studied the pair of birches in our front yard in Jersey, leaning toward each other as if they were in love but too shy to say so.

"I don't get the trees," said Liz, "but whatever floats your boat. What I do get is making art, and this is what you gotta know more than anything: you make art out of whatever crap life is giving you. That's what it's all about. Now I'm not going to make you look at my photos, because I don't want you unduly influenced by the sway of my talent." We leaned forward seriously. "I'm joking, guys. Look, just shoot a few rolls of film of whatever is the most wrong with your life. Get them developed and bring them back in two weeks."

"What do you mean by what's wrong with your life?" Abby asked. "I mean, I feel a little fat, so am I supposed to take a picture of my butt?"

Mark smiled and Eshe laughed out loud. `

"Take your butt and whatever else is messed up. And don't censor yourself. This is about hunting down your life and shooting it."

I nodded, but my mind was already spinning with ideas about where to aim my camera. According to an after-school special I'd seen on TV, the average divorce took about six months. I could document this divorce and turn it into a story that would fit neatly into a photo album. Years from now I could pull it down from the shelf, open it, and casually browse through the pictures.

The divorce, however, never progressed like those divorces on TV, the ones where the kids were always vacationing in the Bahamas with Dad and his new girlfriend, while Mom got a makeover and went out on her first date in two decades. This divorce was strange from the start, largely because Dad never moved out. Instead, he took control of the master bedroom with its private bath and two coffin-length closets.

"Why should I leave?" he hissed, his eyes shaking nervously. "It's my house, too."

"I just think it makes it harder on everyone, you both being here," I replied.

"Why is that? This doesn't affect you kids," he told me. I snapped a picture of him as he installed the combination padlock on the door of his new bachelor pad. Roger stood behind me, wearing too-short pants and a too-tight plaid shirt, calling at me, "When are you going to take my picture? You never take my picture."

I was practiced at ignoring him. Each day I focused my camera on Dad and occasionally on Mom, who hated it when I pointed the viewfinder in her direction. "Oh, for God's sake, not that *mishigas* again!" she would yell as she carried the screaming baby up the stairs.

I snapped portraits of Dad as he lugged in heavy bags of brand new leisure suits, each a different shade of pastel. Where he went in those suits only I knew, because I went with him. The first time he left the house alone I'd raced out after him, bored and still hungry after a hamburger helper dinner that I'd hated. I didn't ask, just hopped into the passenger seat of his car and away we went. From then on, he would tap me on the shoulder and make a clicking sound with his tongue whenever he was ready to go out.

We always headed for the same diner on Route 9, run by a family of Greek immigrants who understood the lure of padded booths and a twenty-page menu. They also grasped the appeal of a rotating dessert case packed with ladyfingers and éclairs the size of men's shoes. I came to think of that dessert case as a glorified nightlight, glowing like a beacon of safety when the world got dark. Although I knew Liz wouldn't find anything particularly wrong with it, I snapped pictures of that case anyway, adjusting my camera to fill the viewfinder with sugary sculptures.

"Put that camera away," Dad would bark at me before greeting the hostess. A small Greek woman, she always wore a long gold caftan with dark trim and a V-neck that emphasized the beginnings of her huge breasts. We tried not to gaze down into that V, but it was hard for my father, at six-three, and me at five-eight, to avoid staring down past the bottom of her face. I could tell Dad had a crush on her by how polite he was whenever she spoke to us.

"Two for dinner?" She smiled up at Dad.

"Yes, and how are you tonight, sweetheart?"

She always answered demurely, "Fine."

Next, he would compliment some minor aspect of her attire. For a man who had never learned to talk this way, he tried his best. I wasn't surprised that he had no idea how to give compliments, since they were as rare as rainbows in the house that Mimi ruled.

"Your watch is very nice," he'd say, "functional, too," or "Your shoes match your dress," as if it were a delightful coincidence.

We devoured bowls of matzo ball soup followed by plates of eggplant Parmesan and turkey croquettes. Then we ordered multiple desserts, one at a time, followed by cups of hot chocolate, so we could spend at least three hours at that diner. The hostess—her name was Fatima—would smile in our direction every so often, which Dad took as encouragement to order more food. He must have believed the higher the bill, the more she would like him.

Finally we stood up, carried the bill to the register, and let her ring it up. Dad pulled out the monogrammed money clip—the one that had recently replaced the thick leather cub scout wallet Roger sewed for him—and peeled a twenty from a thick wad of bills, each a wish for her to want something of him. I wanted to photograph the money, but I knew he would yell at me. Instead I turned my back and snapped more pictures of glass shelves covered with peaks of meringue, glowing in the light.

One night, as we sat in our booth ready to order dessert, I saw Eshe come in. Her companion was a short, Indian-looking woman whose hair was as black as Eshe's but much longer, pulled back from her face with duckling barrettes. I watched them, hoping to catch Eshe's eye so she would say hello to me, but they disappeared into the booth behind us. I didn't have many friends at school since my best friend Cynthia had moved away. If Eshe would only speak to me, it surely would mean something good was about to happen in my life.

"Your mother," Dad was saying, "you know that this is all her fault." He plunged his spoon angrily into his bread pudding. He had gotten into a routine of starving himself all day and then eating all evening. "I ask for a few simple changes, like maybe she can start cleaning up a little better and make me a better social life. The only friends she has over most of the time are hers, and they wouldn't care less if I dropped dead. What about me?"

I had once overheard Mom on the phone with the other Bev, telling her that Dad had insulted all their friends so much that he didn't have any left—but why should she have to suffer as a result? I ventured cautiously, "Hey, Dad, I don't mean to upset you, but you know you used to tell Mom that all her friends were idiots."

"There are more than just idiots in the world," he intoned. I fell silent again, realizing he would continue to say it was all Mom's fault, which might even be true. At the same time I was straining to overhear Eshe's conversation and find out who the other woman was.

"She used to have Bill and Linda over, and they liked me," Dad said. "They thought I told great jokes. But she must have told them something about me, because when I called Bill to say I was finally divorcing your mom, he said he couldn't talk to me anymore."

Eshe and her companion were talking in low voices, then Eshe almost yelled, "Why should I have to fucking cooperate? She's the fucking mother!" It reminded me that Mom kept yelling at me lately, mostly about not cleaning my room or helping her in the kitchen.

"And that other Bev, she's put all these ideas in your mom's head. She was always out to get me, probably because she's so fat," Dad added. "Women like that have no life."

"Please, Eshe, keep it down," came the other woman's voice from behind my head. "Life's given you lemons? What you gonna do? Eat them or make lemonade?"

"I hate fucking lemonade," Eshe answered, and they both laughed. I wished I had someone to say "fucking" to, and then laugh about it. The hostess came by with a pot of coffee. Although Dad never drank the stuff, he turned over the empty cup and smiled up at her. She smiled back, a secret smile like she knew something none of the rest of us did.

As soon as she was gone, I said, loudly enough for Eshe to hear, "I never liked that fucking Bev." I acted nonchalant, as if it weren't the first time I had ever said "fucking" out loud.

Dad laughed like we were old friends. "Of course you don't."

I felt happy and surprised at the same time. I looked up at the new goatee that clung to the bottom of his face, like a gray mouse. I had to admit to myself that he looked creepy this way.

"I know why your dad goes there," Mom began one afternoon. She'd cornered me as I was reaching into the refrigerator, trying to dislodge a pudding cup from behind a casserole. "That tall blonde waitress, the one with no bust. You know who I mean."

I stood up and turned to find her staring at me earnestly, dressed in her white tennis outfit. How could I tell her she had it all wrong? I saw my camera lying on the counter and picked it up. It was an Olympus Dad got me from some sidewalk vendor in the city, or at least it looked like an Olympus. Every time Liz glanced at it in class, she only rolled her eyes.

"Oh, not that again," Mom said.

"But you look good in that tennis outfit," I told her, adjusting the F-stop. Last month I'd found out that Mom and I were the same size, although I was six inches taller.

She sighed. I thought she'd complain about how Dad should wait until he moved out of the house, how it wasn't fair that he went out at night while she was home crying, worrying about the live baby and the ghost of a dead baby. But she didn't. She just stood there, her hands on her hips, staring at me as I snapped a few pictures, the cacophony of the shutter quickly unfurling.

Dropping the screen that often made her seem too distant and unfamiliar to be my mother, she took my wrist between her thumb and fingers and looked into my eyes. "I want you home with me each night. Home," she said.

I had never seen her cry before, although her voice was shaking when she talked on the phone once, a little while after the baby died, telling someone, "I never knew they could make coffins that tiny."

She came up behind me now and put her freckled arms around my bony body, her voice shaking. "I don't want this to hurt you, not to hurt you."

I froze, wishing this scene were just another photograph. She never touched me, not with Roger still climbing in her lap and the baby always screaming from her playpen until Mom picked her up. I tried to remember the last time she told me she loved me, but it was too far back—before we moved to Jersey, before Joshua. I wanted to push her away and run, and at the same time I wanted to melt into her.

"You're my girl," she whispered, and something in me softened. I let her hold me tight, but I still didn't lift my arms. A year ago she'd told me, "You've always been a daddy's girl." She had wanted to take me shopping for a new dress, but I stayed home so I could heat Dad's dinner for him.

I lifted my hand now and placed it mechanically on her arm, part of me wanting her to hold me, part of me wanting her to let go.

Chapter Three

Mr. Lexington winked as I came through the classroom door. "You know," he said, his Louisiana accent sounding like bad Brooklynese, "I just saw on the student roster that your birthday is the same day as mine. We're birthday soul mates, Deborah." He smiled broadly at me in his brown-checkered suit. "Now, what do you think that means?"

Mr. Lexington had been my social studies teacher for two years in a row. I'd had a crush on him since last spring, when he'd handed me the paper I'd written about why philosophy is important and said, "You think good."

"I don't know what it means," I answered. Then I remembered that I was supposed to be gifted for my age, at least according to the school counselor. "Maybe that we're linked by fate in some way, if you even believe fate exists." It was easy to be breezy with him, like a wisecracking character on a sit-com who always got the laughs.

The other kids were filling their seats as Mr. Lexington lifted a small stack of quizzes that were ready to be returned. "Oh, now, don't you think fate just abounds? Look at Arthur over there," he said, pointing to a kid in black leather who was seated in the back row. He always wanted to be called "A-man," but Mr. Lexington insisted on Arthur.

"Isn't it his fate to be named Arthur, the name of a noble knight, while he leads the knights of the cafeteria round table?"

I shrugged and smiled, like I knew what he meant. "And isn't it your fate, Deborah, to dazzle us in your own way?"

A few kids overheard, and as I slid into my seat Josephine called out, "Hey, dazzling Deborah." Great, just what I needed, a nickname. Yet I knew Mr. Lexington intended it as another way to reach out to me, which was something he did on a regular basis these days. Just yesterday he'd said, "Don't let anyone run over you, darling," as I dropped my in-class essay on morality on his cluttered desk. I had nodded like I knew what he meant, but I really had no idea.

That afternoon, I arrived early at Karmic Clothes and walked around the piles of Faded Glory jeans. Some had little patchwork back pockets that I liked, while some had three zippers in front. "I bet you're a denim purist," Liz said, coming in from the back.

I looked down at my Wrangler jeans and then up at Liz, who was arrayed in many shades of orange. I hadn't really thought about style much—I simply wore whatever Mom got me. "You think she'd be interested in some kind of style," Mom had said once to the other Bev, "but Roger's the one who really likes to shop, and he looks so good in whatever he tries on. A little model, that's what he should be."

"What've you got for me?" Liz asked. "I can look at these now, before the others come."

I was a little nervous about what she would think, but I opened my macramé pocketbook—another gift from Mom—and pulled out an envelope of photographs. I placed them on top of the pile of size five jeans. Liz picked up the photos and started leafing through them: Dad at the mall in a light blue leisure suit, trying on a goofy knit hat; Dad waving me away when I tried to take his picture on the steps of the diner; Roger watching TV and reading a comic book simultaneously;

Mom talking on the phone with the baby on one hip and crying a little, something I hadn't noticed until now. There was also a self-portrait of me looking into the mirror, one eye hidden by the camera, the other staring intently at my reflection. I looked older than I had imagined, the way Dad would have looked if he'd been a girl.

"You look sad," Liz said as she handed back the photos. I'd thought it was my mother who looked sad.

The other kids came in all at once. We quickly settled into the back room, swapping pictures and laughing at Eshe's shots of her mother chasing her with teapot in one hand, knife in the other. "She was trying to have tea with me. You know, she's Egyptian and they do that, but she wanted to kill me at the same time."

I looked around, wondering what Mark's photos would look like, and realized he wasn't there. I stuffed my photos, so ordinary looking, catching nothing of what was wrong in my life, back into my bag.

"Interesting things happen all the time," Liz was saying. "You just have to have your eyes open. Tell yourself to look at everything as if it's a shot. Think about how to frame it." She went on to explain why we never wanted to center the main subject of the photo; that was too obvious.

"You want to hang out and groove with your best friend, so maybe you shoot your friend from the level of her alarm clock, making her smaller and time bigger. That's asymmetry. That's what makes kick-ass photos—when you catch something so obvious, yet so unexpected."

I found myself gazing through the door at the hanging jeans, wondering what kind of interesting life each pair would eventually have. I wondered what was wrong with me—why my camera flattened everything into a sanitized version of itself, as if I were aiming at a typical family determined not to lead an interesting life.

To my surprise, Liz looked over at me next and added, "Like what Deborah did when she took a self-portrait. It's off-kilter enough that her sadness comes through, especially the way the shot centers on one of her eyes. Deborah, pass that one around, will you, hon?"

As Eshe leafed through my photos, she nodded approval. Mark walked in, tossed himself into an empty chair, and gave Liz a quick smile to make up for being late. Eshe handed him my pictures. He paused at one of Dad yelling through the car window, forearm poised on the edge of the glass, and looked at me. I smiled nervously, and then bit my lip.

"Sorry I'm late," he apologized, his voice kind and familiar.

"No problem, as long as you bust your ass in this class," Liz retorted. "Hey, I'm a poet, and I know it."

No one laughed, so she launched into our next assignment, telling us it was time to learn about panoramic shots. We had to find a good shot and carefully turn in a half-circle, inching the camera along as we snapped each frame. Then we were to put the images together into a panorama.

"Why am I telling you to do this? Simple, my little friends. You have to get expansive before you can get specific. You have to open up your souls to see the big picture, the biggest picture possible, and then, in that big picture, you'll find the details you often overlook. Get big to get little, and you don't even need to go ask Alice for this." Some of the kids laughed at this and I nodded knowingly, having read the book of the same title last year.

"Like this," she said, opening her beaded fringed bag and pulling out a large envelope. She started slapping down four-by-six photos of red rock, sky, and treetops onto the little table in the middle of the room. At first they didn't seem to fit together beyond sharing the same colors and textures. Then she bent down and arranged them carefully, one photo slightly overlapping another, some a little higher and some lower so that they made a shifting line across the table. "Now what do you see?"

We looked carefully. A canyon with every color of rock, even blue lines that curved across the photos. "The fucking Grand Canyon?" Eshe asked.

"The fucking Grand Canyon," Liz said. "You can't get a shot of the fucking Grand Canyon with one photo. It's too fucking big. I mean, look at this. I have nine photos here, and this is only about forty-five degrees of what I was seeing."

"When were you there?" Mark asked, lifting his hair behind his ears as he bent closer. He had a long neck with a small wisp of hair beneath the spot where his ponytail started.

"Who the fuck knows?" she answered, laughing. "I don't usually do tourist gigs, but about ten years ago my sisters wanted to meet me there. If they got on my nerves, I figured I could just push them over the edge and be done with it. Did I ever tell you I have twins for sisters? Total pain in the tuckus."

She related all this in such a serious tone that we all looked up in alarm. "How gullible are you kids?" she laughed, shaking her head at us. "I'm not going to murder my little twin sisters."

That night, when Dad and I arrived at the diner in a cold rain, our hostess was clearly distressed. Fatima barely said a word as she led us to our booth. As soon as she dropped our menus on the table, she turned on her heels and rushed to the phone. We tried to focus on the task at hand, but we couldn't take our eyes off her back and shoulders, which kept gathering up around her neck and dropping again. While we were sipping our matzo ball soup, one of the waiters rushed forward, yelling in Greek. Everyone in the restaurant turned. Fatima looked completely exasperated. She started yelling fast and low.

"A car!" the manager's voice blasted from the kitchen.

My father's face lit up. He sprang out of the booth toward Fatima, exclaiming, "I have a car!" She stared at him. "Take it," he added.

"No, it is more difficult than that," she said. I watched Fatima, the manager, and my father all gesturing wildly and shaking their heads. Fatima translated the manager's Greek slowly into whispers of English for my father, who nodded enthusiastically. He was so tall that he had to hunch down to hear her. All at once he signaled to me, and I lifted our coats off the hook while Fatima gathered a black cloak around her. It was an adventure—and I had left my camera behind in my bedroom.

By listening to my father conversing on the car radio of the Buick, I learned that a cab in the city was supposed to head east on 177th Street, pick up someone with a name that sounded like Bialy, and meet us in a parking lot near the first exit off the Belt Parkway. Dad kept assuring everyone that we would be there in twenty minutes. Since the diner was at least forty-five minutes away from the meeting place, I wondered how this was possible. But then, I knew Dad.

In no time at all we were zooming north on Route 9 at eighty miles per hour, my father with both hands uncharacteristically gripping the wheel and both feet characteristically cranking gas and brake at once. Once we were on the turnpike the traffic thickened, so Dad steered the Buick onto the shoulder of the highway. After glancing ahead to make sure that no vehicle was using the shoulder for an emergency, he floored the gas pedal. The turnpike lights zoomed over us with little dashes of darkness between them. "No turning back," the motion said. "Into the future. And fast." I imagined taking a photograph of the car moving fast, half on the curb, half on the road, all of it a blur in between now and then. Of course, we were moving far too fast for me to shoot anything.

Fatima sat right next to my father, her hand on his shoulder and her luxurious hair shaking in its pins. My father's shoulders rounded toward the wheel, his head bent forward like a race car driver and his large hands gripping the wheel of our lives as the car neared 120 miles per hour.

Fatima started speaking excitedly in Greek and my father hit the brakes. We snapped back into the right lane just in time to miss an orange Volkswagen parked on the shoulder. The dark-bearded face of a hippie holding up a tiny Volkswagen tire flashed by. I imagined my mother at home, calmly watching TV. *The Partridge Family* would be on, with Roger sitting solemnly in his yellow beanbag chair in the den. Maybe he would be looking for me; we usually watched the show together, although I pretended it was stupid. Mom would be out of her tennis outfit by now and into slacks and a blouse, feeding the baby a bottle. She would be wondering why I wasn't home. I wanted to frame her in the lower corner of a photo, as life without us cascaded down around her.

We emerged from the Holland tunnel just in time to meet up with one of Dad's cabs. Lou, the black driver, had dyed red hair, wore high-heeled sneakers, and always kissed me on the cheek, wagging one of his long fingers and saying, "You look good enough to put whipped cream on and eat." Dad never reacted. Occasionally, he reminded me that Lou was "a fag, but a good one, so why should I have a problem with it?" I was never sure if he meant that Lou was good at being a fag, or a good employee in spite of it.

"I tell you, the police were after me, and I had to do an alley dance to get there, but here we are, and here's your Greek boy," Lou said to my father as he jumped out of the cab.

Dad and Fatima joined a huddle of people while I stayed in the car. All I could see of Lou's cab was an arm holding a lit cigarette, so I turned my face the other direction. The nearby A&P store was bathed an unearthly sunset, deep orange turning into blue. Would I use a wide-angle lens here? How much of the store would I include in the frame, or would it be better to show mostly sky? Maybe a panoramic shot would be best, one that included the taxis butting noses in the foreground.

The door of our Buick opened, and a dark-haired boy bent down and slid into the back seat beside me. He looked a little like Fatima—without breasts, of course, but with her delicate fingers and black hair, and a certain air of aloofness that made him handsome. I didn't expect him to speak, at least not in English, so I was surprised when he looked at me matter-of-factly and said, "Hi, my name is Theodore. I'm Fatima's son," as if he were reading a script.

"Fatima, that woman right there," he added, pointing his finger at her as she opened the front passenger door. Fatima slid over into the middle of the front seat and a Greek man hopped in beside her, slamming the door shut as my father settled into the driver's seat.

"That's my mother, you understand, and beside her is my father," Theodore explained. Fatima was whispering in a terrified voice to Dad, as if her life depended on something. That something, I realized, was the speed with which my father careened out of the parking lot, throwing us all back against our seats.

As if nothing had happened, Theodore continued, "But they're divorced now."

I looked at Theodore. "What do you mean?"

"Oh, where do I begin?" he mused. "You see, I'm not a U.S. citizen—I was born in Turkey, but I've been living here with my dad, and sometimes on weekends with my mom. My dad's family wants me home with them, but hey, would I be able to get decent Chinese there?" He paused and laughed, as if he thought his remark was funny.

"Besides, they moved to Canada—Toronto, more precisely—which is a microcosm of the world from what I understand, except it's colder. I don't want to go to Canada, but that's truly the best option. My dad has a maître d' job waiting for him there, so that's where we're headed.

But since we're here illegally we can't get a visa, so we need to enter through the James Bond school of adventure.

"As for my mother, you do realize that Fatima is a Muslim name, don't you? Her father was Muslim, Turkish actually, but after he abandoned the family she was raised by Greek relatives near Cyprus. You ever hear the song 'A Boy Named Sue'? Well, that's what it was like for my mom, growing up with that Muslim name in a Greek Orthodox family. But hey, the Muslims can't make moussaka like the Greek Orthodox." He lifted his face up and grinned, as if he was doing a monologue on the Johnny Carson show. I pretended to be the audience, laughing on cue.

"Now my father, he's not a citizen either. That's the short version, except to say that we didn't plan to go north so suddenly. One of our disgruntled relatives tipped off the authorities, and that's why"—he paused, turning dramatically around to look out the back window—"the INS should be after us momentarily.

"Our plan is to meet some of his"—pointing to his father in the front seat—"relatives across town, and they'll get us into Canada until we can work out the paperwork to come back here. Would that I could stay here and be an American teenager! But fate is incorrigible."

I blinked, and Theodore explained, "I'm in honors English. I have an IQ of 153. I may look only 13, but I have a more extensive vocabulary than most Harvard PhDs."

I stared at my father's back, hunched into its center as he bore down on the wheel. We zipped smoothly onto the Belt Parkway.

"But like many brilliant people, I lack emotional aptitude." Theodore moved another inch away from me. "Girls, in particular, make me unwittingly nervous."

Just then we stopped at a traffic light, and everyone in the front seat began laughing. As the light turned, I saw two men in brown suits emerge from the car behind us and head straight for our car.

"Dad! Dad!" I screamed.

"The INS," Theodore said casually, yawning for effect. Dad slammed down on the gas pedal and sped two-and-a-half blocks before the men could even get back into their car. We swung down a bluish alley and wound up a few blocks *behind* the INS agents. Just like a James Bond movie, I thought. I wondered if the car would suddenly sprout wings to fly us back to Jersey.

Now we lurched to the right and back onto the beltway, heading north this time. Fatima was crying passionately on Dad's shoulder. No one said a word, except Theodore.

"Do you like John Denver?"

I nodded.

"I like him too, despite his reliance on clichés. Rhyme and reason, it's really an accurate summary of life's purpose, wouldn't you say?"

We were entering the Holland Tunnel. As the lights of passing cars swam over us, Theodore tapped Fatima on the shoulder and started humming a John Denver song. Then she began singing, "You fill up my senses..." It was all a well-rehearsed act—the way she sang, the little pauses in her voice and then the full, clear words. I leaned back and listened, remembering how I would sit in my room playing the eight-track until the smell of burnt lamb chop, and my mother yelling that I should come down to dinner, forced me out of the music and back into this life.

Coming out of the tunnel, the sky overhead filled with bright darkness, I thought of Mr. Lexington and fate. I wondered whether one day my fate would include being held by someone like him, someone who would make smart, sweet jokes and tell me I was good at thinking. I smiled at the thought of Mr. Lexington, imagining him taking my hand, raising his eyebrows at someone as corny as John Denver, and then laughing conspiratorially with me. I looked up and saw that Fatima had noticed my smile. She smiled broadly at me before turning back to Dad.

We drove a few more blocks, dashed down another alley, and came to a stop at the back door of an olive oil import company. Theodore and his father quickly unbuckled their seat belts. "Lovely to meet you," Theodore said, offering me what my friends and I called a "dead fish" handshake. As he got out, he waved to my father, bowed to me, and kissed Fatima, who had also stepped out of the car. Her ex-husband touched her shoulder briefly, but she ignored him and lunged at Theodore, holding him tightly in her arms for several seconds. Once they had released each other, Fatima deflated. The boy and older man walked away, disappearing through the door of the import company. She climbed back into the car and nestled close to my father again, although there was no longer any need to make room for another passenger. I asked my father a few times what was happening, but "later" was all he would say.

By the time we pulled into the diner parking lot, I had been asleep for a while. I barely registered Fatima stepping out, talking to Dad, and disappearing up the diner steps. The next thing I knew we were pulling into our driveway, as if we had just finished another long night of dinner out. Dad was singing along to a country love song on the radio. He seemed thrilled.

I went upstairs, opened my bedroom door, and collapsed on the bed as if it were the middle of the night. Downstairs, I could hear my father walking carefully into his bedroom, then the creak of the playroom door opening across the hallway and my mother sobbing, my father trying to explain, first in rather kind tones and then in angry ones. I heard my name—my mother was saying something about how Dad was taking away her little girl. Now he talked low, angry, in a steady pulse of words I couldn't make out.

There must be something wrong with them—didn't they know they shouldn't even be talking, let alone sharing this house, in the middle of the night? At least that's what I told myself as I hid under the covers, trying to push from my mind the nagging thought that *the* something wrong was me, something I'd done. Maybe talking back to my mother, or ignoring my father all those times when he told me to get him some ice water, because then my mother would have to do it instead. Or not watching the baby closely enough. Something I couldn't take back.

Chapter Four

The fighting at our house spread to rival stereos, one in the living room and one in the playroom. On a weekday evening or a weekend morning, after a flash of words and some door slamming, Dad would march toward the white fake-antique console in the living room and carefully place a Mario Lanza album on the turntable. Mom aimed for the playroom, putting a Barbara Streisand record on our kiddy record player and turning up the volume so high that I could hear "People who need people are the luckiest people" from our mailbox on the street, where I went to escape for a while. I imagined Mom getting up from the green-and-pink striped daybed, surrounded by knob-shaped Fisher-Price butchers, bakers, handymen, and mothers, singing along with Barbra and spraying lemon-scented Pledge on the furniture in her new room. Meanwhile, Dad would be leaning back in his favorite chair (a plaid recliner that Mom had always hated because its arms were worn), smiling broadly as Lanza's baritone voice filled the living room. If you stood between the two of them, you would hear whatever was the opposite of harmony.

Other furniture was soon recruited into the fray. I came home from school one rainy day to find Dad's recliner sitting in the middle of the lawn draped with his finest suit, the one he wore to his wedding.

Although the suit was outdated, he had worn it to a cousin's wedding just last month to show off how thin he'd become. Another day, I woke up to find the coffee table—the one Mom had picked out of a catalogue when we bought the house—upside down beside the mailbox.

Of course I photographed all of it from the driveway across the street, which belonged to a family we saw for only brief moments when their garage door opened and a little white car disappeared into that dark space. I aimed my camera first at the edge of our neighbors' pristine white house, boxwood bushes cut into rectangles, windows gleaming and shades drawn down. Then I shot our denuded rose bushes, some of them dead already, and our overgrown pussy willows. I caught the coffee table on its side, draped with a pale blue dress that my mother had worn only once, and a broken lamp with the glass bottom broken out, as if it had been punched. I ended with our station wagon, its muffler hanging low and the wood paneling scratched, and the other neighbor's weedy yard, which hid a strange little dog somewhere between a beagle and dachshund. "Suburban Disarray," I would title my panorama. It wasn't the Grand Canyon, but at least it was a kind of hole in the ground.

Later, Roger came outside and sat down on the railroad tie that surrounded our flowerbed of crawling juniper and almost-dead rhododendron bushes. He tilted an open box of Lucky Charms cereal my direction, and we munched together on multi-colored marshmallows while staring into the too-bright sunlight. Barbara and Mario blended their voices as if they were singing a duet, but in reality the sound was a life tuned to two frequencies at once.

"Do you think we'll laugh about this when we're grown up?" I asked him. He shook his head and gazed down the street, toward the approaching mail truck.

The biggest fight took place in silence. No one was home that day but me until dinnertime. Then all at once the door burst open and Mom hustled toward the fridge. She tossed old cold cuts at Roger and me, saying, "Here. Eat this. It's good enough."

"Do we have bread? I like bread," Roger said.

"No, just roll it up like it's something fancy."

She seemed more agitated than usual. Missy, on her hip, grabbed for a banana every time they passed the fruit bowl. Roger nibbled rolled-up bologna with his shoulders hunched. I didn't want to eat any of the food, but I was afraid to speak. I knew in my gut that something bad had happened, or was happening now, something like the molecules of the universe untying themselves. So I sat down at the table, sliced off the hard part of the salami, and kept the one edible piece for myself. Mom sat with the baby on her lap, letting her eat a banana. Red leaves fell against the window and then slid downward. I reached for my camera, stepping toward the sliding glass door.

At that moment Dad raced in. He stopped short when he reached the kitchen, fixing his shining eyes on my mother. He reached into the bag he was carrying and pulled out a bottle of Ivory Liquid, snapped open the top, and headed toward the sunroom. My mother kept dozens of plants in there, all going crazy in standing pots or suspended by faded macramé. Dad's maroon leisure suit looked out of place amidst all the greenery. We watched as he methodically administered a dose of liquid soap to each plant. My mother, always the first one to yell out, stood silent behind us.

"Dad," I finally said. But I couldn't help myself. Instead of trying to stop him, I started taking pictures. There might be something off-center and jarring about what I saw through the viewfinder, and I was sure it would make for great photos. There were long wandering Jews with their runners tangled over all the other plants, stringy little stubs of cactus in ceramic bunny pots I had painted for Mom in ceramics class, velvet-leaf African violets carefully raised by Dad's father. Dad continued from plant to plant as I slowly lowered my camera.

I considered running away and hiding upstairs, but my mother was right behind me. I knew that tears were pouring down her small freckled cheeks. There would be no way to avoid seeing that, just like there's no way to avoid seeing the sun on a sunny day.

When he was done, my father lifted his shoulders, looked down on us as if he were a little ashamed, and said, "There, and your mother can tell you why I did this."

Defiant and defeated at once, he suddenly turned to my brother, sister, and me. When Mom's eyes met his, he shook his head at the plants, still so green and shiny, still not smart enough to know they had all just been murdered.

Roger, to my surprise, spoke first. "Will the plants be okay?"

My father sighed, closed his eyes, and whispered, "I'm sorry, son." There was a flash of tenderness between Dad and Roger that I had never seen before, but it evaporated as quickly as it came.

Dad walked right through the midst of us and crossed the threshold between kitchen and laundry room. The next threshold lay between the laundry room and garage, where his car was waiting.

He didn't turn, just quietly said my name. I didn't move. He said my name louder.

I looked at my mother, who was frozen in a sheet of tears as if an ice storm had rolled over her, the very quiet baby still on her hip. I imagined her holding an older baby on the other hip, although he died before this one was born. I knew I should answer my father, "no," but the word wouldn't come. I ducked my head and followed my father over the dirty laundry into the very neat garage that he still controlled, and into his car.

We stayed at the diner until 1 AM, Fatima bringing us desserts one after another and smiling at my father as if he were Jesus. He smiled back like Barney Fife. At some point I saw Eshe come in, but she didn't seem to register who I was, or how she knew me. She simply sat at the counter and drank a few cups of coffee before slamming down a dollar and leaving.

It was so interesting listening to Dad, though, that I didn't mind. He didn't just talk about the incident with the plants but about everything, as if I really were an adult. He explained the elaborate scheme to hide Theodore and his father in crates in the bottom of a ship heading up the Hudson to Canada. Once the ship was out of port, they could come up on deck. ("Like being on a cruise," Dad explained.) He also talked about the divorce.

"It wasn't your mother who wanted the divorce," he said, although I would have had to be blind not to know that. "I couldn't live with it anymore. She was a different woman after the baby died, not that she was easy to live with before. But I've been doing for her half my life. Don't I deserve a little something?"

I wasn't sure how to answer. I sipped on my cream soda and listened to him detail how Mom had cleaned out all the bank accounts, even my Bat Mitzvah money. He had killed the houseplants, but they were only plants. How else could he get her to understand that what she did was wrong?

We cut a Napoleon in half and I took the bigger piece, daintily forking off manageable bites. Mom stole my Bat Mitzvah money, I kept telling myself, the money I was going to use for college. He said she wouldn't talk to him, wouldn't let him near her, wouldn't sleep in the bed anymore after the baby died. She'd slept in the playroom for months, ignoring everything he said and did, no matter how drastic. "I'd tell her she was pretty or that maybe we should go on a vacation. I'd tell her our life was a hellhole. I'd tell her..."

"That she killed the baby." I blurted out and suddenly stung by guilt, but I couldn't tell if it was because of what I had just said, or something else. If I had only watched the baby more closely, then maybe none of this would be happening.

He pushed the remaining bite of pastry away and shrugged. "It was just a way to get her to talk. You don't know what it's like, living with a slammed door for a wife." I pictured my mother, the woman who could talk on the phone nonstop for three hours straight, sitting on the kitchen stool smoking cigarette after cigarette.

"You know," Dad continued, "you're growing up, you deserve better than all this." He looked down at his oversized knuckles, capable of great cracking sounds that always made me laugh when I was younger. "You need to look out for yourself, too. Don't let her do to you what she's doing to me. She takes and she takes. You've got to protect yourself."

I nodded as if the truth had finally been revealed to me at last, now that I was old enough.

"You're turning into a nice young woman, and you gotta do whatever it takes to make sure she doesn't ruin you." He had never talked to me like this before. "She's lost her youth, and women like that, well, I don't need to tell you that sometimes they don't make the best mothers."

He was right. In my mind, I'd collected a stack of memories of Mom screaming at the top of her lungs, her face redder and more uneven than usual, telling me my room was a pigsty, that I would never amount to anything if I didn't stop eating and start listening to her more. All this had been happening for so long, and now it came together like a puzzle I didn't know I was assembling. Whatever guilt I had felt burned clear, leaving me free and light.

"The truth," said Mr. Lexington, "is supposed to set you free, but does it?"

43

I was busy drawing a palm tree in my notebook, placed off-center in the corner of the page as if I had snuck up on it with my camera. I nodded, to show I was paying attention. Mr. Lexington continued, "What is truth in the first place?"

Most of the class was still working on the in-class essay he'd assigned yesterday. Hardly anyone was finished yet except for me and a boy drawing robots at the desk next to mine.

"Deborah," he said, leaning toward me a little. He sat on the edge of his desk, not even five feet away, not even the length of a whole person. "What is freedom to you?"

I sensed a few kids looking up now, maybe sneering, so I tried to talk low. "The freedom to be yourself," I replied.

"Or freedom from something?" He tilted his head a little, almost smiled. I wondered what he knew, what he'd gleaned from my essay. I'd written about how truth could change from one person to another, how it might not be a real thing at all. "Maybe 'freedom's just another word for nothing left to lose,'" he continued, quoting Janis Joplin. A few girls in the back giggled.

Before I could answer a voice called my name over the intercom, instructing me to report to the office immediately. As I gathered up my things, I tried to imagine what might be wrong, my mind reeling out scenes of the house on fire or Dad in a car crash on the Belt Parkway. Everything had been quiet at home lately. Since all the plants had died there had been no music wars. My mother had even, one day while we were at school, emptied the whole greenhouse and washed it clean. As I slipped out the door, Mr. Lexington glanced at me again and said, "Go find your truth."

As I walked into the office, the large redheaded secretary handed me the phone. It was Roger, calling from the hospital where Mom had just arrived with Dad. Within ten minutes I was there, stepping out of the secretary's car as she chatted on and on about how she hoped my father was okay. "God bless," she called after me as I ran inside.

I found Roger in the waiting room at the end of the lobby. "What? Did he have a heart attack or something?" I said, thinking of my dead grandfather, Dad's father.

"No, Mom ran him over." Roger sounded far too casual. He sighed and began again, looking a little more scared this time. "She didn't mean to."

The way Mom told it, after she joined us on the green vinyl bench, it all started when Dad threatened to put her beloved Hummel collection out in the snow. "He was very irrational," she said calmly, lighting a cigarette beneath the "please don't smoke" sign in the waiting room. The baby was asleep on a mustard-colored couch beside us.

"I told him not to take the love seat outside," she continued.

"The love seat? I thought it was the Hummels."

"Oh, that happened later. First he took that love seat—you know, the one my great aunt left me?"

I did remember. As a child, I had memorized its upholstered print of royalty attending a great ball, especially the recurring dark-haired princess in the rose-colored gown.

"So I told him not to, and things got a little heated." A nurse signaled to her to take the cigarette outside. She said, "I'll be right back," and headed for the lobby door.

Roger tried to finish the story, but he was unclear about how the fight over the love seat had escalated. Mom had grabbed the baby and yelled at Roger to "get into the station wagon this minute."

Dad ran after them, but he slipped and fell in the foyer. I imagined the rest, based on what Roger said and didn't say. He'd stopped beside his father's head, afraid to move, but Mom had yanked him out the door and into the car. She had laid her right arm across the top of the driver's seat, turning her small head to look through the rear window as she backed out of the garage. She saw Dad's face a moment too late, felt the vibration of his fist against the car window, and heard him drop to the ground. By then, she had already backed up several inches.

"He's not really hurt," Roger said, swinging his legs under the padded bench. "He's just pretending."

"What did they tell the doctor?"

"That he forgot to close the rear door of the wagon, so he was latching it for our safety. Mom didn't know he was there. They made up the story in the car."

"You mean, they were talking nice to each other?"

"No, not nice. Mom cried and yelled, and Dad just yelled. Do you have any change? There's a candy machine."

I reached into my pocketbook and told him to get some for me, too. I looked over at Missy. Her rumpled hair was neither blonde nor brown. She was longer than I realized, one of her feet dangling off the couch. My mind went over all the details of last summer, before there had been any sign of a divorce. Just eight months ago, they'd called me from this very hospital to tell me I had a sister. My parents were still living in the same house, or at least pretending to. Now that day seemed so far away it was hard to remember that she was ever my sister.

My mother took us to swimming lessons every morning, then we'd hang out at the pool in the middle of our housing development. Roger leaned against the candy stand all day with his friends, stuffing himself with potato chips, while I lay in the lounge chair reading magazines and talking to Cynthia, who had not yet moved to Georgia.

"Look at that woman," Cynthia would whisper, pointing to someone my mother's age with pubic hair sticking out of the edges of her bathing suit. "Please run me over with a car if I ever do that." We tried not to make vomit sounds as other women walked by, their tushes hanging from their suits. "It's always the part that hangs out that ruins it all," I told Cynthia.

"You're so lucky that you're developing late," she said, as if it were a prize to be fifteen years old with no period yet. My mother had given me lectures about how all the women in our family started when they were fifteen or even later, but it didn't matter. Cynthia still rubbed in her maturity by telling me how the Nair stung her sensitive armpits. I might be smarter than she was, but she was a real woman while I was stuck in girlville forever.

Sitting at the hospital, I thought about how to frame that scene with my camera, how to find the right moment to capture what it was to be a girl. Then I remembered something else—today was Liz's class and I wasn't there. I couldn't show them my pictures of Dad killing the plants, something that might catch people's attention as much as Eshe's photos. I started to feel trapped, stuck at this hospital for who knew how long with Roger and Missy, instead of with the cool kids at Liz's. I started counting the blocks from here to Karmic Clothes, but once I figured out that the store was at least five miles away I gave up trying.

Hours later, we rode home in the station wagon as if we were still a family, although my parents were still calling each other schmucks and imbeciles and threatening to call their lawyers. The early November cold had turned the fields and trees beige like the housing developments. Missy whimpered a little, occasionally throwing her head back and dropping off to sleep. Next to me, Roger sat still as a statue, but I knew he was taking in everything.

Without thinking, I yelled at my parents, "Shut up already." Then I added, "Please."

"Young lady, you don't talk to your mother that way," Mom yelled back, turning to glare at me, but I was already focused on what was outside the window. The housing developments, each one a mixture of muted tans, yellows, blues, and greens, spread in familiar clumps on either side of the car. What really drew my eye were the occasional stretches of farmland filled with orderly lines of brown stubble, handfuls of tall trees, and an occasional white house with windows that glowed like night lights. I imagined that these houses were flooded with the smell of apples, and I wanted to live in one of them. I was dimly aware that Mom was still yelling at me, saying something about respect. Dad yelled back louder that a parent needed to earn respect.

"Like you would know!" she screamed.

As we pulled into the driveway, we saw Mimi waving at us angrily from inside her parked Cadillac, a white steamship of a car. She couldn't miss the love seat out in the middle of the yard, right next to the French coffee table she had given them when they married.

"Oh, not *that* woman again," Mom exclaimed.

"Oy, just what we need," Dad replied in true solidarity with Mom. I could tell they both dreaded the hour ahead, when we would all have to act like the story they had told the doctors was true. They were already embellishing the account of my father's fall: he'd slipped on his way outside to refinish the wooden love seat, where the fumes wouldn't bother the baby. They agreed on the details so quickly that it was hard to believe they had spent so many hours fighting over every other detail of our lives.

Chapter Five

The brand new bowling alley on Route 9, located next to the triplex movie theater, was empty except for the three of us. The dimly lit lanes each featured a different shade of orange, yellow, or brown with matching plastic chairs and desks. My father took his carefully polished, blue-and-white marbled bowling ball out of its faux-leather case. I noticed he wasn't wearing his neck brace—he only put it on when my mother was around.

"Ah, such a beautiful ball," said Fatima. I removed my own pink-and-white marbled ball from its worn case. It was originally my mother's, but a year ago she'd told me that she was too old for bowling. The funny thing was that she was never too old for tennis.

"Tennis is a game for your whole life," she had explained.

"And bowling isn't?"

"No, it's a game for couples in their early years of marriage. Once they cross thirty-five, they have to give it up and go play bridge once a week. Then when they get past fifty, they start on checkers." She had blown cigarette smoke in my face, laughing. "You get really old, then there's dominos."

"What about Monopoly, Mom?"

"Doll, everything's Monopoly."

Now here I was, holding a pink marble planet in my hand. I tried to cram my fingers into the slim openings but my hands were too big, so I bowled with my fingertips. Of course, I could have bowled backwards wearing a blindfold and still have beaten Fatima.

Fatima's approach was to demurely carry the lightest ball over to the lane, turning back to my father and smiling as if she were too dainty for such a game. Then she shocked us by throwing the ball overhand at the pins as if she were launching a shot put. Most of the time she didn't hit the shiny wooden lane at all. A few times she did manage to strike the signs for Freddy's Pizza and Earl's Lube Job, high above the pins. But that was only because she got a running start, tossing the ball when she was halfway down the lane.

"It's so difficult to get the ball into that tiny hole," she said to my father, extending her hands as if she were making an offering.

"You mean that big rectangle with the pins inside?" my father teased. She constantly reminded him that softball, the only other American game she had ever tried, was much easier.

At times she went to the other extreme, carefully pushing the ball down the alley in slow motion using both hands and as much force as she could muster. She was lucky if her ball even reached the gutter. Three times the owner had to come and rescue her ball from where it had come to a stop in the middle of the lane.

"With you, it's all or nothing," Dad remarked later, as we munched on fries in the snack bar. Fatima took it as a compliment, and asked me how I was doing at school.

"Fine," I said. "How's Theodore?" I wondered vaguely if he'd ever made it to Canada, where he would be able to do his stand-up comedy routines in Greek for a bunch of willing relatives.

She picked up the last fry, looked at it meaningfully and shook her head. "Fine," she answered, but her eyes turned abruptly away, as if someone had just hurt her.

That night, unable to sleep, I snuck downstairs. I thought I might have a chance to take photos of something in the house I'd missed on previous expeditions. Then I planned to load up a plate of food and park myself in front of the TV. When I turned on the kitchen light, however, I was shocked to find my mother sitting at the counter. She wasn't smoking or eating, just leaning her elbows on the Formica counter as if she had been waiting for me in the dark.

"Sit down," she said, patting the stool beside her.

I sat. "You can't avoid me forever. I know where you're really going with your father. I know he has a girlfriend, and he takes you as his cover. Take a kid along, so how could he really be on a date? But I know."

I'm not a kid anymore, I thought to myself.

"What I don't know is what crap he's been telling you. But I assure you," she said, as she reached into her house dress for a cigarette, "that it's crap."

"He doesn't say much about you." I paused, lifted my camera, and aimed it at her. She was so used to being photographed by me that she didn't notice.

"He doesn't say much true about me, that's what I'm telling you," she said.

I sighed and started to stand up, but she took my arm, pulled me back down and started speaking quickly. "I can tell you what is. I can tell you that your father, the night the baby died, walked out of this house and went to some slut. I can tell you your father blamed me for the baby—for getting pregnant and then for when he died. You think he wanted to have another one?

"And another thing you should know, Deborah. It's not Fat Fighters that made him so thin. It's diet pills. They made him crazy about the business, too, never coming home until god-knows-when. It wasn't my idea, this divorce. I tried everything, Deborah."

Her voice softened, and she paused as I snapped a photo. I caught half of her face with the stove in the background, although I figured the stove would come out blurry. "You remember those Saturday mornings you kids stayed at Leila's house?"

"Why are you telling me this?" I couldn't hide my irritation.

"That was so your father and I could go to marriage counseling at the temple, but you know what? Your father never showed up half the time. He would say it was useless, because he didn't want to be married to me anymore. He wanted a refund, a new wife, a prettier model from the store. 'This one I got from Two Guys isn't as good as the one I could get from Macy's, and I want to try a blonde this time.'"

Now she was going too far. "Leave me alone already, I have school tomorrow," I said, standing up again and trying to pull away.

"No, I have more to tell you."

"I don't want to hear it. Besides, everything you say is a lie." My voice was edgy and strong.

She ignored me, clutching my arm as if I hadn't say a word. "And you know what else? He filed for divorce without even telling me. I had a few friends over for mahjong when the papers came. No warning. No cares. He's ripping my life apart—and yours too, don't you forget it—for what? For some little shiksa?"

I jerked my arm away, breaking her grip on me. "You didn't try hard enough. It's your fault you're getting divorced," I said. Even as I pulled away, I was lifting the camera to photograph my mother with her face turned sharply toward me, green eyes filling with tears, one hand perched and ready to slap me, hard. I winced and waited, but couldn't push the clicker. I lowered the camera.

Once I could no longer see her through the viewfinder, my face heated up. I hated her. I wanted to tell her that, yet part of me believed her and wanted her to hold me. I stepped back in spite of myself.

She stared past me into the darkness of the dining room. In a voice with no trace of either sarcasm or self-confidence, she asked, "That's what you believe?"

"So he's not your boyfriend?" Eshe asked. We were sitting in Mr. Lexington's class trying to stay out of range of Seymour, a redheaded boy who frequently shot paper airplanes around the room, then laughed uncontrollably as if we weren't tenth-graders. I'd caught one of his more recent planes, so Eshe was wondering if it was actually a love note.

"Boyfriend? No way. I'd rather have needles stuck in my eyes. Better yet, stick them in his eyes."

Eshe laughed, and her friends laughed too. They were treating me as some possible cool-girl-in-waiting, who just needed the pregnancies, abortions, or violent outbursts to prove her coolness.

Mr. Lexington returned to the classroom and resumed his lecture on psychological projection. We had covered repression during the last class. Afterward, I had written a long journal entry about my mother, who was supremely repressed and, as a result, had driven my father away.

"Projection," he began, "is when you transfer your feelings about someone to the other person, as if he were the one who felt that way about you." (Did I only imagine that Mr. Lexington looked toward me with a certain tenderness in his eyes, before redirecting his attention to the class?) "For example, when I tell someone she's shy and repressed because I'm shy and repressed."

But I'm not repressed, I wanted to tell him. I'm just going through a lot.

A few days later the first winter storm arrived, and we stayed home from school. I dreaded being in the house all day with Mom, who snapped at me every chance she got, so I begged Dad to give me the keys to his room before he left for work. He handed them over without a blink.

The room looked pretty much the way it had always looked, except that the bureau and the bathroom no longer smelled of Mom's aging Jean Nate collection. The bed was made, the carpet immaculate. Actually, their bedroom never looked this nice, except when company was coming. I pulled open the levered doors to Dad's closet. Inside were many leisure suits, several pairs of those ankle boots he'd taken to wearing, and one pair of neatly arranged gray slippers.

I went to my mother's old closet and discovered old curtains stuffed on the shelf, a few hanging clothes in plastic (including her wedding dress and a hideous orange chiffon gown she'd worn to a cousin's wedding), a few pairs of dyed-to-match lavender and orange pumps, and not much else. I snapped some pictures, already knowing that they said little. Dead pictures and live pictures, Liz had explained last week.

"You want the live ones, the ones that hold some kind of ghost of what they're about. You know what I mean?" I wasn't sure I did, but Mark leaned toward her and said in a low voice, "Yeah, I know *exactly* what you mean." Everyone laughed then, Liz included.

A sharp knock on the door interrupted my thoughts. "Deborah, are you in there?"

I thought about not answering, but then I imagined her filing a runaway report with the police. "Yeah, leave me alone."

"Okay, I just wanted to make sure you're okay. I cooked some bacon and matzo-brei for breakfast, hon. Come on out and have some."

Bacon? She never made bacon, we didn't eat bacon unless we were in restaurants, yet I could distinctly smell its incredible allure. Matzo-fry was Dad's favorite food, a strange mixture of crumbled-up matzo, eggs, and a little water to mush it all together.

"No, I'm not hungry."

"I have plenty."

"I said I'm not hungry."

"You sure? I know you like bacon a lot," she said, more softly now.

"I'm sure," I yelled. I thought about Dad, telling me not to let her do to me what she did to him. She was always trying to manipulate us, I told myself. I added, "And leave me alone!"

Her voice went back to normal. "Suit yourself."

Then silence. I plopped down on the bed in front of the TV and watched game shows all morning. After awhile I lay down, still repeating the answers before the contestants at times.

When I woke up the house felt quiet around me, and I realized I was hungry. I unlocked the door as silently as possible and crept into the kitchen. I could hear my mother upstairs in my brother's room, first talking, then moving furniture around. I raced to the cupboard for a plate, and then to the refrigerator to fill it with leftover matzo-fry, two pudding packs, an orange (because it was healthy and cheerful-looking), a big hunk of salami with a dollop of mustard I shook out of the jar, and a handful of pretzel sticks from the baby's stash.

I had reached the door of my father's room, ready to lock myself in again, when the sound of my mother's voice made me jump. "I'm glad to see you won't starve." Ignoring her, I tucked my food and myself inside the big room for the rest of the day.

Sometime later, as I was watching *Match Game '75* and admiring Gene Rayburn's high cheekbones, I heard a knock at the window. I screamed, grabbed the phone and, with the receiver still in my hand, lifted the curtain high enough to see my Aunt Geraldine outside in the bare pussy willows. Since I had always liked her, I opened the window—but since she was also my mother's sister, I didn't open the storm window.

"What is it?"

"I thought we could talk," she said. "Why don't you let me in?" She had a scratchy voice that always felt both exciting and familiar to me.

She was wearing a forest green hat with matching scarf and gloves that made her red hair glow. It was a red she got out of a bottle, but I didn't care. I opened the window as wide as I could and she swung one long leg over the sill, then pulled the rest of her body inside. I snapped a picture of her standing upright before she lowered herself onto the bed beside me.

"Your mother is always your mother," she said.

"Yeah, I know that," I answered calmly, as if it were true.

"Your mother has always done for you. She's given up anything that kept her from you. Do you know about the tennis?"

"Yeah, she likes to play it, so what?" I instantly regretted sounding bratty.

"And you know she was offered a full tennis scholarship to college, that a coach at our high school said she was Olympic quality? Of course you don't know that. Your mother walked away from it all for that father of yours, and she didn't ever want to burden you with it."

"But she was the one who wanted to get married!"

"Is that what your father told you?"

Geraldine explained that Dad had convinced Mom to give up her dreams, that her own mother had conspired with him to push her into marriage. She told me Mom was afraid of being "pinned down" by my father or any other man, that she lived for the Olympics. I tried not to look sheepish. Aunt Geraldine thought I was just a kid, but maybe I was. I tried to imagine my mother on the Olympic team, playing tennis for a gold medal.

Next my aunt told me about Dad's temper, how he once threw Mom's tennis racket at her so hard that she had the lines of the netting on her cheek for a week. How my mother worked at a shoe store the first year of the marriage and saved all her money so she could take night classes in phys ed, then gave Dad all the money to buy the taxi business from Grandpa. There were the women, too.

"Imagine it, even when she was big as a house, pregnant with you kids, there was always a little someone on the side." The bottoms of my feet itched. I didn't want to hear any of it, and I was suddenly very tired.

By the time Geraldine crawled back out the window (I offered to unlock the door, but she said my mother had no idea she was here and she wanted to keep it that way), my eyes felt exhausted. I opened the small drawer of the night table. Nothing there but a red box of Diet-Aid capsules emblazoned with the slogan, "Add zip, not excess food, to your life." I looked at my stomach, which was still mostly flat, but for how long? I turned on the TV but found nothing to watch except soap operas.

Before I could think of what to do, the phone rang. My father was on the other end, saying he would be working late because of the storm. Could I call Fatima and tell her we wouldn't make it to the movie with her tonight?

"What movie?"

"That teen film. What's it called? *Sherry? Cathy?* No, *Carrie.*"

Why go to a horror film, I wondered, when your life is one already? His voice seemed higher, more pinched, not the voice of someone I wanted to be with all night. I hung up, unlocked the door, and went to the kitchen. My mother was banging a frozen package of lamb against the counter, trying to separate the chops.

"Here, use this." I handed her a letter opener to use to pry them apart. She glanced at me briefly, nodded, and went back to work on the lamb chops.

"You want that instant stuffing you like so much?" she asked, trying not to look too pleased, as if she'd won something.

I nodded and sat down on the couch with one of her women's magazines. Outside, all the around the house, a cold, glassy layer of ice coated the branches. Behind me, I could hear Mom opening and closing cabinets, talking to Missy, yelling for Roger to change the channel to her favorite show. Eventually she called me to set the table. I went right to her, as if it was the most normal thing in the world, and strangely enough it was.

Chapter Six

Fatima looked ecstatically happy, Dad was glowing, and I was bored. We were on the third story of a sloppy brick building in the garment district of Manhattan, watching hundreds of Puerto Rican and black women guiding long lines of fabric under the speeding needles of factory sewing machines. Dad and Fatima were speaking quietly with the only other white person in the place, a short man in a white button-down shirt and tight white slacks. He looked like a bad imitation of Don Rickles. Through the windows of the building across the street, I could see more captive rows of women bent over sewing machines, hands darting up to direct the fabric. Overhead, shaky heaters blasted out hot air every so often, and then the room went starkly cold again.

Fatima and Dad had fashioned a plan: they would buy up irregulars of stretch pants and tops for fat women. Fatima reasoned that these women needed cheap clothing the most. Then they—this actually meant me—would tag the clothing, load it onto a truck, and sell it each Saturday at the Englishtown Auction, which according to Fatima was the biggest flea market in the free world. We had come up with the plan last week at the diner. I was excited about my first real job, which would pay ten dollars a week, plus Dad promised to buy me all the film I wanted and pay for developing, too, no questions asked. This was the best part of the plan as far as I was concerned, since Mom had recently announced, as we picked up my prints at Two Guys, that she couldn't afford the expense anymore. From now on, she'd insisted, I would have to limit myself to one roll a month.

Dad signaled to me to follow the floor manager over to the cutting area, where huge stacks of fabric lay piled on tables. Men in sleeveless T-shirts sliced through the piles as if they were stacks of Sicilian pizza. I lifted up my camera, trying not to be too obvious, and snapped a dozen photos in all directions.

"These," the manager said, pointing to a dozen boxes on the floor. He bent over, opened one, and pulled out a pair of women's double-knit polyester slacks with black and white checks, size 46. The slacks also came in blue, black, bright screaming orange, vomit yellow, dark green, and paisley. Fatima clapped her hands together, my father pulled out his wad of money, and the manager signaled to one of the sleeveless workers to load the boxes onto a dolly. Once we'd sold these, he explained, we could come back in a few weeks for more.

"There's always more," the manager said matter-of-factly. "These girls always screw up. The colored, you know how they are." I looked away from him, embarrassed. I wondered if there was a way to show through my photographs that he was a racist.

As if he had read my mind, he suddenly noticed the camera around my neck and asked my father, "She's not going to do anything with those pictures, is she?"

"Her?" Dad answered. He seemed surprised that I was taking pictures again; it was something he never got used to. "Nah, it's just a school project. And she's a crappy photographer anyway. No one would be able to make out who's in any of the photos." The men laughed and I stepped back, ashamed, although I knew he was wrong about my abilities. I had very clear focusing, according to Liz. The problem was with what I was seeing.

Half an hour later we were back in the car, me riding in the back seat on top of a box. Two more boxes were stuffed under my legs, while the other passenger seat and the rear of the station wagon were packed to the ceiling. Even Fatima had a box nuzzled against her like a square poodle. Four more boxes were tied to the roof rack. As we headed into the Holland Tunnel, my neck ached from bending over to avoid hitting my head on the roof of the car. Yet somehow, hidden among all those boxes, I felt a strange kind of happiness.

Mom, who hated baking as much as cats hate baths, had promised we would bake knishes together that night. When I asked Dad to drop me off, he insisted that we stop at Fatima's first to unload the boxes before it rained. He failed to mention, however, that she lived twenty minutes in the opposite direction. Even with good traffic, I knew we would be an hour late. I considered stopping at a phone booth, but Fatima assured me that I could call my mother from her house.

By the time we got to Fatima's mustard-yellow ranch house, it was pouring. The boxes from the roof felt like wet bags of groceries, but even more slippery. We struggled to carry them across the wet stones of her walkway and into the living room, which smelled of oregano. Several times the polyester clothing spilled into the yard, and we dropped to our hands and knees in the mud. Fatima yelled at us to hurry as Dad hummed and lifted each pair of pants carefully, so as not to unfold them, and I wildly grabbed big bundles of polyester and dumped them in the house. At one point I grabbed Fatima's phone to dial home, but the line was busy. Fatima and Dad kept running up and down the stairs to Fatima's basement, where they hung some pants on clotheslines and stuffed the rest into the dryer. Dad kept muttering that it would only take another fifteen minutes. I started to freak out, but I didn't say a word.

When we finally got back on the road, Fatima kept apologizing as Dad drove, head tilted down, at high speed. By now we were almost two hours late. I kept telling myself that there was no reason to get worked up over being late. Mom never went anywhere, and she could just as easily make knishes with me if I were late rather than on time. But something about my logic felt all wrong, and I knew deep inside that I was hurting her more with each passing minute.

The house was dark when we arrived and Mom's car was gone—or maybe in the garage, I thought hopefully. My father, without being told, stayed behind in the driveway as I got out of the car. Inside the house was that good knish smell, yet somehow it smelled like fear to me now. By the time I reached the kitchen and saw the cookie sheets covered with small, misshapen, cold knishes, I knew I had ruined my mother's life again. Hadn't she been telling me how selfish and inconsiderate I was, ever since I was born? At least it seemed that way. I started crying hysterically, in a way that I couldn't ever remember crying before. It hurt so much that I gulped for air between sobs, grabbing the kitchen door handle before I crumbled to the floor. Why couldn't she have waited? None of this was my fault, but that didn't help. Somehow, it was all my fault.

I knew I had to leave. I couldn't stay in this house any longer, not when Mom hated me so much. I got back on my feet and left the house of knish, walking gingerly to the car as if I were carrying a giant bowl of water and trying not to spill it. I climbed into the back seat, shivering, and lay down right away, curling up into a tight ball to keep warm.

Fatima leaned over me, her hand landing on my shoulder as I hid my face. "I'm so sorry, Deborah. But I will make the food with you."

I tried to nod. I wondered if I should have taken pictures of those cookie sheets. I could have gotten some interesting shots of the knishes, maybe close-ups of the mangled ones. Then I imagined a self-portrait of me collapsed on the kitchen floor. If I had held the camera high above me with one hand, it might have been a good photo, one that would make Liz raise her eyebrows.

I roused myself as we pulled into the diner parking lot. For a moment I thought we were there to eat dinner—maybe I could drink a cola for energy. But as soon as we got inside, Fatima grabbed my arm and pulled me into the kitchen.

"Chicken croquettes, knishes—we will do both. I will be a mother to you," she crooned. Dad sat down at a table to read the paper and I followed Fatima, worried that she could see I'd been crying. She kept her eyes averted out of respect as she got out ingredients.

We didn't talk much. Fatima would hand me an egg, a bowl, and a fork, then swirl her hand to let me know I should beat the egg. I watched how she mashed and shaped the potatoes from the brown hulks we had peeled together side by side, thirty minutes ago. It went on like this, with pots on every burner sizzling or boiling continuously as the fast-moving Greek chef and several waiters milled around us, the wash of heat from the industrial oven flooding us whenever we opened the door, making me feel almost human again.

"You know why I left my husband?" she asked suddenly.

We were pulling a tray of knishes out of the oven and putting the tray of croquettes inside. I shook my head politely, still not wanting to meet her eyes.

Instead of answering, she grabbed my wrist and directed my hand to push up her sleeve. My fingers touched a black mark, more like a smudge of dead skin than a bruise. Then she showed me her other wrist, how it bumped up as if the bone were twisted out of place. She took my hand again and placed it on the base of her neck, pushing my fingers up under her hairline so I could feel the depression, a place where the skin caved in slightly.

"Your ex-husband, the one who went to Canada—did he do this?"

She shook her head. "My first love," she said quietly. "A long time ago. Not here."

"What happened?"

She looked away. "I was young. I was a girl."

"Were you married to him?"

Quietly, so that I could barely hear her, she said, "Yes, but it was far away."

We looked at each other shyly. She turned back to the sauce she was stirring and added, "There is more, some I had fixed." She met my eyes again as she touched the place where her cleavage began. "But some, you can never fix. You think you survive"—she pulled her sleeves back down as she spoke—"but you carry it inside you. Big or little, you carry what happened."

That night, I slept on Fatima's couch while Dad shared the small back bedroom with her. I leaned into the plush of the old sofa and tried to imagine living here, a place where there seemed to be all kinds of ways to prepare forgiveness. The anticipation of something good filled the air. After I fell asleep, I dreamt of learning how to drive and getting lost in a city where I had never been before.

Chapter Seven

Trapped inside my mother's brown station wagon, I whipped around like an animal. Every time my mother put her key in the lock, I lunged over to hold down the button on the car door and keep her out. Standing beside her was my brother, chewing gum and looking at the ground, and a short, bald man who looked exactly the way I imagined a shrink would. He was frowning and talking quietly to my mother, but it seemed to do no good. My mother, her face more crooked than ever, her lip curled to one side, screamed like my animal counterpart, banging on the windows and yelling, "I'm going to get you out if it's the last thing I do!"

"You're not going to touch me, you bitch!" I screamed back. She banged on the door handle. "Stop it. I hate you!" I yelled louder.

In her fur-trimmed green coat and white running suit, Mom was sweating even though the air was freezing. Her face looked like she wanted to rip right into me, but she couldn't speak because she was crying too hard. She backed away and then turned toward the doctor. A moment later the three of them crossed the gravel parking lot and entered a small, neat building. I wondered what Roger was thinking that allowed him to go along with this charade. I noticed he was carrying a new comic book, so maybe she had bribed him.

A week ago, she had started slipping letters under my father's bedroom door during the times when I locked myself inside, generally after school and before dinner at the diner. She wrote that she was sorry she didn't wait for me to make knishes, that she understood it was my father's fault, that she was still my mother. I was so relieved that I started leaving letters for her on the kitchen counter—chatty letters about school and photography, as if I were away at college and cheerfully writing home. After a few exchanges, we agreed to stop at a new photography store one day after school. I looked at it as our way of making up—and a way to get some supplies on the list Liz had given me of what I needed to set up my own darkroom.

At first the outing seemed perfectly normal. The baby was staying with the other Bev, and Roger enjoyed looking at the graphing supplies. ("A genius at math," Mom whispered to me.) The store was bigger than the one in Woodridge, but I quickly found my way to the darkroom supplies. I picked out a thick envelope of contact paper and glanced at the bottles of developer, quickly adding the costs in my head. I told myself it wouldn't be that much, not if I contributed some of the money I'd make at the Englishtown Auction. I turned back to Mom.

"I can set this all up in the closet under the stairs, the one with hardly anything in it. I mean, I could move the other stuff into the garage for you. I already found a good place."

"Fine," she answered. "Haul that old stuff away, but I don't want any chemicals all over the new rug, you got me?"

I nodded and smiled, imagining what it would be like to lock myself inside that tiny closet and print my own photographs under a single red light. In my mind, I was already turning the wooden cartons from our garage into low worktables when a salesman with long hair parted down the middle appeared, smiling as if he knew this would be a big sale. Without missing a beat, Mom said, "Get her suited up, whatever she needs," and headed toward Roger, who was investigating acrylic paints with the rigor of a scientist.

"I was thinking of starting my own darkroom," I told the clerk. He grinned even more broadly and swooped into action.

On the ride home, Mom talked nonstop about how great it was that I had photography as an outlet. I noticed that she was studying the road signs with great interest, as if she were looking for something. "Whenever you go down different roads, like the one we're on right now, there's so much more to see."

"Are you lost?" I asked.

"No, I just need to stop somewhere on the way home. You'll like it."

"Where?"

"You'll see."

I was a quiet for a few minutes, then said, "Tell me where now."

"It'll be good for us," she said. "I've been going for a few weeks, and it's helping me. You know, there's nothing wrong with needing some help sometimes in your life. Everybody, at some time or another –"

"A shrink? You're taking me to a shrink?" We were pulling into the parking lot in front of a small building with a sign that simply read, "Professional Building."

"A psychologist. He's very nice, calm, a sweet man, and he specializes in families like us." She settled into a parking spot near the entrance and eased the transmission into park.

"I'm not going. You said this was just to get photo supplies. I'm not going to see anyone—I don't care what you want to do." My voice sounded strangely calm, although I felt myself starting to shake.

"Deborah, calm down. It will be nice for you. It will be fun—you can even call me names."

"I don't care, I'm not going!"

"Yes, you are going," she said, more sternly now.

"No, I'm not. You tricked me, and you can't make me do anything. You're just like Dad said you were."

"Now young lady, you listen to me."

"Fuck you!" I screamed. I'd never said those words to anyone before.

Before I could unfasten my seatbelt she raced around the car, faster than I thought she could move, and opened the passenger door. I flipped around to kick her away, but she came at me again, trying to grab me and pull me out. This time, I kicked her so hard that she fell over backwards. As my brother rushed over to her I slammed the car door shut and locked it, then leapt into the driver's seat and locked that door, too. Roger helped her up, and they walked into the building without looking back.

I breathed hard, trying to catch myself. Now that they were gone, I noticed a light snow falling. I was still shaking, crying a little too, my whole body like a terrified animal caught in a trap. I wondered how I could convey all of that in a photo, how to capture the contrast between me, scared, and the calm flakes of the first snow. My gym teacher advised us to breathe slowly when our heart rates went up, so I started counting to four on each inhalation and exhalation. I thought of climbing out of the car and running away, but all I saw nearby was an out-of-business gas station and a highway. I had no idea which direction would take me home, or even to a pay phone.

A knock at the window made me jump. It was the therapist; my mother and brother were nowhere to be found. He signaled to me to lower the window, so I opened it a tiny crack and he leaned down. "You don't have to come in and talk to me. It's your decision. I just want you to know I respect your ability to make your own decisions."

I didn't let myself look into his eyes.

"I'm sorry you were tricked into coming here. That was never our intention, but your mother wanted to help you, and she thought this was best."

Glancing up, I discovered that he had blue eyes, a face shaped like an egg, and dimples. I pulled out my camera and took some pictures of him through the glass—bad photos, I knew, but it felt like a way to protect myself, to keep this camera between him and me.

He pretended not to notice what I was doing. "I realize you probably don't want to talk now, but in case you ever do, here's my card." He slipped a business card through the cracked window and I took it, still without a word. Then he turned and walked back into the building.

I briefly touched the card's raised print, then stuffed it into the bag of darkroom supplies and climbed into the back seat with my camera. That was still too close to my mother, so I climbed all the way to the very back where Roger and I liked to sit when we were small, making faces at the drivers behind us.

I curled up with a box of contact paper over my legs to keep them warm and fell sleep, my camera cradled on my belly like a baby. I covered my eyes with the sleeve of a black sweater I found. Very soon, I heard people walking on the gravel, circling the car. I didn't move, and soon, doors opened, Mom and Roger got in, and the doors closed. No one talked. I pretended to be in a deep sleep all the way home. Only after I felt the car turn into the drive and Roger and Mom get out did I sit up, climb over the seat, and drag my new things into my room. I pushed a desk against the door, in case Mom tried to talk to me. Then I hid the darkroom supplies under my bed, buried under an old stuffed Snoopy and some clothes I had long ago outgrown.

Dad wouldn't be home for a few more hours, so I started writing in my journal for English class. I was supposed to turn in three pages a week to Mrs. Levine, who promised not to read what we wrote, but simply count the pages. I wrote that I wished my mother had died, or that somehow I could have a new mother, someone like Fatima who wouldn't turn on me. The more I wrote, the more I realized I wished it were me who had died. At the very least, I wanted to go to sleep for a year or two and wake up after this divorce was over. When I'd finished writing, I ripped the card from the psychotherapist into the tiniest pieces I could manage and dropped them into the wastebasket. Then I took a picture.

On the first Saturday of the Englishtown Auction, the temperature hadn't yet mounted above zero when Dad crept over to Fatima's couch to wake me. Although it was five AM, I could hear Fatima in the kitchen humming, brewing coffee for the thermoses, the lights all over her house strangely ignited. I climbed quickly out of the afghan she had wrapped around me and into my clothes.

By the time we crawled into Fatima's new gold van, adorned with the logo of a now-defunct band called "Shifting Explosion," it was still pitch black. As planned, I stretched myself out across the bottoms of two racks of blouses, the cold metal biting through my clothing, to keep the racks from tipping over. Fatima sat on one box with another under her feet, and several boxes were jammed around the racks to keep them in place.

When we arrived at the auction, it was my job to arrange neat piles of giant pants according to size, starting with 40 and ending with the largest of the large, 52. I concentrated on piling the pants with the folded edge out, each stack an art project. Dad carted the heavy racks of blouses and Fatima disappeared in search of more change. When she returned with a cup of hot cocoa for me in her hands, she looked unbelievably happy standing there at six AM in long underwear, layers of clothes, a black and white fake fur coat, and a wool granny hat. I wore my favorite pea coat, wool cap, and mittens. I had refused—stupidly, I realized now—to put on the long underwear Dad bought me because I thought it would make me look bulkier.

The light slowly made its way to us, and so did the people. A large black woman in a thin white coat asked, "How much?" When I told her, "Two for five dollars," she nodded without looking at me. A minute later she handed me ten dollars and walked off with four pairs of size 44 pants, all in dark blue. I reached under the table for another dark blue stack, size 44, and overheard Fatima happily selling blouses, over-emphasizing her accent as if being foreign made for better clothes. Dad leaned against the building behind us, coming forward only to talk to the most attractive women. Fatima shot him a look as he bragged to a small redhead about what it takes to make a business like this go, and he disappeared.

I discovered that I could sell pants without talking much. One woman, slightly overweight and carting a bundled-up toddler, asked if I would stick three pairs of size 40 pants in the bag.

"What color?"

"I don't care," she said, so I selected the red, the brown, and the black.

The booth next door to ours suddenly sprang to life with a cry of, "EARRRRRLY CALLERS! Come in and buy two shirts for two bucks for two minutes." As I turned to look, a man the size of a telephone pole reached out to me and grabbed my hands.

"Ma'am, I'm really Latvia Larry, but you can call me Boy," he said. Gesturing to the elegant older man, much shorter than Boy, who sat guarding the entrance to the booth, he added, "And you can call him Big Boy."

I hurriedly told him my name and muttered an excuse about getting back to the customers, but he wasn't finished. He yelled out that the strange-looking Slavic gentleman selling low-cut women's sweaters across the way was Sergei. Sergei, who actually looked rather kindly, pointed at me and then to his sweaters, as if suggesting that I come over and try one on. I shook my head and gestured to the piles of pants before me.

Dad reappeared with a bundle of dark blue nylon in his arms. "Parkas," he said, "for all of us."

Fatima squealed and tore off her coat. Dad clapped his hands and I reluctantly removed my pea coat. The parkas were warm and came all the way down to our knees, and the hood helped a lot with the wind. From the back, we looked like a little family of bears in the woods.

The day dragged on with Fatima bringing me food every hour or two: French fries in a small paper bag, tasting better than anything I'd ever eaten before, a chocolate cream donut, chili, some kind of Italian pastry. She was our runner, rushing out into the larger world and shepherding back nourishment. In between eating and selling, Dad and I took turns running over to a barrel filled with burning coals and warming our hands.

Refolding pants after a careless customer had pawed through the pile without buying anything, I thought about last week's conversation with my father's lawyer. He was a tiny man who always called me "doll" and kissed my forehead. Dad kept forgetting his long Italian name, so we called him Manicotti behind his back. He had instructed me as to what I should tell the judge if I decided to live with Dad. If I stayed with Dad, we would probably get to keep the house. The very idea of staying in my own room was reason enough for me to choose Dad—every bit as important as avoiding Mom.

I hadn't spoken to Mom in two weeks, but I watched her sometimes through my upstairs window. She carried the baby to the car in the morning, yelling at my brother to follow; at night, she'd walk out to the sidewalk in her bathrobe and sit down at the edge of the begonia garden, smoking cigarettes and staring at the empty street. My heart softened as she tossed the butts away, and I wondered if I should try to talk to her. Then I remembered the look on her face as she tried to drag me out of the car and into counseling. That look always locked me away again.

Returning to the barrel of glowing coals to warm my hands, I wondered what it would be like to be an orphan in some unpronounceable Slavic country, getting through the long winter by my wits. Just then an old man with a heavy accent sidled up next to me, completing the picture. "Eh, cookie, cold today, very cold," he murmured sympathetically. I recognized Sergei and felt thankful that he was the grandfatherly type, with a face that looked like an old potato gone soft.

"Big girl, good way to be, you come to my booth? I keep you warm," he continued, winking and patting his groin.

His words brought me back with a jerk to real life, where everything was unscripted and dangerous. I turned away and ran back to our stand, my home base every Saturday from now on.

Chapter Eight

Fatima and I walked through the auction together in early spring, just after the afternoon rush. She was talking fast, leading me past pickled pig's feet and giant salamis in search of a dress I could wear in court. The first stand we visited had nothing but strapless beaded gowns that reeked of old popcorn, vinegar, and cotton candy. I snapped a few close-ups of the wares.

"It's important you look old enough to make your own choices. You know what I mean." I nodded, as if we were co-conspirators. "Tomorrow, I can show you how to do makeup. Not a lot, because you still want to look young, but just something to help a little." I pictured Fatima's bedroom, where one whole bureau top was covered with lipsticks and eye shadow, the vast numbers of cosmetics further multiplied by the bureau's giant mirror.

We next passed a nest of sweater dresses, Izod shirt dresses, and giant floral muumuus hawked by a tiny girl with long yellow hair who cried, "Muumuus, get your muumuus, cheap and big!" Fatima steered me into a cocoon of racks that held business attire, stiff navy suits with double-breasted jackets. I let her pick out something for me and hold it up against my torso with my camera still poking through. All the while I was staring at a rack of tea-length dresses, particularly an off-white one with little roses at the bodice. I might wear that very dress to prom next year. I would lean over the ledge of a white balcony as Mr. Lexington brought me a glass of champagne. "Sorry about your life lately," he'd say. Then he'd bend down and kiss me lightly on the lips, his hand holding my chin.

On the way back to our booth, my new jacket and skirt secure in a bag labeled "Lulu's Headshop," Fatima and I didn't say much. I was still imagining my evening with Mr. Lexington, who would drape the silky weight of his blazer over my shoulders whenever a breeze swept across the patio. We would pose for a photograph, the two of us leaning toward each other against a brilliant sunset. Fatima stared straight ahead.

When we reached the booth, Dad handed Fatima a thick pile of money and disappeared into the crowd. Meanwhile, someone placed two five-dollar bills in my hand. I looked up to see a large blonde woman who was almost in tears. Clutching four pairs of black stretch pants to her chest, she exclaimed, "Thank you. You people are the only place I can go to get something to wear so I can leave the house. Bless you for bringing me back out in the world."

"What the world needs now," Boy sang, loud and clear next door, "is love, sweet love."

Although I tried to focus on the piles of pants, I spent most of my free time daydreaming about Mr. Lexington. I imagined him asking me to help him get supplies after class. He would turn to me in the dim supply room and whisper, "Listen, I'm not getting married after all, because I'm in love with someone else."

"She must be pretty lucky," I'd answer coyly.

"Yes, but there's a hitch. She still has two years and two months of school to go, but if she could only wait for me"—he'd gaze at me, his blue eyes shining like they had sun behind them—"I will love her forever." With that he would kiss me, and we'd walk back to the classroom carrying our boxes of pencils.

I wasn't deluded enough to actually believe in my fantasies, but it helped during those afternoons when I sat invisible in the back room of Karmic Clothes, listening to Liz and Eshe fire quips at each other as they reviewed Eshe's sharply focused photographs of her gentle father and furious mother. It helped whenever I fell asleep to the strains of my parents screaming at each other downstairs, right below my feet. It helped when I stood at the clothing booth for hours, my feet aching and burning before I even got home. I had polished my fantasy to the point where I had every detail worked out, including the hours leading up to and following that kiss and promise.

Needless to say, I was shocked when one day Mr. Lexington turned to me in the middle of class and sent me to the supply room for chalk. I obediently rose from my chair and walked into the hallway, as if I were in a dream. When I opened the supply room door and clicked on the single light bulb, I was disappointed to find that it was nothing more than an overgrown closet. As I reached for a box of white chalk, I felt the heat of another person at my back. It was Mr. Lexington, and he was smiling. I started trembling.

"Oh, Deborah, I forgot to tell you, we need an eraser, too. Bill tossed ours out the window yesterday."

We laughed rather nervously as he reached over my head to pluck an eraser from the top of a chalky pyramid of erasers. There was a smell on him that reminded me of clothes on a clothesline, with sweat and cologne mixed together.

We retreated from the supply room and walked side by side back to class. "So, fate got your tongue lately?"

"No, but the cat does."

He smiled. "Good one, my dear, but there's no reason to let the cat keep your tongue. You can talk," he said, leaning slightly toward me as we walked, "to me."

"Oh, it's hard to begin," I said. "Things get so complicated."

"Try me."

He wanted to be there for me. A little song ran happily up my spine as I tried to think of something I could say, without sounding like the whiny daughter of divorcing parents.

"I can tell when one of our great future philosophers runs out of philosophy," he teased.

I wanted to tell him that I was a photographer, not a philosopher. Philosophers knew what they were doing. Artists didn't, according to Liz. Before I could form the appropriate words we were back in class, and he was joking with the students that he couldn't leave for a minute without them missing him horribly, his focus far away as if we'd never spoken.

Against my better judgment, I asked Dad to drop me off at a school dance the following Friday. It was my sixteenth birthday, but my mother hadn't said a word to me. I looked around the kitchen to see if my relatives had sent gifts, but didn't see any. I finally reminded Dad what day it was as I climbed out of the car. He looked guilty for half a second, then pulled out his roll of money and peeled off a twenty. I stuck the bill in the pocket of my hip huggers as I walked away. "Don't let the boys feel you," he called after me.

His words startled me so much that I jumped, but then I continued walking as if nothing had been said. I had my hair pulled back in a ponytail, which made me look a little older. At least that's what I told myself as I stood in front of the bathroom mirror, trying some of Mom's blue eye shadow and then wiping it off because it made me look like her.

Once inside I found a table with Tina, a girl from my social studies class. She had clearly perfected the art of eye shadow and those dangerous-looking eyelash curlers.

"You like that paper airplane guy?" she asked me.

"No, of course not." Tina wore a low-cut red shirt and a matching choker with a little dangling cameo. I wished I dressed like her. She was small and shapely—okay, I wished I looked like her.

"Oh, too bad for you."

"What do you mean? He's a nerd."

"He's rich, though. His grandpa invented something, I think the paper towel."

We both laughed a little, Tina hunting through her purse for a cigarette. I looked out over the dark terrain that served at various times as cafeteria, gym, and dance floor. There were just a few clumps of people talking excitedly. The band was starting up, a small group of guys called the Fireballs. In a moment the room filled with noise as kids gravitated toward the center of the dance area. They stood there moving slightly, as if they were mainly interested in talking but couldn't keep their bodies from pulsating a little.

When Tina slipped out with some other girls for a smoke, I tried to act as if sitting at this lunch table watching the dancing was all I really wanted to do. I hoped no one could see me. That's when I noticed Mr. Lexington next to a woman with thick, wavy hair pulled back with gold barrettes from her heart-shaped face. They smiled at each other knowingly. After seeing me, he waved enthusiastically in my direction and whispered something to her.

"Wow, she's a fox," said Linda, a girl from math class who had sat down beside me. She was considerably short and wide and didn't have many friends, so I guessed that's why she came to my table. "But then, that's what you'd expect with someone like Tom."

"Tom?"

"Mr. Lexington. His first name is Tom. Don't you know that?"

If I left now, I would have to walk right past Mr. Lexington—Tom—and his girlfriend, and then I would have no place to go. So I sat still, wishing I were against the wall where no one could see me. The kids on the dance floor started moving a little faster and talking to each other a little less. My head hurt, the music was too loud, but I tapped the table anyway, acting like I was into it. I don't know how many songs came and went, but eventually even Linda got up to dance. I decided it wasn't bad to be here, just boring.

Then I heard a familiar voice. "*The* birthday is here. Aren't you my birthday dance partner?" It was Mr. Lexington, and of course he knew it was my birthday, because it was his, too.

I was nervous, but somehow I made it to the dance floor anyway. I was afraid my body would suddenly jerk or twist the wrong way. Whenever I rehearsed in front of the mirror, I looked stupid if I tried to be sexy so I moved like a robot the rest of the time.

As we stepped onto the dance floor, we were enveloped by the sounds of Dianna Ross's "Do You Know Where You're Going To." Mr. Lexington, without missing a beat, pulled my body against his, put one arm around my waist, and held out the other and clasped my hand. I draped my free arm around him, although it felt awkward.

He was actually an inch or so taller than me, but somehow it seemed as if we were the same height. My hips lined up with his hips, my shoulders with his shoulders, my chest pressed into his chest, my thighs brushed against his thighs. We rocked around the dance floor just like the other couples, the ones who were planning on having sex later in the back of a car. Out of the corner of my eye, I saw Eshe pressing up against some guy as she balanced on six-inch heels in a pair of low-cut jeans. She laughed deeply, shook her head, and acted drunk as she clutched her partner's bottom to pull him closer.

The dancing went on for three and a half minutes. I learned that fact the next day, after I bought the album and timed that song. It was the best part of my sophomore year. When it was over, Mr. Lexington thanked me as we backed away from each other abruptly. I rushed to the bathroom, ready to call Dad to come get me. The moment I'd dreamed of had come true. As I walked past the mirrors over the sinks I saw myself glowing, my face lit up by more than the florescent lights.

But when I turned to look at myself head-on, I noticed that the neck of my sweater was off-center, and the light blue that had seemed so feminine actually looked like something a junior high girl would wear. Aside from my height, I really was nothing more than a junior high kid: my waist didn't go in enough, I had no hips to speak of, and no curves, even though I did put a few tissues in my bra. My appearance was all wrong, and in a moment someone appeared to confirm it for me.

Eshe unexpectedly burst from one of the stalls, moving fast. "Hey, screwing your social studies teacher?" she asked. She pulled her shoulders up fast, exhaled, and slammed the bathroom door behind her before I could think of a reply. Ashamed and confused, I shook a little as I headed toward the pay phones.

Later that night, I wrote in my English class journal about dancing with someone who resembled Mr. Lexington. I didn't name him or mention his age, just in case Mrs. Levine cheated and read my entry. After writing for a while, I remembered Eshe's comment. If she could see it, couldn't everyone? Couldn't he?

My thoughts were interrupted by my mother's screams. When I ran to the top of the stairs and looked down, I saw my father dragging her wedding dress outside. She ran after him and I quietly followed with my camera, tracking them around the house to the backyard. There, he pulled the gown from its plastic casing and reached into his pocket for a lighter.

"Don't," she cried. "It's mine, you can't do this. You can't destroy what's mine."

He shook his head as if she were merely a child, lighting one sleeve of the dress as she tugged on the other. Eventually the dress ripped apart with one half burning, the other half covered in mud. I was just in time to capture the whole scene on film.

A few days later, I showed Liz my latest series of "domestic destruction photos." She flipped through them before the other students arrived, telling me I had a good eye and an offbeat way of framing things. Once class began, she referred to my instinct for finding "the picture in the picture."

"You want to do that, too?" she asked the other students. "Then you need to drop the way you usually see things, get naked so you see exactly what's real." I flushed with embarrassment at how she ended a comment that had started with me.

"So you gotta be naked to make art?" Mark asked. He hadn't brought any new photos to class for several weeks.

"Hey, I'm always naked when I make art," said Eshe. She winked at me to show her approval of the burning wedding gown. "Burn, baby, burn," she muttered, making everyone laugh again.

"Hey babes, it's all about anticipating the anticipation. No mind games, no pretense. You just drop your shit at the door and show up for the photo," Liz said, passing around a box of jelly donuts.

As I bit into the sweetness, I wondered if the bitter taste of what I was photographing could be passed around and shared with other people. I wasn't sure I was naked enough to see what I was capable of, but then I realized that maybe even thinking this was a way to be not just a photographer, but also an artist. Despite my life, I smiled. Liz pointed at me, and said, "See? What did I tell you: get naked and eat donuts. That's all it takes."

Chapter Nine

At seven thirty in the morning there was still a slight chill in the air. I picked up my camera, my yellow social studies notebook, and the textbook I'd never opened the night before and trotted down the stairs. For some reason I felt happy for a change, maybe because school would be over in a month, or because the court date was only two days away and then everything would all be settled. Fatima said there was no need to rush—after the divorce she would stay in her own house, which made me realize they must have been talking about getting married.

I was halfway out the door when I saw the gray silhouette of my mother in the shadow of the living room. She wasn't smiling, and her arms were folded across her chest. "And where do you think you're going?"

"School," I answered calmly, as if it hadn't been weeks since we'd talked.

"There is none." She seemed smaller, her face tighter than usual. I couldn't stand looking at her.

"Sure there is, there's always school," I joked, fidgeting in the doorway.

"No," she said. "It's an in-service day. The teachers sit on their fat asses, eat danishes all day, and complain about you kids."

I paused with one foot on the threshold, one foot still in the house. I dreaded the thought of staying home with my mother for the whole day, not knowing what she would try next. I casually said I was going to take a walk, a long walk, good exercise, you know.

"I'll put your books away upstairs," she offered, sounding strangely upbeat as she reached out for the stack in my hands, her breath close enough for me to smell the cigarettes she was living on lately. "Oh, and Mimi is coming over later, just a little visit on her way home from Florida. She'll want to see you."

A visit from Mimi required me to sit by her side, prepared to run to the kitchen whenever she wanted seltzer water, a cracker, or the blue eye shadow that she applied to my lids to "make me look right." I would watch the grandfather clock to determine when I had spent enough time with her. Usually, I calculated the interval at thirty-five minutes—"almost an hour," I would tell Mom later.

I started stumbling after excuses, something about having a lot of homework to do, but Mom pried the books out of my hands. "No, go take your walk." She started up the stairs as if she were just a mother trying to help, although of course she saw, out of the corner of her eye, that I still had my camera with me, as I always did these days.

I went outside and walked, listening as the hidden birds made their noise. It felt easier to be alive once I was away from Mom, and Dad, too. Yellow irises were blooming in front of virtually every house on the block, as if God had ordered the neighbors to plant them, and the comforting blue sky was overhead. Yet something still felt vaguely wrong to me. I photographed the irises, trying to include a car bumper in some of the pictures to show that I knew life wasn't so beautiful. Liz would like this, I thought.

I was shooting the big cluster of yellow irises in front of Linda Finkel's house when I suddenly realized why something felt wrong. Last night, I'd absent-mindedly stuck my English class journal inside my yellow social studies notebook—the very notebook my mother had just removed from my hands. I raced back to the house, hoping against hope that the baby had distracted Mom enough to keep her from opening the journal immediately. Some mothers might respect their daughter's privacy, but I knew better. The sidewalk bumped up and down under my feet, the camera striking my chest with every stride, my breath loud ahead of me, everything too hot to bear.

Even as my hand touched the doorknob, I knew I was too late. Mom was screaming into the telephone receiver. As soon as she heard me walk in, she dropped the phone and came running at me. Her next words confirmed my worst fear: she had read the passage in my journal when I wrote about wishing that one of us were dead.

"You want to kill me? You want to kill yourself?" One of her eyes bugged out wider than the other.

"No, it was just a joke, something I wrote to freak out the teacher."

"A joke?" she yelled, loud enough for the other Bev to hear her, even with the receiver resting on the linoleum floor.

"Yes, it was a joke!" I yelled back. Why had I let my mother ruin what could have been a perfectly good day?

"You wanna kill someone? I've taken care of that. You just sit here and we'll take care of everything." Now she was trying to act calm, but she had a scared look on her face, like she could start crying at any moment.

"It was a creative writing assignment," I went on, embellishing my lie. "We were supposed to imagine the worst thing that could happen. It was just a stupid assignment."

Her eyes narrowed to show me that she was not taken in by my story. She moved slowly toward me as I backed into the couch. I sat down gingerly. Mom sat across from me in the lazy boy recliner, prepared to leap up and block my flight if I tried to run. I wondered which of us was stronger. Something about the way she stared at me, however, kept me frozen in place. She made no move to retrieve the phone, although I could hear a tinny voice from the receiver saying, "Bev? Bev? You okay?"

The screen door opened, and as soon as Geraldine's tall shadow fell across the room my mother sprang into action. The two women rushed at me together, Geraldine holding what looked like a rope, of all things. They were both crying out in a kind of terror I had never heard before.

Instinctively I dropped to the floor, my camera banging the carpet, and charged between Geraldine's legs. A moment later I was on my feet and running out the door. As I rounded the lawn and hit the street, I saw Mimi step daintily out of her Cadillac. She was right in the middle of reapplying her lipstick when she caught sight of me.

My camera had fallen off my neck when I hit the floor, but there was no way to go back for it. I ran until I reached a bend in the cul-de-sac and then ducked into a garage, pushing one of the twin doors just high enough so that I could crawl under it. When I turned around slowly, there was enough light to reveal the lawnmower parked neatly in a corner and a pegboard of immaculate tools. At least I have weapons, I thought—and then I nearly burst out laughing at how crazy everything seemed, as if I were watching a television movie.

Hanging quietly in another corner of the garage was the thing I needed most: a slim brown telephone. I dialed Fatima but got no answer. Then I tried Dad at work. Adonis, the dispatcher, told me that Dad was getting bagels for everyone, since he thought he was the only person who knew how to choose the good ones. I tried to laugh at his little joke and even managed to say, "No problem," when he asked, "You okay, baby?"

I slumped down onto the cold, smooth concrete and tried to think. I didn't know who owned this house, or what they would do if they came home and found me. All the cars were gone, and there was no vehicle in the driveway. What if I crept into the house and waited there all day? Or called the police to report my mother, saying she'd gone crazy and I needed some help?

To keep myself from shivering, I wrapped myself in an old bathroom rug, rust-colored and shaggy, that I found on a shelf, but the more I shivered, the more exhausted I felt. Here I was, needing to make a big decision, and all I could do was fall asleep.

When I woke up, I couldn't remember where I was or how long I'd been there. I didn't know if Mom was still looking for me, or where she would try to take me. Rather than risk an encounter with her, I opened the door that led into the house, which was fairly easy since there was no lock. The door opened into a laundry room, which led in turn to an immaculate kitchen nook with an octagonal table and chairs. I could see the clock on the avocado stove and took a few steps closer until I could read the time: 11:34 AM. The window over the sink faced the back yard, which displayed a red, white, and blue swing set with the word "Bicentennial" inscribed on the frame. Unlike at our house, the patio with its glass table was swept as clean as the kitchen floor.

The only sound was the ticking of a clock—not the stove clock, but the big grandfather clock that stood around the corner in the formal dining room. When I was small, I used to climb into our clock and pull the door closed as if I were in a vertical coffin. I loved hiding in there the same way I loved sitting under the pine tree, its branches drooping to the ground so that the soft green needles enclosed me.

I returned to the kitchen and opened the refrigerator. It was empty except for a few cans of Tab, a small glass bowl of jellied cranberry sauce, a container of Parmesan cheese, a carton of eggs, and packets of soy sauce from a Chinese restaurant. The freezer was full of TV dinners, pot pies, ice cream sandwiches from Carvel, and steaks wrapped in white paper with neat labels that read "flank," "ribs," and "T-bone."

I closed the freezer and realized that a man was standing behind me. Or maybe a boy. I screamed. He screamed.

"What are you doing in our house?" he asked. He was tall, with an angular face and soft brown eyes. He didn't sound angry.

"My mother," I began in a halting voice. "She—no, it was actually my fault, because of my journal." My face burned as the tears fell. What if he called the police and had me arrested? He reached out and took my arm, making me feel even more scared. What if he raped me? Didn't I deserve it, for coming into his house like this?

But instead he led me into the living room, where we sat down politely on the red crushed-velvet couch. I tried to look at his face to show him that I was normal, not the kind of person who breaks into people's houses and looks in their freezers, but my eyes kept drifting to a black velvet painting of a little girl that was hanging on the wall behind him. She was dressed in blue, with a single teardrop on her cheek and a white flower in her hand, and her eyes were inordinately large.

He saw me looking at the painting and said apologetically, "Yeah, my mom has gross taste. I don't know why she likes that shit, but man, it doesn't do it for me. You like art?"

I told him I liked photography, and he replied that he preferred oil painting. In fact, he had a studio in the basement. "Come down and look."

I thought it over for a moment. This was what every after-school TV special warned against, going alone to the basement with some guy when no one else was home. He must have sensed my objections, because he said, "You're the one who broke into my house first!" We laughed, the tension broken, and I followed him downstairs.

"Is your name Carrie?"

"No, I'm Deborah."

"Oh, sorry. There's some Carrie girl who's been calling me and then hanging up. She asks to speak to me, says it's Carrie, and then hangs up on me. Weird."

By the time we reached the darkened basement, he had one hand on my shoulder to guide me. I liked how warm his hand felt. I imagined swinging around and falling into his arms, but then he turned on a light. I saw the painted dragons everywhere: hanging on the walls, piled against tables, resting on easels. Every dragon was black, but the backgrounds of the paintings varied—there were pink and blue clouds, dungeons, gray fields, and mountains covered with tiny pink flowers.

"I'm Chris, by the way. Now, do you wanna tell me how you got in here?" I noticed he was wearing one tiny earring in the shape of a cross. I tried to remember what Lou had told me about how men wore their earrings. One ear was gay, one wasn't, but did it make a difference if the earring was about Jesus?

"You see, my parents are in the middle of this crazy divorce," I said. I decided to describe the whole scenario in an entertaining way. "My dad won't move out of the house, and my mom is a psycho. Today she went really crazy and started chasing me with a rope. She read my journal, and I wrote in it how I wanted to kill her. Not really kill her, you know, just be free of her. Nice shadowing," I added, pointing at a dragon perched on a mountain.

"Were they gonna try and catch you and get you locked up or something? Put you in a straightjacket, just because you said you wanted to kill her? Man, I want to kill my mom every day."

We laughed again, then sat down on an old couch whose tan floral upholstery matched the shag carpet beneath our feet. He stretched out one arm strategically as we leaned back, so that the arm wound up around my shoulders. I let myself lean into his armpit and relax, not wanting to think about anything: my mother, what I was doing in this house, what might happen next. It was like a dream, where I could act cooler and braver than I really was.

He reached into his pocket and pulled out a white cigarette, tighter and narrower than any cigarette I'd ever seen. Instinctively, I knew what was happening: this was one of those moments everyone talked about, when you get offered your first drugs and you try to say no, but then peer pressure bears down on you from all directions.

"A little M.J. to make the day go by faster, or slower if you like."

I smiled, pretending I'd done this kind of thing before. He held a yellow-and-black "keep on truckin'" lighter to one end of the joint and sucked on the other, his thick lips pouting a kiss. I reminded myself that my mother had just tried to catch me and take me to the loony bin. If that wasn't a good excuse to try drugs for the first time, then what was? Giggling a little as he put the joint into my hand, I placed the damp end against my puckered lips and tried to suck in, but instead I blew out.

He laughed. "No, take a deep breath."

The best I could do was to purse my lips, half-close my eyes, and act like I knew how to smoke. I tried to smile broadly every time I handed him back the joint. He smiled, too, and didn't seem to notice that the cigarette shrank only after he sucked on it. When the joint was merely a stub he laughed a little, a deep happy laugh that made me laugh, too. He pressed the burning end against the side of the lighter, blew on it thoroughly, and dropped the stub and the lighter into his pants pocket. We leaned back on the couch, eyes closed—in his case because he was high, and in mine because I suddenly felt very strange, as if my legs and arms were stretching out a little, growing right there on the spot.

His hand started rubbing my left shoulder, and then started moving up and down my upper arm. "Hey," he said, putting his other hand under my chin, bringing my face up to his to kiss me. I had never kissed anyone before but I followed along, praying he wouldn't notice how little I knew.

When his lips opened a little, my lips opened a little. His tongue slipped across my lips, so I let my tongue slip around his as I tasted the funny flavor of the joint, if a smell can truly be a taste at the same time. He pulled me closer to him, his other hand rubbing my arm more vigorously now, his chest pressing against my chest. Our lips moved like water or electricity against each other, a little harder, then a little softer. I felt an odd sensation in my nipples, a kind of stretching out or a diving down.

When his hand cupped one breast, my open, good feeling suddenly turned on itself, and fear was everywhere. I knew I wasn't supposed to be doing this, but how could I possibly stop it? He moaned and leaned into me harder. I was falling backwards underneath him as something hard in his jeans pressed down on my legs. He took my hand and pressed it against this mysterious lump, which felt like a hammer wrapped in denim. I never knew that a body part could get this hard. He pushed my shirt up, pushed his hand up my bra, and grabbed at the nipple so it hurt. I knew in a moment he would pull off my clothes and aim that hard thing into my body. He would push and push, just like his teeth were pushing against my neck now.

I tried to remember his name, Bill or Chris, but I couldn't. He was moving so fast and hard that all the heat was draining out of me. "Think about what you're doing," I told myself. "Think of a way out." But I couldn't. All I could do was lay very still, and not touch anything.

I tried to cry low enough that he couldn't hear me, but as I got colder I started gulping air. Eventually a sob flew out of me, which he mistook for happiness or desire. Something got hotter against my left thigh. He sighed loudly and then yelled "ugh," as if someone had kicked him in the stomach, collapsing fast with all his weight on me.

A moment later he sat up, apologizing, "I'm sorry. I'm sorry. I didn't mean for it to happen this fast. I'm really sorry." As I lay on my side, shaking and crying silently, he leaned over me and stroked my hair. "I meant to do something for you. Baby, I'm sorry, it's just been so long, and you got me so horny."

The word made me nauseous. Like "fag" and "retard," it was one of those terms everyone made fun of when I was in junior high. I stopped crying and lay very still while he scratched my back lightly under my shirt. "Oh, baby, I'm glad you understand," he said, but he seemed to be reassuring himself, not me. "Next time it'll be better. Yeah, next time, I won't smoke so much weed."

When we went upstairs a little later, he asked, "Would you like something to eat, now that you know what we have to offer?" I knew he was referring to the sex, but I felt a rush of shame, all over again, that he'd seen me looking inside his freezer.

"Flying saucers," I replied about the ice cream. He took out two, one for each of us, and opened the sliding glass door. We ate the saucers in the back yard, sitting on the swing set.

"Have you done that a lot?" he asked me.

I shook my head.

"It was my first time," he said nervously. In the house, his thick brown hair and high cheekbones had made him look older—at least eighteen, almost a grown man. I'd figured that was the reason I hadn't seen him in any of my classes at school. But as he continued to rock back and forth on the baby blue swing set, eating ice cream, I could see that he was only a boy.

"How old are you?"

"Fifteen," he replied, "and you?"

"Sixteen."

We swung for a while without saying anything much. He offered to let me stay and watch TV all afternoon, but I told him that all I really needed was a chance to make a phone call. "My mom's gone bonkers," I told the boy again, like it was some kind of an old joke between us. This time, I reached Fatima right way and instructed her to pick me up at a gas station a few blocks away.

As I started walking down the street to the gas station, the sunlight was everywhere. Strangely enough, everything felt shiny again as if nothing had happened. The heat and light made me feel like my skin was forgiven, but the rest of me knew better. Underneath, there was a war going on, and I couldn't even tell what it was about.

I didn't plan to say anything to Fatima, but I fell apart as soon as I got into the front seat of her gold van. She handed me a tiny bag with a piece of baklava inside as I cried and shook. As she drove, she reached out and held my hand as tightly as if I were her daughter. I managed to tell her the parts about Mom, but I was too ashamed to tell her what happened with the boy.

When we pulled into her driveway, she twisted around and grabbed me in her arms. I cried and gulped, feeling ashamed and stupid. In her living room I collapsed on the couch. She wrapped me in a blanket and tucked three small, crocheted pillows under my head, then brought me another blanket. She dimmed the lights in the room and lit a tall white candle in a glass container.

"The *kandili* is for the Panagia, Virgin Mary," she explained. "She weeps for you. She weeps even for Jewish girls, for all girls with good hearts." At that I cried even more, knowing full and well that something was very wrong with my heart.

As I watched the yellow flame moving around inside its white container as if trying to escape, I gradually stopped crying. I was nearly asleep when I heard Fatima on the phone, saying, "This is what that woman has done to her, and this is why you will never give your daughter up to that monster."

But it wasn't just about my mother. When I pictured the crazy scene at the house with Mom and Geraldine, it seemed no more real than an episode of *I Love Lucy*. No, it was what happened with that guy, how stupid I was to go into his house, why I didn't try to leave as soon as I realized that someone was home. It was me who did all of it, it was me who deserved what was coming to her. I fell asleep wondering what bad thing would happen to me next.

When I woke up, my father was in the kitchen. I heard whispers, and then Dad said, "Chinese for tonight, it's still warm," gesturing at the white cardboard boxes on the table. I obediently sat down and spooned clumps of meat and vegetables onto a foothill of white rice. Fatima and Dad each took a seat at the yellow table, watching me like I was their tiny baby.

"Well, if you want to live with us, we can –" Dad began.

"You're getting married?" I interrupted, putting down my fork.

My father smiled nervously, and Fatima looked away, her expression very sad.

"We'll see about that, but we will be together"—he looked at Fatima and adjusted his expression to match her sad one—"forever." The "forever" had the ring of an "amen," as if to say, "this prayer is over, you can go now."

"Right now we're concentrating on you. Where do you want to live? You're a big girl now, and you can decide."

I glanced at Fatima, who was peering at me through her lashes even as she looked down, pretending it didn't matter. I looked at Dad, who seemed anxious. I didn't understand the way they were acting, but it was already settled in my mind.

"I'll live with you." I tossed the words out casually, even as I wondered why Dad was asking me. We'd already planned it all out with the lawyer, what I needed to say so I could live with him. Then I cried anxiously,

"What about my camera? I left it at Mom's. What if it's broken? She might have broken it or something."

They were too busy smiling at each other to hear what I was saying. "Dad," I said, tugging on his arm, "my camera."

"Forget about it," he said. "I got it wholesale on Fulton Street, a good deal. I can pick you up another one tomorrow." I tried to relax, but I worried about the roll of film stuck in the camera. I couldn't remember if there was anything on it besides the irises.

"The court date. That's what counts now," he said in a more reassuring tone. "Then your mom moves out, and we start our new life." Fatima glowed as he kissed her on the cheek, something I'd never seen him do with Mom.

So it was settled. The court date was so close, like a birthday I both wanted and dreaded, flying across the windows of everything we did over the next two days.

Chapter Ten

I broke open the plastic egg to unfurl my new panty hose and carefully inched them up my thighs. I stepped into the new red skirt Fatima bought me, pulling it over my feet and up to my waist. Linen, she'd said, fresh and light, just the thing to wear. Then the button-down white shirt, so unlike anything else I wore, angular and stiff in all the wrong places. At least it fit, and I managed to tuck it into my pantyhose to keep it anchored, as Fatima told me she always did. Finally, the jacket with the silky lining. As it slid on I instantly felt older and somewhat famous, as if I were living a life that required a lot of late-night dinners in the city. The down side was that I was missing the show-off-your-best-pix (and twenty percent off all jeans) party at Karmic Clothes. Weeks ago, when I'd told the photography class I had to be in court that day, the other kids had seemed impressed—until Eshe mentioned that she'd gone to court dozens of times.

It was an hour until court, and ten minutes until we had to leave, when Fatima put a touch of eye shadow on my lids. "Nothing too much, you're still a girl," she said, painting some pale pink lipstick on me with her lipstick brush. She herself was wearing a white suit, just like mine, but the jacket was shorter and fuller, and her shirt was a silky red V-neck, cut just low enough for a little cleavage to show through. We looked like reverse images of each other.

"Wait," I said, getting out the new camera Dad brought me yesterday to snap our photo as we stood side by side in front of the bathroom mirror. I knew I couldn't take any pictures in court (Dad had told me that if I took that "cockamamie" thing into the courtroom, he would smash it), but this shot would tell something of the story. I stuck the camera in my pocketbook and wondered how different we would look on our way out of court in a few hours.

When we reached the courthouse, Manicotti put his arms around me and Fatima. "Such beautiful women in your life, Harold," the lawyer said, "you're a lucky man."

He led us into a small, wood-paneled conference room where the three of us sat down in velvet chairs. "It's all as we said, and I think you'll be smelling like a rose by the end. Remember, doll," he said to Fatima, "you need to be in the balcony where the wife can't see you. No sense giving her any ammunition. And you," he said to me, "you don't need to take the stand unless the judge asks you to, so just sit by your dad, look innocent and sweet, and smile nicely at the judge if he looks at you."

I had already rehearsed my lines with the lawyer's secretary, a patient woman from Trinidad, and by now I had them memorized. As we walked to our places, I went over the speech in my head: "I'm here because I want to live with my dad. He's always been a good father to me, and I'm sixteen now, old enough, your honor, to choose."

That was all I was supposed to say. If they asked me why I didn't want to live with my mother, I was supposed to put my head down and act like I was crying, while Dad's lawyer passed forward the Polaroid of the bruise left on my arm when Mom and Geraldine tried to grab me a few days ago. If pressed, and only if pressed, I was supposed to say, "Please don't make me live with that woman. I'm afraid she'll hurt me again." My father's lawyer would tell the judge about her kidnapping me to the psychotherapist, so the judge would understand just how distraught I was. According to Manicotti, it was likely that my brother would be testifying against Dad today, so I should just stay calm.

But when we entered the courtroom—alive and busy like the auction, only with everyone all dressed up—the first thing I noticed was my English class journal in the hands of my mother's lawyer. He carried it over to Manicotti, who read a few pages hurriedly. As my father and I sat down, I felt all the life draining out of me. Manicotti handed the journal back to the attorney, shook his head, then crossed the room, took my hand, and kissed it.

"You're a good girl," he said soothingly, "a good sensitive girl. They're just a bunch of bullies, but bullies always lose in the end." I held my stomach in tightly and bit my lower lip so hard it started to bleed. This was the worst moment of my life, and there was nothing I could do to stop it.

My mother's lawyer, a tall man with reddish hair and a double-breasted brown suit, smirked at us. Then he carried the journal over to the court stenographer, who sat at a little table typing on something the size of a calculator. With no expression on her face, she opened the notebook and started to type. The pain in my stomach sharpened and I started crying in spite of myself, the tears falling so hard that my face burned. It was all I could do not to make a sound. I felt an arm around my back and a hand patting my shoulder as I held my face in my hands, head bent low, trying to disappear.

Then a miracle happened.

"Put that away! That is not to be entered into the record!"

I sat up and took my hands away to see what was happening. The judge, an old man with no hair, banged the gavel, and said, "We shall recess to my chambers. I want the brother and sister now. No counsel, please."

We seemed like figures from a dollhouse as we stood up, my brother rising parallel to me in the far universe beside my mother. He wore the same suit he'd worn for my Bat Mitzvah, even though the pants were now too short. Our parents looked stunned as Dad's lawyer whispered, "Now this is wacky," just like Johnny Carson did. My mom's lawyer mumbled something similar, but with more syllables.

The magnetic pull of the judge drew us forward and we followed him—a tiny man, an elf really—into a small mahogany room. He directed us into red velvet chairs balanced a body length apart. Roger and I were so scared that we dared not look at each other. The judge took off his robe to show us he was just a man and leaned forward, balancing his elbows on the desk.

"I won't have a brother and sister testifying against each other," he said, with the voice of God.

At that moment I felt something wet seeping out of me, soaking through my panties, my panty hose, my smart red skirt, and, I worried, into the velvet cushion of the chair.

"No child should be put in this position," he continued. "If I could, I'd take you both home with me."

I couldn't believe a judge would say something like this out loud. I couldn't believe my body was leaking, either—was it blood, finally my period? Did all the crying make this happen? What was I supposed to do now?

"So I ask you to choose, and whoever you choose, I will see to it that you reside there for the foreseeable future. Now in a year, if you happen to change your mind –" He was making it easy on us, while I was permanently staining his chair. I knew it, even as I nodded at him.

"Roger," he began, "with whom do you choose to live?"

If only we could choose our parents at birth, like desserts. Now it felt like a wedding ceremony. I heard my brother answer, "My mother." He said it so easily and sounded so young that I hated him.

The judge nodded, wrote something down, and turned to me. He said my name, looked into my eyes without smiling. I tried to meet his gaze, but my face betrayed me. I was crying without tears, shaking without movement.

He said my name again, softly, as if trying to wake me from a deep sleep. My mouth was twisting into a Picasso painting, and everything pointed to the center core of my body where I was bleeding.

"You have to choose," he said gently, "your mother or your father. You only have to say one word."

A few moments later he would be called away, and I would burst out crying so hard that my brother, who knew nothing of women and blood, would rush out of the room and beg the court secretary to help me. When she and I were alone, I would tell her everything: about the divorce, the guy in the basement, my diary, the blood, the new suit. She would nod, put her arms around me, and lead me to the bathroom to clean up while she took care of the red chair without a word.

But that was still minutes away. Now, my voice crackling with static, I could only manage to say, "My father."

Part II

Chapter One

The Melmac dinnerware looked cheap and stupid, like kiddie play dishes. How was I supposed to change my life with those? I took pictures of them anyway as Dad talked about how much better they were than breakable dishes. I was already tired of shopping and irritated by Dad, who wanted to choose everything himself.

"Melmac will last forever," Dad said.

"But it's just not that pretty," I answered.

We had filled two shopping carts with almost everything we needed to outfit a home: serving spoons, frying pans, pots, potholders, a plastic red-and-white tablecloth, matching dishtowels, flatware with yellow plastic handles (my choice), coasters with smiley faces (his choice), a toaster oven, a dozen purple and blue towels of various sizes, a four-piece canister set decorated with blue flowers and green leaves, a shish kabob set, a fondue pot, an electric mixer, orange plastic mixing bowls, and a spice rack that came complete with twenty-two spices. We had worked our way diagonally across the store, starting in bedding and hitting every department in our path. Our last stop was dishes, and I was leaning toward the rose-colored glass set. I could tell they wouldn't photograph very well.

"Those glass dishes won't last a day when your sister and brother visit."

"So? We'll buy more," I said. "Or maybe we can get two sets to begin with."

"You think money grows on trees? You think it's easy paying your mother out the nose?"

The sales lady stood a safe distance away, waiting for us to finish bickering. We had been in Two Guys Department Store for more than two hours now, which surely made us her sale of the day, if not the decade.

"I just like these. And if I'm going to be doing the cooking, shouldn't we get my choice? I mean, you chose almost everything else. Let me at least figure out the kitchen. You want me to act like an adult, so you should treat me like one," I said, proud of my logic.

Dad sighed and shook his head. I was sure he was about to give in, but instead he hoisted the ugliest of the Melmac sets—the one with an orange and brown plaid pattern—and settled it into the cart, careful to avoid the drinking glasses. I grabbed the set and placed it back on the shelf without looking at him, and picked out the daisy pattern instead. I wanted to cry, even though it was just dishes, but maybe that was because I was so tired.

The settlement wasn't good, Dad said. Mom convinced the judge that Dad and Fatima were making a killing at the auction every weekend. The accusations of adultery didn't help, and the taxi service had enjoyed a record year in 1975, which really screwed us over. The end result, he told me, was "the highest alimony in the state of New Jersey." When I thought about all the really rich people—the ones who lived in elegant old houses set back on lawns that were always freshly mowed—I found this statement a little hard to believe.

Dad's end of the deal included me, the house, my brother and sister on weekends and every Thursday night, my bedroom furniture, the master bedroom furniture, and the grandfather clock. Gone were the kitchen table, plastic-covered living room furniture, and the contents of every drawer and cabinet in the kitchen. Fatima was gone, too, off to Greece for a month to arrange for Theodore to move to America, leaving us alone in this big, empty house. We stood in the foyer, surrounded by twenty-two bags of our new life.

That night, with the Melmac neatly stacked on the red-checkered contact paper we'd used to line the cabinets, I broiled four hot dogs and opened a bag of chips. I tried to fry sauerkraut the way Mom did, but since I didn't really know how, I managed to burn it. As Dad studied the back of the laundry detergent box like it was the Old Testament, I set the table with our new flatware.

We quietly ate our first meal together as this new creature, this daughter-wife and newlywed-father living in the house of the mother. Before cooking the sauerkraut I'd been confident I could handle everything, but now I was having my doubts. Dad told me that he would do the laundry because he needed clean, wrinkle-free clothes for work, and I would probably just screw it up. But he wanted me to clean the rest of the house—I knew how to use the vacuum, right? I was barely listening, wondering if I could finally set up my darkroom now that I had the closet empty and Mom out of my hair. Maybe I could even set it up tonight.

"Deborah? I'm talking to you." He looked irritated.

I nodded, thinking of everything I'd already done that day. I had put away the new towels (purple for me, blue for him) in the bathrooms. In the living room, I'd set up the blue-and-orange woven lawn chairs and the matching lounger. ("Just until we can get a real living room set," Dad said when we bought them.) Then I had arranged the new folding table with its four matching chairs in the dining room, where they stood like a lonely brown island in the middle of a giant sea of gold and orange shag carpet.

"We did a lot today," he said, continuing his monologue. "You know, those seashell soaps you picked out look good in those little dishes. You could be an interior decorator—that's a good career, flexible hours, too. This photography thing, that would be a big mistake for you." He looked around at the walls, empty except for a school photo of Roger mounted with a thumbtack, probably something he did as they were moving out. He shook his head and walked abruptly into the laundry room.

Those soaps and little dishes were practically the only things he'd let me pick out myself, I thought as I stacked my empty Melmac plate atop his Melmac plate, also empty. I walked dutifully to the dishwasher, pulled it open, and loaded it with the pieces we'd used, but even the dishwasher looked lonely. I poured in the powdered soap and pushed the button anyway. So far, so good, I told myself, now I just need to get the hang of cooking. If only I could remember the details of how Mom did it.

Chores done, I raced upstairs and removed the contact paper, developer, and beige-colored trays from their hiding place under my untouched bed. In my desk were some green plastic clothespins, and my closet held three wooden crates I'd shepherded home from the auction. It took me two trips to bring everything downstairs, but I was amazed at how fast I got it all set up. There was no sink in the closet (something Liz said was necessary), but I planned to carry in trays of water. With an extension cord, already bought and ready to use, I hooked up the red light and hung it from the ceiling of the closet. In less than an hour, I had a darkroom. I didn't feel like using it yet, but maybe it needed time to sit and turn into itself into something more. I smiled in the dark at the idea of a closet changing into something else, something so much better.

I went outside and stood in the middle of the little patio. Emptied of the grill, planters, and lawn chairs, the cement seemed to have been beaten by the sun until nothing remained. I found a shady place to sit between the pussy willows and the side of the house. From there, the quiet stopped being so quiet. I heard crickets, grasshoppers, and other jumping insects all around me, buzzing and chirping and disturbing the grass. As I sat there, I couldn't remember exactly what my mother looked like, only that she had freckles and a small face, smaller than my dad's hand. "She's not in right now," I repeated politely to myself as I lay down in the overgrown grass, huddling on my side to stay within that small pool of shade.

Some time later I woke with a little start, remembering the last time I'd seen my mother. She was leaning toward me and away from her team huddle with Roger and the lawyer, as if she wanted to say something. Maybe she was sorry about the journal—but the moment I pictured it changing hands in the courtroom, I pushed her face away. She was just a speck in my life now. Dad had told me Mom was dead to him from now on. She was going to be dead to me, too. I didn't need a mother anymore. Nearby, someone revved up a lawnmower. A cricket sounded. I fell back into a hard sleep.

The next time I woke up, the air had cooled to satin blue and the sky looked like it did in a photo I took on a summer night. My arms were covered in goose bumps and one side of my face was matted with grass. How long had I been asleep? It felt like hours. I sat up quickly and felt the sweat all over me, followed by panic over what I had done. I rose and lunged into the house.

Dad was in the living room, sitting in the new lawn chair and watching the news. "So, you decided to come home?" he asked sarcastically.

I was about to reply that I had gone outside to be alone for a while, but I'd accidentally fallen asleep. Then I noticed that he'd eaten the package of Mallomars that we'd been planning to use all week for dessert. "We can have one a day," Dad had told me, "and still stay in shape." He was also drinking a beer, something I had never seen him do before except at summer barbeques.

"You ran off with some boy."

"No, I was right here in the back yard. I fell asleep next to the house. When did you start drinking beer? I thought you hated that stuff."

"You were petting with some boy," he said, then added, "And don't tell me what I should drink. You're not my mother, just a tramp off with some boy."

"No, I wasn't," I said, mustering a little outrage in my voice. "I was sitting against the house, just outside your window as a matter of fact, and I fell asleep. Want to come see?" I was nervous about revealing my hiding spot, but it seemed like my best defense.

"I can smell it. Don't lie to me."

"But I'm not. I don't even know any boys I would—I mean, I was just outside."

He shook his head and glanced around like an animal unaccustomed to its cage. "A lot of dads wouldn't tolerate their daughters being sluts, but not me. Not when I have a daughter who appreciates how much money I spent making a nice house for her."

"I'm not a slut! I was in the back yard the whole time." I continued my protest, but I could tell he wouldn't believe me. How could he even imagine I had time to think about boys? "I'm not, Dad, I promise, I'm not."

Knowing even before I said the words that it meant pain for me, I added, "I don't have time for boys or even friends, with how much I'm doing for you at the auction and around the house. Didn't I just spend the whole day shopping with you and helping you set up the house? Didn't I?"

He walked over to the refrigerator as the woman on a shaving commercial crooned, "Take it off, take it all off." "'I'm not a slut,'" he said, mimicking a girl's voice. "Yeah, tell me another one."

He abruptly changed his tone. "Your uncle Sheldon called tonight." Sheldon was his older brother who had made it big in the drapery business and now lived some place far away, Utah or Nevada. "You know what he said?"

He looked straight at me as he unwrapped the apple pie we had bought at the supermarket, the one we were planning to eat tomorrow night with cool whip on top. I shook my head.

"He said, 'To hell with you.' That's what he told me. He said if I couldn't be man enough to do for my kids and wife, I wasn't worth his time."

We hardly ever saw Sheldon and his quiet wife Lenora, who came from Sweden or someplace like that. All I could remember was that they had five daughters, all very good singers and all older than Roger and me. A long time ago, we had seen them perform some kind of Gregorian chant at our temple, except it was all in Hebrew. They took their little show all over New Jersey, which made them seem like the Von Trapp family, only Jewish.

"He couldn't mean that," I said. "I mean, you guys always made up."

Dad liked to tell stories of following Sheldon through Brooklyn on hot summer nights, going from one place to another playing practical jokes on people, like putting whoopee cushions on their chairs or dropping fake spiders in their soup. One year, Sheldon was named the best practical joker of Flatbush in a contest. The two brothers also conducted screaming matches during Sunday dinners at Mimi's, usually while she was out of the room. Dad would always turn to Mom and said, "Bev, get the kids ready to go now. We're finished." The next weekend we were all back at Mimi's, eating leg of lamb or orange-glazed duck as if nothing had happened.

"Sheldon disowned me, and you know what else?" He looked sad for a moment, and much younger than I wished. "Mimi called and said if Sheldon wanted nothing to do with me, neither did she—but I better keep sending her those monthly payments from the taxi service, or she'd see me in court. She always took his side."

I looked down at my hands, wishing I had my camera in them, anything to put between us. Dad didn't seem much like Dad anymore, but more like someone my own age. If Mimi had abandoned us, Sheldon and Lenora, too, then who did we have left? I hadn't heard from Mom's family at all since the divorce, except for one card from Geraldine. She said I could always count on her, but it would be better if I didn't get in touch for a while. Nana and Grandpa had moved to Florida, and with Nana in and out of respiratory care at the local hospital, they had all but vanished from my life. The neighbors didn't talk to us, either, probably because—as Dad said yesterday—Mom turned them all against us. Dad and I were alone on this big island.

He had thrown his shirt on the family room floor next to his shoes, and my flip-flops lay nearby where I had kicked them off. He saw me looking at the messy floor, and I could tell he was probably biting his tongue the way he always did before he yelled at Mom. "This is yours to clean now, and I'm not living with another slob," he told me angrily, "so you better keep up with this, or I'll send you to live with your mother."

At the mention of her name, I felt the same flash of ragged-edged pain that had surged through me when I saw my journal passed around in the courtroom. "I don't want to live with her," I said, and then, getting a little braver, added, "and if you gave me up, you'd lose this house. You know you only got it because of me."

Before I had a chance to react, he slammed the pie toward me. He missed, and the pie struck the cheap plastic clock on the wall. "You ever talk to me like that again, you're going to be out of this house! I'll send you back to your mother so fast you won't know what hit you," he said in a much higher pitch, and then bit his tongue. He walked quickly to the front door and slammed it so hard on his way out that all the air in the house shook.

I stood frozen in the kitchen, listening to the sounds of the car starting up and pulling away. When the sounds were gone, I started crying. What had changed my father into this guy who would talk about women with me at the diner as if I were a peer? What had I done to make this happen? And where could I find the recipe for undoing it? As a daughter I was worthless, that was clear.

It was still early, only half past eight. Although the air conditioning was on, it felt suffocating in the house right now. If I could just take a walk, maybe I could do whatever I needed to do to make this home mine again, to make my father happy again. I opened the sliding glass door and slipped outside. Maybe if I ran away he would feel so guilty that he'd stop acting like this, or maybe it would be better if I left, because I was bad luck. All I knew was that I had to get out of this house.

The outside air had grown cooler and I wished I had taken a sweater, but if I walked fast enough it was okay. I headed over the hill behind our house and then across the neighbors' yards, looking into houses where kids and parents watched televisions in orange-lit rooms. Each window seemed to frame a television show of its own, which made me feel better and worse at the same time. I was safe, I was on solid ground, but I was on the outside now, outside of a family, outside of this whole housing development, and I didn't see how I would ever get in again.

Walking aimlessly, I saw my old elementary school up ahead, the one I attended the year the baby died, the year my parents started slamming doors so hard the whole house trembled. I would go to the swings and I would swing right off this planet. I would go higher than ever before, and when I was good and ready, I would go home again and quickly clean up the whole mess. Or maybe I would just stay here all night and to hell with school tomorrow. My temples ached, but I moved faster and faster toward the swings.

That's when I saw a bunch of Jewish-looking kids, all vaguely familiar, including Abby and Mark from photography class. I would have run away or ducked out of sight, but they noticed me at the very moment I saw them. They rushed toward the window, which they tried to open but couldn't, then signaled for me to meet them at the front door while the kids behind them watched with interest.

"It's Deborah," Abby said as she let me in. Her hair was held in two braids that made her face look older, and she was wearing orange hot pants and a matching orange tube top.

"Yeah," said Mark, "Come on in. It's a little late, but not too late. Sy was hoping some new people would come."

"Sy? Who's that?"

"Oh, he's the youth group advisor, but this is his last time with us. The new rabbi is taking over in August," Abby said.

I tried to think of a way to tell them, politely, that I hadn't come for whatever this was, but I suddenly felt very tired. Inside one of the classrooms, the youth group from our synagogue was assembling bags of food for the poor, using what they'd collected during a recent food drive. It was easy enough: I just put two boxes of this, three cans of that, and a package of the other into a bag before passing it on to Abby. She added a special card that she had made, then passed it to another girl who added a giant wooly pompom, and finally to Mark, who put in a donated pet rock. The starving, I thought, would obviously be living on Rice-A-Roni and hamburger helper. I hoped they would have some hamburger to go with it.

When I first arrived, they were busy talking about Mr. Morris, the new gym teacher, and how gross it was that he had a thing for teenage girls, especially redheads. Then someone mentioned "Saturday Night Live" and imitated the guy who'd imitated Gerald Ford as he tripped over his plastic dog. They talked about getting their driver's licenses—one large girl already had hers, along with a white Olds 442 that her parents gave her for losing seventeen pounds last year, although she confessed that she'd had to do laxatives for the last few days before the big weigh-in.

No one asked me anything, which didn't surprise me because that was how it seemed to be everywhere lately. By the time the evening ended, the large girl had at least registered my presence sufficiently to offer me a ride home in her car with a bunch of other kids.

I thanked them as I climbed out of the car, but they enthusiastically said in unison, "No, thank you!" The house looked just the same but with all the lights on downstairs, including Dad's room, which thankfully was locked. I made my way to the kitchen and cleaned up every trace of mess, using half a roll of paper towels that I stuffed into the wastebasket. Worried that Dad would get upset over the full trash bag, I hauled it outside to the curb. On my way back I noticed the moon, just a sliver inside a pale cloud, hardly visible. I remembered seeing a full moon just a few days ago, but that couldn't have been right. Nothing made sense any more, but I was too tired to care.

Chapter Two

Going to the auction without Fatima was like school without Mr. Lexington, or shooting photos without Liz to critique them. No one cooled us down by fetching ice pops or colas every twenty minutes, or by attaching miniature battery-powered fans to our hats. Worst of all, no one covered for us when it got busy, and in the summer it was always busy. School was out, photography class didn't start again for a few more weeks, and I saw Roger and Missy only on Thursday nights. We would visit the diner and then go bowling, where I would be forced to hold Missy and distract her with lollypops that made her sticky and irritable. Meanwhile, Dad instructed Roger on the secrets that made a man a good bowler: "Aggression. You gotta remember that the pins are the enemy, and your ball is your only weapon."

Roger threw gutter balls, seemingly on purpose, and hounded me for change to buy candy. Missy made me read *Curious George* to her repeatedly, then cried when she saw Roger eating red licorice until I got her some, too. I checked the clock often on those nights, reminding Dad that Mom probably needed the kids home early. He always bought into any excuse to deposit them back at Mom's townhouse, a place Roger said was "as big as Dad's house, only vertical."

"What does that mean?" I had asked him.

"It has a lot of floors, and a living room with a super high ceiling." He smiled rather smugly at me, then shrugged his shoulders.

Dad was at home a lot less on weeknights, usually working until ten. He said he was training a new girl on dispatch, plus business was always crazy this time of year—and then there was the Bicentennial right around the corner. I met the new girl once, an Armenian woman as petite as my mother but with dark hair and olive skin. Lou said she had a wicked laugh, as in, "That girl there has got such a wicked laugh she could make faggy men cross over." Dad's absence made preparing dinner a lot easier, but it also left me with huge blocks of free time in the evening. I would wander through the housing development and the surrounding fields, shooting roll after roll of film. Realizing I hadn't captured anything special, I developed none of it.

Every Saturday at six AM, I helped Dad unload clothing racks that left my hands smelling of rust. I got to where I could balance a huge box of clothes on my thighs, hugging it into my body as I hobbled toward the display table. I always imagined someone taking aerial photos of my feat, preferably from way above. Dad always got nicer toward the end of each week, because he knew he had to have my help at the auction. By Saturday morning we would be working together like a congenial team. Every so often, though, he slipped away to make phone calls without telling me why.

Over the summer I planned to put together a photo essay about the auction. It would be a surprise for Liz, who always encouraged us to find real life, gritty and unprocessed, wherever possible. I figured that the auction was as real and gritty as it got in central New Jersey. One morning, as I pulled the camera out of my pocketbook, I heard Boy yelling, "Caps! Caps for sale! Fifty cents a cap!" in a fake Czechoslovakian accent, imitating a children's story that I grew up with and that he evidently grew up with, too.

"I loved that book," I told him. He replied, with a winning grin, "Oh, baby doll, one day we won't have to carry all these caps on our heads all the hot day long. One day we'll sit under trees and eat a good meal and let the monkeys sell the caps."

"Or take them," I added. Sometimes, when I was making change for a customer, I'd see a shoplifter out of the corner of my eye. Usually it was a young black man who stuffed one of Boy's shirts into a dingy paper shopping bag while Boy was looking the other direction. Even if Boy didn't catch the culprit, however, he always seemed to know, yelling, "May I help you, *professor?*" in a melodramatic way.

"Now, whenever I say 'professor' or 'scientist,' I mean a jungle bunny who's gonna steal us blind. You got that?" Boy whispered to me.

"That's prejudiced. Just because someone's black doesn't mean anything." I looked up as I aimed the camera at him.

"I love that innocence!" he yelled to the world in general. Turning back to me, he whispered, "And back when I was young and the world was gay, I thought that way, too. But then I learned that some people buy the caps, some people sell them, and some monkeys steal them. And you best not let any of them see that camera," he added. "That would buy a big bag of Mr. Marijuana."

"Oh, no one is going to steal this. I keep it really close to me," I said, pointing to my pocketbook.

"Not close enough if you get a rush and you're busy making change," he said. "Or you might find yourself watching that camera instead of the goods, while professors walk away with those snazzy big pants you've got."

"Each according to his need," I said defensively, quoting Karl Marx from Mr. Lexington's class last semester. I casually took some photos of the tables laden with sweaters, but I didn't like the idea of people stealing from Dad.

"Ah, you're an 'each according to his need' type of girl."

"I don't know what type of girl I am," I confessed. I didn't really know what I believed or where it would lead me, or why I said what I did.

"I know," Boy said, placing his giant palm against the side of my face, "exactly what kind of girl you are: the type that will make a good mother."

I snapped my head away, pretending I had to fix a tumbled pile of pants, but I felt like spilled paint had mixed together into a sickening gray green pool in the pit of my stomach. Last night my mother had called, with her usual impeccable timing, as Dad and I fought over how I had burnt the steak, and how the dishes weren't clean, and was that too much to ask when we had a dishwasher? My father dangled the phone in front of me, saying, "Here, it's your mother, she's just like you, go live with her."

I twirled away from him like a dancer in a TV special I'd seen, but as I unlatched the screen door I heard him telling her, "What can I do? I told you she refuses to take the phone. In fact, she...." My refusal seemed to amuse him so much that he was actually laughing as he told her about it. I ran down the sidewalk, down the driveway and out into the empty street, with all the neighbors tucked away inside after the afternoon rain. When I came to a stop, breathing hard, past the edge of the housing development and near a field of green corn, I felt as if my whole body were still moving. The wind had picked up. Maybe that's what God is, I had thought, not some entity but wind. Maybe God was holding me. Maybe God was letting me go.

Boy started singing, reminding me I was at the auction. I turned to watch him sing "The Sound of Music" as he straightened out a pile of Izods.

I looked down at my camera and had decided to put it away safely in the truck when Dad yelled, "I'm going on break." He disappeared before I could even say, "Get me a Tab." The wind had picked up and the heat and the crowds that had filled the stand all day were gone. I leaned back against the brick wall, which Dad said we were lucky to have, considering that our stand was new.

Out of boredom, I decided to start taking pictures again. I turned my camera on Sergei, who'd been selling women's sweaters with fake jewelry on them in the same spot for fifteen years. He waved at me as he tried to convince some girl she was getting a good deal on sweaters. When the girl laughed in his face and turned away, I saw it was Eshe. I tensed up and lowered the camera.

"You, " she said, "you're Deborah, right?" She looked down at my camera and added, "Nice." Although I had brought the camera with me to class, she'd never even noticed it. "Look, is this your stand?"

"Well, it's my dad's," I said lamely, admiring her deep voice and dark tan. "It's sorta fat women's clothes, you probably wouldn't find anything you like."

"Clothes? No, I got plenty of clothes. What I want is a job. I need a car, I need some money, and I need to get an apartment away from my bitch mother. You hiring?"

Just like that, the most beautiful and mysterious girl in our class was asking if I could get her a job. "I don't know, I mean, we might be," I mumbled. "The people we usually do this with are in Greece."

It slowly dawned on me that she might be good at this job, which meant maybe I could stay home in bed every Saturday. The moment Dad returned, Eshe turned to him and said, without missing a beat, "I know your daughter from school, and she said you might need someone. I can count, I can fold, I can carry, and I can get my ass here on time every Saturday. You interested?"

"How much are you talking?" asked Dad.

"Twenty-five a day, and I'll be here from set-up until tear-down. It has to be under the table, too—I don't pay no goddamn taxes." Of course, neither did Dad.

"You crazy? I only pay that one ten dollars a day," he said, gesturing to me. "Tell you what I'm going to do, I'll give you fifteen."

"Who's the crazy one here?" she shot back, stepping a bit closer. "You pay me and your daughter twenty dollars a day and," she said, smiling slowly, "the rabbit lives."

"What the hell's a rabbit got to do with it?" he asked, before he realized she was joking.

That's how Eshe got hired, and my salary doubled, right there on the spot. While Dad was showing her the ropes and giving her a bundle of dollar bills and fives for change, I went on break and tried to figure out whether I was terribly happy or scared shitless.

By the time I returned Eshe was already working the stand like an old pro, yelling, "Women's pants, two for five dollars, step right up, ladies, and get your slacks!" She stacked up piles of bills from customers while I was still hesitantly counting out change or straightening up stacks of fallen pants. During the quiet moments, she yelled random questions over to Boy: "Every part of you giant, Boy?" He turned red and answered, "Hush, ma'am, I ain't used to such forward young females like those of youse today."

With me she was polite but distant, devoting all her energy to selling our ugly clothes. She joked with the overweight customers about how pretty they were and told them their babies were "just dolls, gorgeous little dolls." She called out these strange confessions to Boy: "Oh, if I don't have me a little baby like that soon, I'm just gonna die. Hey, Boy, don't you want a baby, too? Your own Little Boy?"

"Now, ma'am," Boy replied, starting to play along with her act, "you know I'm the big man on campus, but my fraternity don't allow me to mix with the eager young women. You're a smart woman and you need a real professor."

"Maybe I need to be the professor myself," she answered, not realizing what he meant by "professor."

When Eshe went on break the following Saturday, I watched her amble toward the bathroom, smoking a cigarette, as she casually rolled up some bills and stuffed them into her pocket. It was easy to steal from a job like this one. The meaner Dad got at home, the less inclined I felt to blow her cover.

"You, you're the one, you're the two, you're the six foot baby blue," Boy sang to me, then bent over to whisper, "but I'm onto her, and I'm onto you, and believe you me, you're nothing like her, thank heavens." He straightened up quickly and sang out into the crowd, "For little girls! Hey, step up for the Maurice Chevalier special. Ask me for a shirt in a French accent, and it's yours. Two for two bucks for two minutes starting in two seconds!"

I shuffled back to our racks, straightening the blouses that kept slipping off their hangers. "What's up?" Dad asked, stepping toward me.

"Nothing."

"Where's Eshe?"

"On break."

He started to turn away, then paused to tell me, "Fatima called last night. She's staying another week. July, mid-July, that's when she'll be back."

"Did she get Theodore?"

He looked puzzled. "I don't know. Hon, I'm sorry about things lately."

He looked embarrassed for a moment. Then, telling me to watch the stand, he headed toward the nearby building that housed the auction's only bar. I felt like I was watching my father turn into a teenager, trying out alcohol and girls for the first time. I let Eshe cover the stand while I followed him at a distance. When I saw him go into a phone booth, I ducked around the corner behind the pinball machine so I could hear him. At first, his voice sounded sweeter than I remembered it could be.

"Sounds good. I can pick you up at ten, if that's not past your bedtime," he said, almost giggling at his attempt at flirtation. A pause, and then, "Of course. Yes. Okay, gotta go. See you later."

I heard him dial again and then bark into the receiver, "It's me." All the sweetness had evaporated. "I don't care what you think," he said. A pause. "You can just go to hell then, and when you die, I'm gonna dance on your grave."

He hung up, put his hands in his pockets, pulled out his money and started counting it. He must have called Mimi, I thought, but then why had he told me he wasn't talking to her anymore? I watched him walk away, disappearing into the big world where anything could be bought, sold, stolen, or maybe given.

Chapter Three

I leaned forward in the swivel chair in the taxi office, balancing my elbows on the desk. I had learned the hard way that if I leaned back, the chair fell over. "Yeah, we can get a car to you at Thirty-seventh and Broadway in about ten minutes," I said, then pushed another button on the phone to call a driver.

"Okay, I got it," answered the new guy, a Pakistani who needed all the fares he could get in order to bring his mother-in-law to this country. When I'd told Liz I would be missing some classes so I could work dispatch at the taxi office, she told me to shoot whatever life gave me—especially if it entailed going underground with a United Nations host of characters. I had already taken portraits of several drivers as they leaned against the cement walls. I called the collection "Driving All Night," and focused my camera on the graininess of the street and our dimly lit garage.

I'd been sitting in the office for three hours now, my toes freezing in the ultra-cold air conditioning, while my father whisked in and out with a car salesman. He was trying to buy three more cabs, but negotiations clearly weren't going well. Through the glass walls of Dad's office, I watched the tall, gray-haired salesman nod and smirk as my father's face turned stone serious. I was trapped on the wrong side of the glass, surrounded by gray walls and cement floors, covering the phone for six more hours. I cursed myself for forgetting to bring my colored pencils so I could draw while I fielded calls. All I had was an old copy of *Time* magazine that featured the Bicentennial and the tall ships that were to descend on New York against a background of fireworks. Roger was going down to the harbor tonight with Mom, Geraldine, and even Missy, although she was too young to remember what she would see. The thought of what I was missing made me wish even more that I were above ground instead of down here.

Something had happened to the new Armenian dispatcher, Dad said, and she had to leave the country quickly. He needed me to fill in until he found someone good. "Someone I can trust. The dispatch is the heart of the whole operation," I heard him tell Lou, who tossed out various possibilities: "Seymour's mother-in-law, she'd be good," or "What about Johnny's ex-girlfriend?"

When I caught Lou plugging a quarter into the candy machine for a box of Raisinettes, I asked him why the last dispatcher left. Lou shook his head and said something about her boyfriend finding out. As he walked back to the garage, it all suddenly made sense to me. Dad must be having an affair with this woman, cheating on Fatima. I glared at him in his glass cage, wondering how he could do such a stupid thing, risking everything for him, for us. As I watched him bargain with the salesman, slamming both hands on his desk to intimidate the guy, I suddenly hated him. I didn't want him home in the evenings or anywhere around me, even if it meant that I was left alone with my camera and the TV for company.

The phone rang again, and this time it was Mimi.

"Your father said you would be here," she snapped.

"I thought you weren't talking to us," I countered, surprised at my boldness. For the first time, I felt like I was on the same level she was.

"Don't be ridiculous. Give me your father." Deflated, I felt myself fall back into my usual role as the obedient, and invisible, granddaughter. I wondered why I couldn't have the kind of grandmothers I saw in the TV commercials, the ones who actually liked their grandchildren.

I signaled to Dad and he picked up the phone nervously, as if he'd been anticipating her call. I watched him through the glass office wall, expecting him to slam down the receiver with a guilty but satisfied smile. Instead he nodded, looked down at the floor, and wrote some notes on a pad. He said something to the salesman that made the man sigh and leave quickly with Dad right behind him, trying not to look too worried. Lou popped into the dispatch office and took over the phone, summoning a relatively new driver—one we both liked, because he told outrageously dirty jokes—to pick us up in five minutes. Dad headed straight for the bathroom without even looking at me, yelling over his shoulder that we were going to meet Mimi at the Russian Tea Room.

Twenty minutes later, the Pontiac Grand Prix stopped in front of the restaurant and we got out, still laughing over a joke that involved a nine-inch pianist. I'd never been to the Russian Tea Room before, but I imagined Mimi must have chosen that place to meet because it sounded dramatic, and she wanted some drama to make her point. I expected her to ask my father, once again, to beg my mother's forgiveness. ("Not that she's the most suitable woman in the world," she'd add, "but stop this crazy nonsense called a divorce at once.") I rehearsed in my mind how my father would tell her once again that it was final—and none of her business.

We entered the grand room, too nervous to even look at each other. The red wallpaper had gilded edges, the wide floor was full of white linen-dressed tables, and the glass chandeliers shimmered in golden light. I wished I had brought color film. Right in the center of the room sat Mimi and her sister, a well-preserved specimen who liked to be called Auntie T. My late grandfather's unmarried twin sisters, Rosie and Ruthie, were there too. Their faces drooped a bit more than they had the last time I'd seen them, at my Bat Mitzvah, but they wore their usual pancake makeup. The last member of the party was Uncle Leo, the champion bowler regarded by the elderly members of our family as a settled family man, with a seldom-seen wife and five children stashed away somewhere on Long Island.

We took our seats quickly, our eyes darting back and forth like pet store fish trapped in plastic bags of water. Mimi beckoned to the waiter and whispered some instructions, then adjusted the brooch she wore on her red dress and patted my head in a way she never had before. Her companions were practically tripping over themselves in their rush to offer us compliments—how pretty I'd become, how trim Dad looked—but my grandmother stopped them with a look.

"I'll get to the point, Harold, because we're all busy people. A divorce, which I'm told is now final, is inevitable sometimes."

Dad and I exchanged a quick glance as we waited to hear Mimi's proclamation.

"We only wish that you had gone through the Jewish court to do it right. Get a get," she said, turning her hands open like it was joke. "But bygones are bygones. What I brought everyone here to press upon you is this request: we want you to give the girl to us to raise."

My spine turned to shivers and my mouth got so dry that I couldn't taste my tea. I would run away first, I told myself, before I went to live with her.

"I have the apartment in Queens, as you know," Mimi continued, "and when I'm in Florida for the winter Auntie T can look after her. School in the city means private school, of course—we can't have her with the coloreds, but I can take care of the tuition. A man shouldn't raise a teenage daughter alone. We all agree that if her mother isn't suitable to raise her, she should be raised by the women of our family."

The waiter brought over a huge tray of desserts, chocolate and strawberry things swirled with whipped cream, but I couldn't eat a bite. The twins giggled as if on cue. Auntie T, who had never spent more than ten minutes talking to me, chimed in, "A girl needs to be raised by women, or else how will she know how to be a woman?"

They seemed like characters out of a gothic horror novel, these four old women—all of them widowed or never married, their days planned around beauty appointments and manicures scheduled when the cleaning ladies came. I thought of our house in Jersey, my home for six years now. It seemed like a life raft, the only familiar thing left to me from before the divorce, and I knew I would do anything to stay there.

"Deborah just won't be safe with you. A man has appetites, and he's not always able to govern himself," Mimi declared, gazing at the wall above my father's head. Dad had gained back some of the weight he'd lost, something not lost on Mimi. "Now, what date do you have in mind for having her belongings sent to Queens?"

"No date," my father answered, looking like he was about to cry. To my amazement he stood up and took my hand, and we walked out without another word. The last thing we heard was Leo, prompted by Mimi, calling out, "But, Harold, it's for her own good. Think of your daughter for a change."

The Grand Prix took us straight back to the garage, with no jokes this time around. A good cabbie, my father liked to say, knows when to shut up. Then we drove home. Somewhere on the turnpike, Dad turned to me and said, "This never happened." I nodded gratefully, leaning my head against the cool glass and telling myself it was okay, over and over, until I finally fell asleep.

After that, summer settled into a strange but somewhat regular routine. We had the auction every Saturday and visitation with the kids on Sunday, when we'd either go bowling or watch a bad Disney movie, the awkward silence broken only by the munching of popcorn. Monday through Friday I usually slept until noon, ate a bowl of chocolate pudding (the instant kind) with some cool whip (or a cup of apple yogurt, if I were following a diet), and settled in to watch TV game shows. I won many washer and dryer sets, matching couches, and vacations to the Bahamas, plus enough cash to carry me for the rest of my life.

The big break in this domestic routine came on Wednesday nights, starting in late June when the "Shoot Your Life" class began. Dad balked at paying the sixty-dollar fee, but when I told him it got me a discount on the jeans I would need for fall, he gave in. Since he wasn't usually home in time to take me to class, I walked to Karmic Clothes with my camera around my neck, a pocketbook just large enough to hold a pile of photos, and some cash for dinner. I'd climb the hill behind the house, cut through the yard of a ranch house, walk down a long lane, and emerge from a small stand of trees onto the shoulder of Route 9.

The highway was busy and always tricky to cross. I looked both ways a few times and then ran fast, singing the line "sprung from cages out on Highway 9" off Springsteen's *Born to Run* album. On the far side of the highway, I walked along a field of tomatoes and passed an auto parts store, three gas stations, the shopping mall, and a field where something that looked like stubby corn was growing. By the time I reached the parking lot of the strip mall for Karmic Clothes, I had been walking close to an hour. Dad said it was five miles and I should just take a taxi, but there was something about getting there across that expanse of heat-holding pavement, under my own power, that felt right to me. Incidentally, I also learned that it was impossible to take good photographs of speeding cars.

I liked to arrive a few minutes early, leaving myself just enough time to buy a large coke on ice from the air-conditioned bagel shop before class. My right hand would pull out new photos for Liz even as my left hand was opening the door.

"What you got for me, little pixie?"

"I'm not a pixie or little, Liz," I reminded her, handing over the photos as she waited behind the register. I had only the auction photos with me today; the taxi shots would have to wait until next week, when I had time to get them developed. Something about that strange meeting with Mimi made me keep putting off developing the new roll of film.

"Nah, you're too tall. But you're sweet enough. You're still one of the innocents."

"I don't know about that," I said, wondering if she could tell I was still a virgin. Maybe non-virgins could sense that in people like me.

She held up my pictures: Boy singing to the sky, his arms extended and head thrown back; Eshe leaning against the wall, smoking a cigarette and counting money; Big Boy holding on his lap a much younger blonde woman who covered her mouth with both hands to keep from laughing. "Now these are great. I like how you're getting the faces."

"What do you mean?" I asked, trying to see these pictures anew. I had barely glanced at them when I picked them up from the photo counter at Shoprite. I knew I should be developing my own photos by now, but for some reason I just couldn't make myself go into the closet and get started.

"I mean that in this one," she explained, pointing to Boy, "you show he's both in love with the world and fucked over by it, too."

"How can you tell?"

"How can I tell? Look there," she said, pointing toward his face. "He looks like he could be crying or praying. I love that."

"But he was singing."

"All the better," she said. "And Eshe, this is pure Eshe. See how sweet and tough she looks at the same time? She's just a normal girl crying out for love."

I took a step back, turned my head toward the floor, and inhaled sharply before looking up. Liz was nodding at another of my photos, but I could tell she was only doing it as a tiny act of mercy, as if what she had just said didn't reveal everything about me.

Chapter Four

"What is plutonium?" Roger said out loud, using a question to answer the television screen, although he knew the game show host couldn't hear him. He would have won, too, since the contestant (a narrow man with scruffy blond hair and a twitching eye) didn't have a clue. We were watching *Jeopardy* in the family room. According to Mom, Missy couldn't come that evening because she was sick, but Dad and I were getting suspicious—we hadn't seen her in three weeks. I had to admit, however, that life was easier without a toddler to chase after and protect from dangers like the stairs and the toilet bowl, into which she dropped my new soaps whenever possible.

"What is an injunction?" Roger announced without looking up, his eyes still focused on the book in his lap.

"How do you know that?" I asked him.

He shrugged. "There's nothing else to do in this family but read." He still liked comics, but now he often read hardcover books he checked out of the library. During commercials he read so intensely that he never heard a word I said. He had discovered his own way to get through the desert between childhood and adulthood—and along the way he was memorizing a handy list of game show tidbits.

"So, do you mostly read science?"

He shook his head, his large blue eyes now fixed on the television. His hair had gotten darker—dirty blond, Mom called it, comparing it to hers when she was a kid—and curlier, too. He liked to keep his kinky, dirty blond hair trimmed short, close to his head.

"What else?" I asked.

"Lately the Brontë sisters."

"You mean *Jane Eyre?*" I had fallen in love with the blind and passionate George C. Scott on my tenth birthday, when Mom and Geraldine took me to see the movie version of the novel. Mom thought it was overly romantic, but Geraldine wept through the last hour, clutching my hand emphatically every so often. I looked over at Roger, who still hadn't answered me. "Hey, I asked you a question."

"Oh, not really *Jane Eyre*. I like *Wuthering Heights* the best."

"Why?"

"Because it's harder to figure out, and it's more like life."

"What do you mean?"

He turned toward me slightly, one eye still on the book and one ear directed toward the television. "I mean, life doesn't always work out so well, and it takes a lot of pages to get to an ending." Then, without missing a beat, he addressed the television again: "What is a symphony?"

Roger was only eleven, but with his game shows and books he already seemed like an old man. I imagined him carefully packing up his quiet life in bunched-up newspapers and carrying it around in an invisible briefcase that only he was able to see. When we were grown up would we become friends like Mom and Geraldine, or would we act like we had never known each other?

I went to the kitchen and took out some frozen pork chops that I had wrapped in foil, which turned out to be a mistake. I had to run the package under hot water until I could scrape the tiny pieces of foil off the meat. Next I put the chops under the broiler. Dad had left for the store hours ago ("back in a few minutes," he'd said), but I was used to his disappearances by now. He would show up just in time for dinner and then drive Roger, to whom he'd scarcely spoken to all day, back home to Mom's.

I opened a box of scalloped potato mix and started to follow the three easy steps. I read the calories per serving on the back of the box: 430, including the butter and milk. That number would upset Dad, who had taken to reading labels ever since his doctor told him he had to stop the diet pills or risk a heart attack. I didn't care. I was bored and craved something heavier and creamier. Then I looked down at my stomach and saw it sticking out slightly over the waist of the new jeans I'd bought from Liz. Suddenly I found my body disgusting. If I continued this way, would I end up just like my father?

Over the past few weeks, we had settled further into the routine of disgruntled husband and inept wife. The complaints came at me faster than Roger's answers to *Jeopardy*. Dad would say the same things regularly: "This ice water glass isn't big enough." "The meat is tough. I told you to read up on marinating." "There's a frozen spot in the middle of my corn." "You're just like your mother, only worse. She could cook."

It was his old song and dance, only this time I happened to be the one sitting across from it. At first I got upset and tried harder, but lately I merely nodded and recited to myself the evening television lineup. Tonight, in only eighteen minutes, it would be *All in the Family* and *Sanford and Son*—not a bad night ahead.

Most nights, when we weren't tagging clothes, Dad went out alone. If I asked about going with him, maybe suggested bowling or a movie, he told me I had my shows to watch and dishes to do, adding that he just needed some time alone. He seldom returned before I went to bed at midnight. We had turned into a boring old couple— grown apart from each other without ever being close.

One night, as I rinsed dishes and stacked them into the dishwasher, I paused, pulled out our biggest knife, so big we never used it and held it against my chest, the point touching the bone between my barely existent breasts.

Just as I did this, I heard my dad yell, "Don't forget, we need more laundry detergent." I wondered what trick of speed it would take, what strength it would require to push the knife right through me—it probably wouldn't kill me right away and the last thing I needed was another mess to clean up.

Our phone remained silent day after day. None of the neighbors spoke to me when I stepped outside. If I waved at one of them while picking up the mail, he or she turned away as if I didn't exist. I couldn't figure out why Fatima was taking so long to come back from Greece. I didn't even feel like taking photos or developing my exposed film. Dad and I were alone, enclosed in a miniature universe like one of those snow globes in the gift shop, the kind you picked up and shook until the snow whirled up from the plastic ground to make a winter scene.

"I can't take it anymore!" Dad shouted at me one evening, out of nowhere.

"What do you mean? What am I doing to you? I'm just breathing."

"Yeah, and taking up space. Why don't you go back to your mother? She likes to breathe and take up space, too."

He must be acting this way because he'd started gaining back all that lost weight, I told myself. "You know I can't do that. I chose to live with you."

My words sounded irritable, even matter-of-fact, but deep down I wanted to run out the door and never come back. The only problem was that I couldn't go back to my mother, not after what she did to me.

"Goody for me," he said, grabbing the unread newspaper and cursing under his breath.

"Yeah, it's all for you," I retorted quietly, but not quietly enough. He turned and stared at me with his tongue between his teeth.

"What do you know about me?" he demanded. "All you know is that I'm some kind of meal ticket. Well, I don't need this anymore, do you hear me?" He was screaming now. "I don't need this shit anymore. I never asked for you."

"I never asked for this, either. I thought we would have Fatima living with us and a brand new life, not me having to be your slave!"

The words came out faster than I could stop them. I could see right away what would happen next, his arm snapped out fast, knocking me to the ground. As I fell, he kicked my knee to make the fall harder. He stormed out of the room, but not before saying, "I never wanted you. Ever."

The whole scene unfolded just the way I imagined it would. I watched myself go through the motions and then lie sobbing into the multi-colored shag carpet. I watched myself slowly scramble to my feet after he was gone, climb the stairs to my room, open the door, and walk over to the bed. I saw myself go back and lock the door, lie down on the bed, then get up again to wedge my desk chair under the door handle to keep myself safe. I froze each step in my mind, as if I were shooting a photo essay about a girl crumbling.

When I woke up the next morning, still dressed, I was thirsty and hungry. I reached into my pocket and found a crumpled five-dollar bill, enough to buy a meal at the diner. I washed my face and headed out the door. The sun was hot, the walk long, and my legs tired, but I kept going, thinking how good it would feel to eat chicken croquettes. Was it noon, or later? I started to cry when a sprinkler started up, the water shooting over the sidewalk and hitting hard against my legs. No one was watching, which was good, I supposed, so I kept walking.

I ate my lunch at the counter, idly reading the menu just for something to do. It was close to one o'clock, leaving hours of safety ahead of me. I could work in the darkroom, start developing that old film. When the waitress came back I pointed to the apple pie, having determined I had just enough money to afford dessert. As I returned to my menu reading, however, a large black man in a crisp, long-sleeved white shirt, an elegant straw hat, and a black silk scarf sat down a few stools away.

I stole glances at him as I ate my pie, hoping that he would not catch me looking. He drank a cup of coffee and talked in a low voice to the waitress about his order. By now I was sure that it was Clarence Clemons. He looked exactly like he did on the cover of *Born to Run*, except bigger than I imagined. Anyone who could play the saxophone the way he did was sent from another planet to enlighten us, according to Liz. It would have been rude to take his picture even if I'd had my camera, so I contented myself with quick looks every few moments.

When I got up to leave, I laid my five-dollar bill on the counter, but the waitress waved it away. "He took care of it for you, sweetheart," she said, clearing away the plates. Clarence turned his head to me, tipped his hat, and smiled.

"Thank you," I said, edging past him on my way to the door.

"Hey," he said, the timber of his voice stopping me in my tracks, "don't let anyone break your spirit."

I was astonished that even he could see my sadness. I nodded hard, and tried not to start crying again as I headed home.

That night Dad came home happy and excited, as if nothing had happened. I had decided not to mention Clarence Clemons—I knew he wouldn't believe me anyway. Instead, I listened as he explained how he was going to add a dozen more cars. It was a big investment, but if he pulled it off we could do special things, like maybe travel around Greece with Fatima, let her show us around. And all the Bicentennial hoopla everywhere seemed to be giving everyone new confidence. He'd be a fool not to take advantage of this sort of opportunity. Then he told me I was doing a great job, especially for a kid—but considering what a head he had for business, it was no wonder that I could run a house on my own when my good-for-nothing mother never could.

He took me to a late showing of *Monty Python and the Holy Grail*, despite the fact that he called *Monty Python* an idiotic TV show whenever I watched it at home. He laughed so hard at the man who got all his limbs cut off that people turned around to stare. "And that killer rabbit," he said, as we were driving home, "that was hysterical." Looking at his profile as he drove, I could see what he must have looked like as a teen: the over-long nose and short forehead, the young face wanting to connect with someone who loved him but not knowing how, even today. He scared me the most when he was like this, because I never knew when the trap would spring and the steel teeth would clamp down again.

Photography classes had turned into the best part of my week, now that Liz took us to the diner after each session. Eshe seldom came along because of her boyfriend, who waited for her outside Karmic Clothes in a decaying orange Datsun. ("Look at that idiot grin on his face," Eshe would say, winking, as she slipped out the door. "Probably thinks he's gonna get some, and know what? He will.") Mark didn't go either, saying something about how he had to get home and help his dad, while Abby lamented that the diner was just too tempting for someone living on 800 calories a day. That left Taz and me—and since Taz spent most of his time sneaking up with his camera on unsuspecting patrons as they were about to take a bite of apple pie or beef tips on noodles, Liz and I had plenty of time to talk.

One night in July, as the temperature wore itself out at 100 degrees, Liz rolled her eyes at me as the manager chewed Taz out for disturbing his customers.

"But I was making art," Taz protested.

"Go somewhere else," the manager said. Liz smiled as she watched the scene unfolding near the dessert case.

"Don't you want your diners to be exposed to art?" Taz insisted.

The manager must have thought art was a person, not a life calling, because he grabbed Taz's shoulder and walked him out the door. I twisted around in the booth as Liz started laughing, but I missed this part.

"You think that boy is just a little too over the moon about photography?" she asked. I shook my head as we pushed our water glasses aside to make room for her lasagna and my chef salad. The waiter set down a large basket of bread and we started grinning like Eshe's boyfriend. "I tell you, girlie girl, I live for starch. Starch and grease, the building blocks of life."

"Me too," I answered. "Besides, I get sick of cooking at home."

"You do all the cooking? What about your mom?"

"She moved out after the divorce. It's just me and my dad."

"I was wondering how long she could stand having the furniture thrown on the front lawn. Did he ever set the couch on fire?"

"Nah. Besides, it's covered in plastic, and it wouldn't burn."

"Hey, that plastic might explode with enough heat. You never know what chemicals they put in it." She paused and gave me a hard look. "So you do the cooking? And clean the house too?"

I nodded. "And you're, what, sixteen?" I nodded again.

"A regular wife," she concluded.

"That's kinda true," I agreed, acting as if it were her idea, although I'd had the same thought many times.

"You like it?"

"No. Actually, I hate it. I hate having to broil those big frozen steaks, which is almost impossible to do without burning the meat. I hate the dishwasher because we use so few dishes that I never know if I should run it or not. I really hate vacuuming, but most of all I hate cleaning his bathroom. It's disgusting—and he keeps old *Playboys* under a stack of *Cues,* which is even more disgusting."

I was surprised by how fast the words came pouring out of me. "The neighbors don't speak to me. When they see me get the mail, they look the other way or go back into their houses. As soon as I'm old enough to leave, I'm going to move far away from the suburbs." I suddenly remembered Liz lived here, too, and added, "I mean, I know there are some good neighbors out there, and sometimes the houses are nice, but –"

"Hey, babe, don't make nice on the 'burbs on my account. I fucking hate living here too. I would move to the city in a heartbeat. Well, that or a farm."

"Yeah, live in the country or the city. Not this in-between shit." I tried to keep myself from smiling self-consciously as I said the word "shit."

"I'm with you there," Liz said. "Now, what about your family? I don't just mean your mother, but your grandparents and crap—you see them, right?"

I shook my head and ate another dinner roll, hoping she wouldn't ask me to explain. I kept my head down, pretending to look for the butter, but I could hear her turning things over in her mind. I imagined a satisfied look on her face, as if she understood everything about me now.

In the end, though, she merely concluded, "Being a housewife sucks."

I nodded again and changed the subject. I didn't want to talk about my life anymore.

Some mornings I woke up so tightly woven in my dreams—especially the recurring dream of being held by someone who loved me—that I forgot where I was. I would look around in a daze at this strange room where I lived, and then I would remember. No mother. No kids downstairs. No lover beside me with his lacy smile, his muscular arms holding me through the dark night.

"Oh, it's just another day," I'd tell myself, as if the days couldn't help but keep coming. But sometimes I would think about getting into the car late at night, after my father went to sleep, and doing whatever you were supposed to do with the tail pipe and the carbon monoxide. Considering that I cooked all the meals, I wondered if it might be more appropriate to go the way Sylvia Plath went, with the help of the gas oven. I'd read Plath's novel and concluded that all you could really do, when you lived in a bell jar, was try to shatter it. Then I read *I'm Okay, You're Okay*, a book my mother left behind, but "I'm not okay, you're not okay" seemed to fit my life better. The guy who wrote about those adult, parent, and child roles would surely have something to say if he visited our house and saw me failing at all three.

In the evenings I tagged clothes, sitting in the living room surrounded by lawn furniture, slipping the needle of the tagging gun into each polyester armpit that came my way. Perched in the middle of a spoked wheel of clothing—eight piles of pants, eight piles of shirts—I would start at size 18 and keep going until I reached size 52.

One night I put *Blue* on the record player and listened as Joni Mitchell sang "Canada," feeling excited that there were only six days left until Fatima came back from Greece. Dad was out again and didn't even want dinner this time; he said he had it covered. I still had 200 tags in front of me, each one needing "$2.50" written on it with a black marker. When I finished, I was going to take photos of the piles, maybe close-ups from off-beat angles, so that no one could recognize the clothing right away. Liz had once shown me a photograph of a cow taken up close, and I'd thought it was a landscape. Surely there must be a way to do something like that with polyester pants.

The doorbell rang and I jumped up, eager for any distraction. When I pulled the door back, however, I recognized Chris, the guy from down the street. I hadn't seen him since that horrible May afternoon in his basement.

"Hey, you, so this is where you live. I brought a little M.J., and I thought you might like to partake of it with me and maybe relax together."

I remained firmly planted between the door and the threshold. "Oh, thanks, but I need to work." There was something wolfish about his smile.

"All work and no play makes a dull girl."

"I guess I'm just a dull girl, then. Thanks anyway." As I started to swing the door closed, his hand shot up and blocked the door's motion with a hard thump.

"Don't thank me. Let me in." The way he said it made my skin seize up, as if he were determined to get in or else. "It'll be good for you this time," he added, his voice softening. "You'll really like it."

"No, I can't," I said. I was trembling because his foot was wedged on the threshold, meaning he could easily force his way in. Think fast, I told myself, think of something very fast.

"How about I get you a soda? I have a whole lot of cream soda."

"Soda? Well, I guess."

He relaxed a little bit, just enough to loosen his grip on the door. I threw all my weight against it, slamming it shut and locking it quickly. He started kicking it from the outside as I ran to the laundry room door and checked it—it was locked. I ran to lock the sliding glass door next, then barred it and closed the shades. I ran into the garage to make sure both doors were locked, then frantically checked the locks on the downstairs windows.

My efforts were unnecessary, however, because he left as soon as I locked the front door. When I realized this, I sat down at the kitchen table and drank a cream soda myself. I was not crying, although I told myself that this was the place in the story where the girl cries. Something in me had sealed shut, and I could see the incident only as a series of pictures: the creep trying to push the door open, me slamming it shut, me running in a blur to lock the doors, me sitting very still right now. Yet even when I tried to put all the pictures together, they didn't really begin to tell this story.

Chapter Five

One afternoon when the sun beat down so hard on the auction that all the shoppers left, Dad took off with a pile of pants "to do some business." He told Eshe and me to "watch the fort" until five o'clock, when he'd come back to help us pack. He and Fatima used to do this often—take piles of pants off somewhere and return with bartered goods like new dishes, figurines, or long underwear. Dad handed me a bundle of money for making change. As soon as he was out of sight, Eshe and I shoved aside the piles of pants and sat down on either end of the long table.

"You know, you would look good with short hair," Eshe mused.

"I like it long," I answered, surprised that she was taking an interest in me.

"Nah, it would look cool if it were shorter."

"Well, maybe a little shorter."

Within five minutes I was in a lawn chair Eshe borrowed from Sergei, and she was cutting my hair. Next door, Boy howled "Going to the Barber" to the tune of "Going to the Chapel."

Eshe assured me that I was a lot prettier than I looked and not to worry, she was just going to take a few inches off, but I saw long strands falling to the ground. "Your hair is your karma," she said. "Cut it off, and you're free."

"What's karma?" I asked.

"Karma? It's like all your shit, all the stuff that pulls you down. My karma is to get messed up with fuckhead boyfriends who fuck their brains out with acid and rip me up. And my karma is to live with my old lady, who chases me around the house with a screwdriver and calls me a whore."

"Can't you change your karma?"

"Sure, but it takes time. That's why I'm working here—gotta get the bucks to move on out. Once I have my own place, I won't have to crash with schmucks who ruin my life, just to keep my mom from killing me in my sleep."

"But this job doesn't pay that much," I observed—rather coyly, since I knew Eshe's secret—as my hair continued to fall. "How are you gonna get all the money you need?" It felt good to finally talk with her like an equal, like I was a normal person.

"This job is fine," she answered quickly, and then changed the subject. "So why don't you talk to your mom?"

"How do you know what I do with my mom?"

"Your dad told me," she said. "Actually, I think it's pretty cool. He said she tried to hurt him in the divorce by hurting you, but you just said you didn't need her."

"Yeah, I guess I don't."

We were quiet for a few minutes while she snipped at the back of my neck. I felt lighter, almost happy again. When I stood up and shook the hair off the black polyester pants she'd used as a towel around my neck, Boy and Big Boy applauded. Eshe said this haircut made my eyes shine. She even took a bunch of pictures of me, first with my camera and then with hers.

Big Boy, who hardly spoke to me, walked over afterwards and touched my forearm. "You're a good girl, a pretty girl," he said. "Just take good care of yourself. Don't let anyone pull your chain, you know what I mean?" I nodded, although I had no idea what he meant. He bent over and kissed my head, and although he hardly knew me, he said, "I love you, baby," before walking off.

Later, I went to the bathroom and saw myself in the mirror looking older, more interesting. I pulled the roll of money out of my pocket and, without thinking, slipped three fives out of the middle and stuffed them deep down in my other pocket. I actually did feel a little happy.

When Dad returned, he had us pack up the truck since the heat was keeping customers away. The racks were so hot that we wrapped shirts around our hands before touching the metal. Within twenty minutes the truck was loaded and Dad paid Eshe. She winked at me, which made him look my way.

"What happened to your hair?" he asked.

"I cut it," Eshe announced proudly. "Doesn't she look cool?"

Dad nodded politely. As soon as she was gone, he said in a sympathetic whisper, "It will grow back." Then he told me to crawl into the back of the truck and lie across the racks to keep them from toppling.

"But those racks are burning hot. And I just have shorts on."

"I don't care. It's your job to keep the racks upright."

Boy and Big Boy pretended to be talking about their wares, but it was clear that they were listening to everything we said.

"I'll get scorched."

"I don't care," he repeated, staring hard into my eyes.

Much to my surprise, I heard myself yell, "No! I won't do it."

"Yes, you will."

"No," I repeated quietly. I started walking away. The short-haired version of me did not put up with shit, I told myself. It was over four miles to our house, but I had covered twenty miles once in a March of Dimes walkathon. I would walk all the way home, and he couldn't stop me.

"You turn around this instant and get in the truck."

I kept moving past the other vendors, feeling a slight breeze that cooled my skin as I pushed my way through the hot air. Once I reached the corner, I turned down an aisle where he couldn't see me. Soon I was running, not fast, but enough. I felt something lift inside me, a sensation of speed that zipped out of me as if running were my natural state. I reached the outskirts of the auction and ran alongside a pine forest that would take me all the way down to the road. He was going to throw me out of the house for sure now, but I didn't care. Cool air spun from the trees and my thighs ached a little, but not enough to slow me down. Ahead lay the side road I would follow all the way down to the busy highway, then cross over to reach the edge of our housing development.

The sky was dimming slightly at its edges. Up ahead lay a shopping center that, like all decent shopping centers in New Jersey, offered pizza, Chinese food, and the obligatory bagel shop. I stopped at Tony's Pizzeria and had two slices with a giant Tab. I continued my walk refreshed, feeling hot, raw, and yet much stronger than I had imagined I could feel after a day at the auction.

When I got home, Dad was sitting in the living room on the lawn chair, staring at the carpet. He started when I walked in. The old fear flooded in again, and I felt myself breathing faster.

"So you're home."

I nodded.

"You get any dinner?"

"Yeah, I brought some money with me from home, and I used that."

He suddenly stood up, his tone changing. "You mean you stole some money."

"No, I brought some that you paid me last week."

"Don't lie to me. I gave you exactly eighty-five dollars when I left this afternoon. When I got back, you handed me eighty dollars. Now, based on sales on a typical afternoon, you should've returned about $300 to me. So where's the rest of the money?"

"What are you talking about? No one came, except Eshe sold something to some lady. I used the five dollars for fries and a smoothie."

"Eshe said you took some change from her, and that's why she only had a ten to return to me from the thirty dollars I left with her." The veins in his long neck were flaring and I could tell he was breathing hard.

"That's not true," I cried. "Ask Boy. Ask Big Boy. And if you don't believe me, look in my pockets. I only have ten bucks. I didn't take hundreds of dollars from you."

He stared me down, but I could see it dawning on him that Eshe was probably stealing and maybe I was, too, but it was only small potatoes and he couldn't prove much. He sat back down, picked the newspaper up off the floor, and said, "Go to hell," in a low voice.

There was no way to prove to him that I wasn't a thief. None of the things I could imagine saying—"I didn't, why won't you believe me!" or, "Go to hell yourself, you asshole!"—would work. He might make me live with Mom, and then where would I be? I tried to come up with some words, some tone of voice that would convince him, but as it turned out I needn't have tried so hard. The doorbell rang, and Boy was there, explaining to Dad that his truck had broken down. The mechanic was waiting for a part from out of town, so he was stuck in Jersey for the night.

"We have plenty of room. Stay here," Dad offered.

"I just need a floor to sleep on, carpeting preferred. My father is staying at a friend's, if you know what I mean," Boy said. "But I could sure use some tidbits to eat, ma'am, begging your pardon."

I led Boy to the kitchen. On the one hand I felt like I'd slipped back into my role as haggard housewife, put upon yet again by her demanding family, but at the same time I was relieved to be delivered from my role as bad daughter. Soon the men were seated at the kitchen counter while I opened the freezer and pulled out two frozen steaks wrapped in white paper. I saw a third white package in the corner, but I didn't want meat. I avoided eye contact with Dad as I cooked, but after a while the whole house was so filled with Boy, so overwhelmed by his size and his stories, that our problems no longer found room to bother me. When we finally sat down to eat, there were potatoes, steaks, a lopsided salad with more croutons than lettuce, some frozen corn heated up, and a big pile of bread. I figured Boy would eat a lot.

"Jimbo's been there the longest, since '65," Boy reminisced, as he cut off a hunk of meat. "That's why he gets the choice spot. Me and my dad, we're just toddlers, only been there since '69. And you, well, you're still in the fetus stage."

The idea of a fetus stuck in that filthy, windy place made me shiver. I spooned myself a plate of potatoes and poured pepper over them. I was just an accessory to their meal. As soon as I was done, I carried my solitary plate to the sink and walked upstairs.

My head ached, my eyes wanted to close, and the bony edges of my feet hurt from being rubbed by my sandals during the long walk. I had a hard time staying awake long enough to take off my clothes and put on an oversized T-shirt, the one with Goofy at the beach. Mom had bought it for me only a year ago, back when I was still a kid. I fell asleep immediately and drifted into dreams of standing next to a long table selling pants, as if I were still at the auction. "It's not fair," I said aloud in the dream, "I already did that all day." But the dream didn't have to play fair.

When I couldn't stand it anymore I sat up, turned on the pink light next to my bed, and stared at the night sky, which seemed darker with the light on. I suddenly remembered that we were going to the airport today to meet Fatima's plane at two o'clock. That meant I could always go back to sleep later, so I went downstairs, opened the door to the darkroom, and flicked on the red light. Along with my equipment, which included the enlarger Dad bought for me at an underground photography shop near the garage, I had Liz's instructions thumb-tacked to the wall—and practically ingrained in my memory by now. I pulled out a roll of film with nothing special on it, just some rooms in our house, the kind of thing Liz had suggested we use as we learned to develop our own pictures. ("And if you fuck up," she added cheerfully, "you can simply step out of your darkroom and shoot it all over again.")

Once I opened the canister, however, I realized that I had picked up the wrong roll by accident. I panicked for a moment, worried that I would destroy some pictures I couldn't afford to lose, but I reminded myself that all I needed to do was proceed from step to step. I wrapped the film onto the reel, remembering how Liz had demonstrated this technique for us in a brightly lit room. (She'd said it was cool to ruin a roll of film if that's what it took to help us save the world with photography). Then I dropped the roll into the developing tank, mixed the chemicals together, and followed the steps she taught us, setting the timer so that I knew when to put in the stop bath, and when to set up the fixer solution.

I watched Fatima's face slowly emerge inside the tank, outlined against the backdrop of the auction. She had a face a little like one of those finely drawn horses on a Greek vase—high, wide cheekbones and large, dark eyes. Her lips were too large for her face, especially in this photo where she was neither smiling nor frowning, just staring right through the camera and me. I moved the print to the stop bath for five minutes and then to the fixer, letting my hands work through the steps of the process. By the time I'd hung the prints up to dry on my little clothesline, I felt as if I had crossed into a new land. This is what photographers did, people like me—or the people I was trying to be, at least. I covered the tanks securely and emerged from the closet into the dim light, heading for the kitchen to pour the used stop bath down the drain.

"What doesn't scare you makes you stronger," said a strange voice from near the floor.

I jumped, almost spilling the fluid all over the shag rug. Boy was leaning against the living room wall, his giant silhouette a looming shadow in the dark. When he stood up, I saw he was wearing red-and-white striped pajama bottoms and no shirt. His chest was covered with reddish hair and seemed to go on forever.

"I heard you moving around in there, but they say light ruins everything with photography, so I didn't come in."

"It's fine, once I'm at this stage, to open the door a little." I waited a beat to see what he would do.

"So we can open the door?"

"Sure," I said. I opened the darkroom door and turned some of the photos around so he could see the images. He was too big to lean in very far, but he recognized faces: his own, Fatima's, his father, my father.

"Those are definitely her eyes," he said, peering into the dark rabbit hole of my darkroom. He backed out and so did I, handing him the contact sheet.

"I know. This is my favorite shot," I said, pointing to a stamp-sized image on the sheet. He agreed, saying that I had chosen the best one to enlarge.

"Why do you think so?"

"Just look at her. She's very comfortable being herself." Even though he wasn't looking at me, I suddenly felt embarrassed. He continued earnestly, "Here's what I want to say. I know this can't be easy for you. I see Eshe. I see your dad."

He reached out a huge hand and placed it on my leg, the way a big dog rests its paw on you before falling asleep. I wondered if he was making a pass at me, but the idea seemed ridiculous. "How old are you?"

"I'm sixteen. You know that," I said cautiously. "And you must be what, twenty-four or so?"

"What makes you think that?"

"I don't know, you just look like that, I guess."

"I just turned eighteen." He looked into my eyes. His were blue and looked beaten."

"But that's almost my age."

"You want to know my story? Mom died when I was eleven. Dahlia, that's my sister, was sixteen. She was the one who was supposed to take care of me, bring me up in the world.

"My dad was on the road buying irregular clothes all the time, and then doing the markets—Wildwood, Philly, one north of New York. You see, he had us at something every day, seven days a week, as soon as Mom died. He couldn't stand being home without her."

"So you never saw him. What happened to Dahlia?"

"Dahlia was a mess. She took drugs. She hung out with men who showed no respect for her. She was almost grown, but I was the one taking care of her. I cooked her dinner, I cleaned up the house while she was out shooting up whatever she could find. When I was fifteen, she got pregnant. It was a miracle that baby came out in one piece. But you see, after that baby was born, Dahlia really fell apart. She stayed in her room and cried, ate nothing, and refused to take care of her young one."

His story surprised me. Where was the man who liked to yell out mock commercials in an Italian accent ("give me money, and I give you sweater!")? He seemed like such a different person than the character he played at the auction.

"I had to get up at night with that baby, rock it to sleep, sing to it. I found an old woman down the block who watched the baby when I went to school, but I changed its diapers. I fed it formula. It was me or no one."

"Where's the baby now?"

His formerly granite-like large face was soft and close.

"That's just it. I was in ninth grade. The baby—we named him Tony—was four months by then. I had two weeks of school left, just two weeks, and then I could be with Tony all day. I was learning about the Civil War when it happened. They called me out of class."

I felt so cold and worried that goose bumps rose on my arms.

"Tony died. No one knows why. He was sleeping at Mrs. Shain's house in the playpen, like he did every afternoon, and he just stopped breathing. Dad flew home from Pittsburgh that night. Dahlia wouldn't even look at us when we told her."

"Did you do an autopsy?"

"Sure, we did. Dad wanted to make sure it wasn't foul play, you know, but the coroner said he just died. Sudden Infant Death Syndrome. No one but God knows why."

"And you still believe in God?"

"Of course. Why wouldn't I?" His blue eyes were so earnest that I realized I truly didn't know what I believed any more. If there was a God, then why did he let babies die?

"I don't know," I replied slowly. "My brother died of SIDS too."

"I know that." He picked up the contact sheet again. "I like this picture of me. It makes me look all slimy and business-like."

I shrugged. "Whatever happened to Dahlia?"

"She's out west somewhere. We only hear from her when she needs money."

"And you send it?" I picked up the photo Boy liked, and clicked on the overhead light to get a better look. His face, wide and white, seemed to tell a different story than the one his hands were telling at that particular moment.

"Of course I send it. She's family, and family is family for life. That's why you need to call your mother."

"What do you know about my mother?"

"I know a girl has to have her mother. Dahlia didn't have her mother, and look what happened to her. You're smart and you're strong, too, but if I were living your life, I'd be moving to my mom's house pronto."

Anger flashed so quickly that I couldn't think of a reply, but I had to say something. "Don't tell me what to do." I leaned back and took a breath, surprised that I was so upset. I tried to sound nicer. "Look, I'm just really tired."

It was true, I told myself, but inside I was remembering the knishes, and the journal. There was a long list of reasons why I should avoid her.

Boy didn't look the least bit rattled by my outburst. He quietly took one of the trays from the darkroom and followed me to the kitchen, and together we poured the chemicals down the drain.

Eight hours later, Boy and I were sitting in the back seat of a speeding taxi, a Volare this time. Fatima was in the front seat with Dad as he drove down the turnpike from the Newark airport. Going to meet her plane an hour ago, I'd been tired but happy. I would have a mother again, Dad would calm down, and I wouldn't have to do all the cooking and cleaning, or even most of it. I could go back to being the rather ignorant, carefree teen I had been just a few months ago. But as soon as I saw her coming down the escalator with a crowd of people from the plane, I knew something was wrong. She half-smiled in my direction but didn't hug me. She didn't touch Dad, either, except to hand him a carry-on bag. She didn't acknowledge Boy at all as we made our way to the underground parking lot. Dad, Boy, and I carried her luggage, so heavy that the handles left deep lines in the centers of our palms.

I glanced at Fatima as we loaded the luggage into the trunk of the taxi. She was staring blankly into the dark of the garage. She didn't look angry, just sad, as if most of the abundant life inside her had leaked out in Greece, and she had returned with what little remained. Maybe she just needed time, maybe she was tired, I whispered to Dad. He nodded quickly, as if he believed in such an easy fix. I wondered why he wasn't more disturbed, what he knew that I didn't know. I couldn't shake the feeling that the world was once again falling apart around me.

The ride to Chinatown, where Dad had invited Boy to dine with us after the trip to the airport, was long and quiet. Boy stared out the window at the refineries. I looked at my hand on the seat, barely half the size of his hand. If he was a fallen giant, then what was I? I heard Fatima say, in a low and distracted voice, "I don't care," as Dad turned onto a street lined with red lanterns. Chinese characters in red paint were scribbled across every window.

The restaurant he chose seemed more alive than we did. There were huge Chinese murals on the walls with swimming goldfish and men playing chess in pavilions of beckoning friends. I sat down next to Fatima, wishing I had brought my camera.

"The auction's been slow," I told her, "but now that you're home, it should pick up." She nodded but still wouldn't look at me.

Menus were passed out. Boy tried to start a conversation several times, eventually grabbing Dad's interest with the story of the fire that had burned through the Englishtown Auction several years ago. "That old building drew that fire in faster than professors can lift a few sweaters out of my stand."

The mention of professors made me turn away from Boy and back to Fatima. "When does Theodore get back?" I asked her, trying to look interested in what she loved, trying to bring her back to me.

She stared into my eyes, clearly angry. Then, without looking at Dad, she asked him bitterly, "You didn't tell her?" She stormed out of her seat and disappeared into the bathroom. I looked at Dad.

"He was, uh, taken back by his father to Greece," he muttered. "The only way she could keep him was to stay in the country."

"But you said it would work out. And what about Canada?"

"So sue me! I was trying to be an optimist. For her sake. For yours. Anyway, Canada just didn't work out."

Boy launched into a subdued rendition of "Cockeyed Optimist," which didn't help the mood at all. I gave him a sharp look and he stopped singing.

"So let me get this right. Fatima gave up her son to be in this country? Why would she do that?" I asked the question as if I had never heard of a mother giving up her children. Then I looked down at the table, biting my lip.

"Not to be in this country, but to be with someone," Dad said, smirking.

"You?" he shrugged, as if he were too embarrassed to answer.

When Fatima returned, there was a long, no-eye-contact meal of terrible food that burned my tongue. After the tea and fortune cookies arrived, Dad started talking up his newest venture. "I have a line on halter-tops, crocheted halter-tops. And the auction's planning to open on Sundays—cheap tables, four dollars a day on the outskirts. Someone," he said, looking at me, "could make a killing."

I looked back at him. "Someone?"

"Sure, why don't you try running your own business? It'll teach you what I have to go through in mine."

Fatima opened her eyes and looked at me, as if she had just arrived. "You could sell halter-tops, Deborah. You and me. We could sell them together, you especially with your young body."

"But you're the one with boobs!"

She laughed a little. Dad laughed too, watching my face turn red. On the drive home, I dozed while Boy sang songs from the fifties and Fatima talked with my father like she did last spring, like we were all good again. At least that was what I told myself, trying to find a thread of hope each time Fatima laughed.

"Give her some time," Dad kept telling me, over and over, in the coming weeks.

That first Sunday was hot, ninety-six degrees in the shade, so I sat on a pile of halter-tops to keep my bare legs from touching the hot wood of my chair. I ate a cherry snow cone, careful not to drip on the orange and green crocheted halter-top I was wearing. Fatima wore hot pants and a thick, white bandanna-style halter-top with a built-in bra that she found at Sears. In the past few days she had returned to her old self. She talked fast, laughed easily, and even tousled my hair occasionally. I smiled broadly at her as the little hamster of hope raced wildly around inside me on its wheel, no matter how much the wheel squeaked.

Our new booth was a long way from Boy, who sold his wares in his usual spot next to Dad. Dad was selling pants and shirts, as usual, with Eshe's help. At the diner Sunday night, Fatima and Dad joked about having thousand-dollar weekends from now on. Fatima patted Dad's arm, newly tanned. He looked slightly orange in his lime-green leisure suit, but neither of us was unkind enough to tell him that.

"We're rich. We're rich. We're fabulously rich," I said, mimicking Mr. Howe from *Gilligan's Island*.

No one pointed out that working Sundays would prevent us from seeing Roger and Missy. I spent my weekday evenings tagging until Dad picked me up and took me to Fatima's house for dinner. We spent most evenings sitting on the couch, watching TV together and joking about the business.

One night, as I washed dishes at Fatima's house, she put her arm around me and said something in Greek that sounded very sweet. "That means, 'just like a daughter, my daughter,'" she explained.

I beamed right back at her, in English.

Chapter Six

"Now, there's intercourse, oral sex, and anal sex," the rabbi began, while the temple youth group members stared nonchalantly at the carpet. Fortunately, the shaggy sea of green, orange, and brown with yellow specks was so hideous it was hard to look away. "Intercourse you all know about."

We nodded. The boy next to me, with blond ringlets and a freckled nose, pretended to be taking notes as he drew giant guns with little Martians holding them. A girl with long black hair, parted in the middle and straight as a Breck commercial, looked the rabbi in the eye as if she really did know it all. Underneath the table, I could see her platform shoes bouncing up and down nervously. Abby, Mark, and a few of the kids who had packed food for the hungry a few months back at the elementary school were there too.

Fatima had insisted I go to the youth group to meet young people, learn to socialize. She was concerned that all I did was take pictures, watch TV, tag clothes, and hide in the closet moving sheets of contact paper from container to container, waiting to see what appeared. Last night, over dinner, she said I had to stop disappearing into that closet and spend time with other kids. Fatima talked about a church group I might like, too, if things didn't work out at what she called my "Jewish Church." Since I knew some of the kids and they had always been pretty nice to me, I decided to go for Fatima's sake.

When I stopped at the temple with Dad to find out when the youth group met, the rabbi shook our hands knowingly as he ushered us into his small, dark, wood-paneled office. He was large and lumpy, with hair down to his waist and long skinny legs. According to the tittering temple secretary, he had just been thrown out of a New York City synagogue for being "too radical."

"Tea?" he asked, flashing a collection of herbal tea bags. We shook our heads, but I was nevertheless entranced by the smell of the apple-cinnamon tea brewing in his "McGovern in '72" mug.

"I see you're looking at my cup. Yes, I worked for McGovern. Since I lived in Rhode Island, I was campaign manager for the state for two years. What a job! But it's what got me back to rabbinical school."

"Back?" Dad asked.

"At least Rhode Island's a small state," I offered.

"Yes to both of you. And back is right. I was thrown out of rabbi school for challenging the patriarchy, but isn't that what Judaism, at its heart, is really all about?"

As soon as he got a chance, Dad explained some things to the rabbi, using terms he'd probably heard on one of his radio talk shows. "And we believe Deborah's clinically depressed, that she needs some activity to help her recover, and that religion would be good for her."

"And 'we' means your wife and yourself?" The rabbi had a high-pitched voice and a huge stomach above his stick-like legs. It was easy to imagine him laughing or screaming hysterically.

"No, sir, I mean, Rabbi. My wife and I are divorced. Deborah lives with me."

"And the 'we'?"

"That would be myself and a woman I date, a woman who's like a mother to Deborah."

The rabbi leaned back in his chair and sighed, as if the phrase "a woman I date" told him everything there was to know about me. "I'd like to talk to your daughter alone for a few minutes, if you don't mind."

I didn't mind at all. In fact, despite the fact that we had just met, I felt as if I had known this weird rabbi for a long time. He seemed like someone who had seen it all and yet wasn't turned off by other people the way I was.

"Fine," Dad said, standing up. "I'll be in the hall."

As soon as the door closed, the rabbi leaned forward on his elbows and looked into my eyes. His own eyes were green and his face, although mostly covered in hair, looked younger than I imagined a rabbi's face could look. He would look good even if he was photographed in natural light. "I've seen some shit," he began. "You can talk to me."

I started to shrug, but stopped myself. I began to say, "I'm okay," but that seemed pointless, too. I felt suddenly stupid. What was my problem? I wasn't sure how to put it in words, but if I could show him some photos, maybe that would work.

"It all just seems so pointless," I finally managed to say.

"What seems pointless? Your parent's divorce? Your dad's girlfriend? This talk with me?"

"I don't know. I guess I mean my life in general."

The rabbi breathed slowly. There was something about the way he breathed, and how sad his eyes looked, that made him seem familiar. I had the feeling he'd been my neighbor for years, always joking around with me about my bike or the new baby. Inside me was a whole island of fear and dread, hidden behind those good meals and dish washing with Fatima. As I started to cry, I felt something reach through the air between us and gently place itself on my forehead.

For a second or two, I didn't realize that this imaginary hand was real. The rabbi had actually reached out and placed his palm on my forehead, like he was going to push me out of this world. But he didn't. He simply watched me with a quiet intensity.

"My name is Lyn," he said. Seeing I was uncomfortable with that, he quickly added, "but you can call me Rabbi. And I'd like you to come in and speak to me each week for a while."

We arranged it so that I would meet with him an hour before the youth group, which he usually led. Now he was finishing his talk to the group by explaining what cunnilingus and fellatio were, and how anal sex could be particularly painful if enough lubricant wasn't used and should be pursued only if both parties were in full agreement. Although no one said anything, I could tell that just about every girl in the room (and a few boys, too) were ready to throw up.

He leaned back in his chair. "Now that was a lot of information. Why don't we take a break so you can absorb it, and then you can come back and rap with me. I still need to tell you about homosexuality. Then ask me anything! Next week, we'll talk about drugs. And believe me, I've done it all!"

We filed out to the kitchen. The girl next to me, so small she could have been in third grade, yelled out, "That is SOOOOO disgusting! I will kill anyone that ever tries to put his putz in my ass."

She noticed me standing next to her and smiled. "Hi, I'm Amy, and that's Sam, short for Samantha," she said, indicating a redhead in pink hot pants who was making gagging sounds and laughing.

Amy handed me a stack of paper cups. As I uncoupled them to prepare pouring lemonade, I wondered why the temple needed two industrial refrigerators and a counter as large as a car, when no one ever ate a real meal here.

"Kill? I would die," said another girl. "I would just die."

"I would turn into a lesbian first," Amy volunteered.

"What do you think lesbians do?" Sam asked.

"I don't want to think about that, it's too sick." The other girl shuddered.

Just then the blond curly-haired boy snuck up behind them, singing the jingle from the local furniture store. "'You gotta see Seaman's first, see Seaman's first!' Seaman—it's just like semen, get it?"

"Get outta here, Randy! You're gross!"

Standing beside that big white counter, drinking lemonade and eating graham crackers, I felt like someone from another planet. I was sad to see that Mark had already left—he seemed different from the others, older somehow. The rabbi walked in with his teacup and opened the refrigerator.

"Echinacea," he said, holding up a vial of something cloudy. "I grow it myself, for the immune system. Anyone want any?" No one did, so he plucked out an apple, closed the refrigerator door, and left the kitchen.

"How old do you think he is?" Randy asked me.

"I don't know. Maybe thirty."

"My mom," interjected Sam, "was on the hiring committee. She says he's thirty-five, but he looks younger. He was thrown out of a synagogue in the city for screwing around with someone's wife."

"I heard it was because he protested the war," said Randy. "My mom was on that committee, too, and she loves him."

"I hope not too much!" Sam shot back.

Although the rabbi had introduced me as "Deborah, a beautiful person," hardly anyone spoke to me or even looked my way for the rest of the evening. I liked that—it made the evening feel more like a scene I was shooting and would develop later, in the comfort of my own closet. After we sat back down in our nervous chairs and listened to the rabbi talk about how homosexuals could have beautiful and meaningful relationships, I felt even more invisible.

"Now, any questions?" No one said anything. The rabbi started breathing slowly again, a trick he must have learned somewhere along the way. Maybe I needed a trick like that. It made people feel like they had to talk.

Jon, a football-player Jew whom we all considered a bit of an anomaly, blurted out, "How do fags do it?"

"First of all," the rabbi began, "'fags' prefer to be called 'gay.' Second of all, if you remember all the things I told you about sex, how it can be intercourse, oral, or anal, you'll see that two out of three apply to gay men. As for women, who prefer to be called 'lesbians,' there are mouths and artificial devices. And we all have hands."

Without thinking, most of us immediately took our hands off the table and sat on them. The gesture was so sudden that everyone in the room broke out laughing, including me.

"What about you?" asked Abby, whose long, straight hair was parted perfectly down the middle.

"You'll just have to use your imagination," he replied. "Even better, don't. Now, any other questions? I covered sexually transmitted diseases and birth control earlier in my talk. If you have any questions about those topics, let's rap."

Someone asked him to explain what "margin of error" meant, but before the rabbi could answer, someone else said, "That's what you are," and we all laughed again. He told us how condoms were made, how IUDs were mysterious but effective, and where Planned Parenthood was located. Then it was time to go home. On the way out, the rabbi caught my eye and winked.

"So you think he's a gay? I mean, how else would he know this stuff?" asked the kid just ahead of me. Sam, the redhead, answered, "Nah, there's that story about him being with someone's wife." The curly-haired boy whispered, just loud enough for everyone to hear, "Could've been someone's husband," and everyone laughed again.

On the drive home, Dad asked what happened at the meeting. I thought for a minute and then said, "We talked about health stuff. It was kind of boring." I smiled to myself.

"Well, you must have talked about something specific. What was it?"

"Dad, I've only been there once!" I protested.

"Well, I was just asking." To my relief he didn't push me, but then he added, "I mean, a girl should have girlfriends. You should be going to the mall, buying nail polish with the money you steal from me, begging me for new dresses."

I leaned against the window, which was icy cold from the air conditioner. I was just a thief to him and a failure as a girl (probably a failure as a thief, too, although he didn't realize it). I pretended to be sleeping as I imagined what I would say to the rabbi next time we met. For this first meeting, I had given him the story version of what happened, starting with the dead baby, the divorce, Fatima, and Dad's temper. I could have been describing images in my photo album: here's Fatima coming off the plane, here's Mom crying as she carries her last garbage bag of clothing out of the house, here's Roger reading while Missy fusses at him. There were a few snapshots of Dad throwing Melmac plates at me, telling me I couldn't even heat up chicken right.

Did the rabbi think I was handling it all pretty well? Or was I messing things up by staying with Dad? I couldn't be sure at first what he thought, because no matter what I said he simply asked, "And how did that make you feel?"

"Like I have to do better?" I ventured. He shook his head.

"Like I'm not good enough." He leaned toward me, still listening.

Hours later, lying in bed, I watched the full moon through the upper pane of my window. It was contained in a rectangle of glass, framed right in the very center. Its white light poured over the bottom half of my bed, light that came from a source on the other side of the planet. I picked up the camera and leaned out the window. I knew from previous attempts that night shots were impossible with this camera, unless I wanted to buy a certain kind of lens that Liz said cost more than a nose job (which she also didn't recommend). But there had to be a way to catch some of that light. Rather than shooting through glass, which made everything blurry, I decided to slip downstairs and out the patio door, the one that didn't make much noise.

At bottom of the stairs, I heard a sound coming from Dad's room. Someone yelling, someone crying, everything muffled, urgent and sad. I headed for the darkroom, crawling past the crates I had set up to balance my supplies, until I found the place where I used to hide as a kid. Amidst where we used to store bowling balls and winter coats, the empty suitcases and vacuum cleaners that didn't work anymore, I returned to the refuge I used to visit whenever Dad and Mom fought. Now the coats were gone, but the back of the closet still smelled faintly of mink stoles and vacuum bags, of stale perfume and my mother. I missed her. I almost coughed. I didn't miss her.

I heard Dad talking. "It's not as bad as you think. We can find a way out of this." He paused, then said, "It was just once, it didn't mean anything."

Fatima must have found out he was cheating on her, like he cheated on Mom. My stomach ached, in a blurry kind of way, and my throat, too. I could rush into their room and ask her to take me with her. I would do whatever she wanted. I could imagine living in her house, part of a whole new family, everyone speaking Greek and joking around with me, maybe feeding me those grape leaf things that Fatima popped into her mouth at the diner.

"Enough!" Her voice, not angry, sounded too tired to say anything more. I heard the mattress squeak and the light click off. The crying continued—it was Fatima, sounding just like Mom used to sound. And breathing, soft and steady, from Dad.

I lay down in the very back of the closet, and to my surprise my cheek pressed up against an old fur wrap from Nana, one she had given my mother years ago. I put my head on it and smelled my grandma's perfume mixed with my mother's Jean Nate. I knew why Mimi never called, but why didn't Nana want to see me? A few months ago, as we waited in traffic on the turnpike, my father had reeled off a list of relatives who said he was crazy and selfish, while I was obviously stupid and brainwashed. Was Nana on that list?

The sound of light sobbing seeped through the wall, little cries that a puppy makes when it is fast asleep. All these women in my head, I thought, all this time buried here and all the years I'd spent in this house, swept away to nothing.

Chapter Seven

Fatima and I hit it big on the third Sunday in July, reeling in over $700 in exchange for our rapidly depleted pile of halter-tops. It was over ninety-five outside and plenty humid, but the auction was buzzing. Someone was selling girdles right next to the Orange Julius stand, funnel cakes behind the plumbing supplies, and peasant shirts from India were everywhere.

Fatima and I both wore big pink straw fedoras. Hers was decorated with seashells and the logo "Avon-by-the-Sea," while mine had a real starfish, dyed green. It was big enough to startle customers as they walked by. "That a real starfish?"

"Yes, and since you guessed, you get two halter tops for only five dollars. The usual price is three dollars each, but you're a lucky winner!" Fatima would announce. She wore dyed-to-match orange platform sandals with orange hot pants, and a bright yellow shirt with a V-neck that dipped down almost to her belly button. When kids yelled, "Hey, disco queen," she just laughed.

"Whatever it is, I still got it," she told me that afternoon as she counted the money. We'd hauled in over $600 by that point. Since I worked on commission, I was fantasizing about another shopping expedition to that fabulous art and photography supply store I'd visited with Mom last year. Meanwhile, Fatima and I were getting browner by the minute, thanks to the baby oil Fatima always brought with her. Finally, around four, we started piling the shirts into boxes, careful not to brush our arms, covered with freshly applied baby oil, against the merchandise.

Fatima stopped suddenly and raised a stack of halter-tops above her head, as if she were making an offering to the gods. At first I expected her to start dancing around, joking with me about how silly these halters were, but instead, head tilted up as high as it would go, she closed her eyes and started praying in Greek. I could see dark green mascara running a little around her eyes, so I knew she must have been crying. Her tears and fervent pleas made me suddenly furious with Dad all over again.

When she was done praying, I said angrily, "He's such a bastard."

She didn't seem surprised by my outburst. "No," she said slowly, "he just wanted to take what was his."

"How can you think that's his?"

"It's his, too, what he needs, even if he hurted me." Her English had grown sketchier in the emotion of the moment.

"What do you mean? You leave for a little while, and he can't wait for you? That's horrible!"

"I mean that my son is not just from me. He is from God, and he is from his father. He is from Greece. He belongs to others."

She started shaking a little as other possible implications of my words began to sink in. "What do you mean, he couldn't wait for me?"

A sick feeling in my gut told me I had just destroyed the romance between my father and Fatima. Now they wouldn't get married, they wouldn't make a new life together—and I wouldn't get Fatima, who was just about the same size as my mother, but so much nicer. I couldn't stand to be alive.

"What are you saying, Deborah, that he couldn't wait? Who was it?" she asked. "He said he was crying himself to sleep every night because I was gone. You must tell me now."

The heat around us hung in mid-air, but my face was on fire because of my words, because of what I had just done. Think, I urged myself, make up something to make all this go away.

"Well, I don't know for sure. I never saw anything," I said, honestly enough.

"Tell me!" Her eyes never left my face.

"Look, I don't really know what I'm talking about," I pleaded weakly. "I heard you fighting the other night, and I wondered if maybe you thought he was seeing someone else. I'm an idiot—I watch too much TV, you know that. You know, I think it would be good to get a cold drink. Aren't you thirsty?"

"You know who it is." She slammed the halter-tops she'd been holding into a box and didn't seem to care that she got baby oil on some of them.

"I don't know," I hedged. "Mostly he talked about you, how much he loved you and missed you."

"He has a girlfriend, and you know this. Children don't lie."

"I'm actually almost all grown up, so maybe I do lie sometimes."

She glared at me. Just before closing the box, she grabbed the bottle and squirted baby oil all over the pile of halter-tops. I was afraid she was going to set a match to it next, but she didn't. She just closed the box quickly and left it for my father to load into his truck. After Dad had packed up his own booth, he carried all our boxes to the truck by himself while Fatima stared silently at his back. When he was done, she told my father to follow her van.

"Fine," he said, a corny "Mayberry USA" grin all over his face, "but where are you taking us?"

She walked away fast and got into her vehicle without answering. Under her breath, I heard her say, "To hell."

I sat next to Dad in the front seat of the truck. When we got to the road where she normally turned off to her house, she went straight instead, veering down a country highway that narrowed as it passed through cornfields and tomato farms.

"Yessiree," Dad said. Ever since he'd put a CB radio in the car and adopted "Hillbilly Hank" as his handle, he liked to try out a fake country accent every so often. "Yer can never tell with a woman where yer going to end up."

Fatima sped up to eighty miles an hour and we sped up, too, the truck rattling and bumping down the road. "Muffler, smuffler," Dad said. "Gotta keep up with her." He didn't seem the least bit concerned that there were hairpin turns on the road up ahead, or that by now we were miles from our house.

Then she did something that surprised me. She braked suddenly and stopped. We stopped behind her. She made a quick U-turn with the van, although she surely knew that we couldn't make such a tight turnaround, on such a narrow road, with Dad's truck. Once the van had reversed direction she sped past us, her face a study in determination. Dad looked a little concerned, but still not scared yet. He pulled into a nearby driveway and, after carefully looking both ways, backed out again and went after her.

What Fatima seemed to forget was that Dad was the king of speed chases, and there was no way he was going to lose this one. I tightened my seatbelt. He rode roughshod over medians, laughing about the flexibility of the old truck and chuckling about how smart he had been to fill the gas tank that morning. We sped wildly down country roads, then smaller highways, and finally onto the Garden State Turnpike. Instead of going back north, toward home, Fatima headed south. I curled up and tried to sleep, hoping to somehow wake up back in time, back before my thoughtless words had ruined everything.

Two hours later, I saw the exit signs for Wildwood and Cape May. Fatima must have seen them, too, because she pulled off at the Wildwood exit and zoomed down a maze of streets to the beach road. She turned south and kept going, but all the kids coming home from the beach forced her to stop often for traffic lights. Through the rear window of her van, we could see the back of her head nodding up and down, like she was talking to herself—cursing, I imagined, in Greek. My chest hurt, my stomach too. What if she hurt herself? There was no way to tell Dad what was going on, or he would throw me out of the house for sure.

At the end of the beachfront road, she turned sharply into a tavern parking lot that ran down to the beach. I realized she was heading for the ocean. Dad was too fast for her, though. He zoomed around the other side of the tavern and blocked her in. She slammed the van into reverse, but before she could move he leapt out of the truck and planted himself behind the van.

"You going to do what my wife did to me?" he yelled.

She stepped out of the van and yelled back. "Maybe she had good reason, yes, *very* good reason!"

He moved faster than I'd ever seen him move. He grabbed her from behind, holding her arms behind her back, while she tried to kick and bite him. Somehow, he got an arm across her neck and managed to lock her against him so she couldn't fight, but this took a while. I watched from my front row seat as this woman I loved screamed at him in Greek, twisting and pulling and occasionally yelling in English, "Get away from me, you bastard! Get away from me!"

Once he had her immobilized, she dropped her head and started crying uncontrollably. "You took my baby away," she sobbed. "I lose him for you, and now what?"

He stood behind her looking like a statue of a policeman, like someone I had never seen before in my life. He still held her, but it wasn't a hold of love. It was a hold of imprisonment. As her sobs and screams of, "You took my baby away!" got fiercer and louder, some of the guys from the bar, teenagers just a little older than me, filtered out the back door to watch. Eventually, they shook their heads and walked off.

Through it all, I remained frozen in the front seat of the truck. I thought about running out to stop him. I could put my arms around her, too, but in love. I could hold her small body, her much older soul, and let her sob until she slept. I would be the good daughter who covered her with afghans and cooked something good to eat. But guilt stopped me—she knew I was the one who had ruined everything.

The rabbi told us once about dropping acid, how it made him want to claw his way out of his own body because it was so painful just to be himself. I knew what he meant now. I opened the glove compartment, hoping to find something sharp to stick into my hand, but a howl from Fatima jolted me. I looked through our windshield into her face. She was still shaking herself back and forth, screaming and crying.

Here, this is what is most wrong with my life, I would tell Liz as I showed her my picture of what was happening. I would shoot it from an angle that showed a little of me, a lot of Fatima, and none of Dad. A voice inside me kept saying, "You shouldn't be seeing this. This is what happens when adults break." But it *was* happening, and I *was* sitting there, watching a woman have what my father told me later was a mental breakdown. ("Not a nervous breakdown, because that would have landed her in the hospital, and she would have needed medication to calm down, but a mental breakdown, kind of like a little break from reality. She's fine now, though.")

Worst of all, I was losing the woman who should have been my real mother. I was losing my one chance at a real family, at a little piece of security. I'm not okay. You're not okay. I was losing her even as she cried. She eventually stopped and, still standing there in his arms, fell asleep. He carried her over to the back of the van, laid her across a few boxes, and locked all the doors so no one would disturb her. He cracked open the windows and left her there. He looked a little shaken, but he was trying to hide it from me, so he smiled.

"Let's eat," he said. "I think there's food here."

"But what about Fatima?" I imagined putting her head on my lap, being there for her when she woke.

"It's fine. I have her keys, and we'll leave her a note." He acted like nothing had happened, but I knew that something buried and hidden had come to the surface now. I wandered after him, terrified and exhausted. Everywhere I went I could smell the ocean.

Chapter Eight

I was staring at a white cinder block wall decorated with posters of Israel that came from some travel agent. The rabbi's office was being re-carpeted, so we were sitting side by side in the hallway farthest from the main office with cool gray tiles under us, smooth cinder block wall behind us. It was four days since Fatima's breakdown, and I hadn't seen her since. Dad went to her house sometimes at night, but he told me I needed to stay home ("And clean up this pigsty, while you're at it") until he straightened things out with her. He swore she was getting better, that she liked the chocolate-chip cookies I made for her, the ones you sliced off a giant roll of dough and baked. He claimed she liked the photograph I'd made for her, too, the one with a tall tree lit from behind at sunset. And she read the little note I sent with the photograph: "I miss you. I'm sorry. I love you. Love, Deborah."

"What is it, Deborah?" the rabbi was asking me, because I'd been silent for so long. "What do you feel about your life?"

"That I'm just watching it go by. I mean, I'm in this life, I'm moving around and doing stuff, but it's not really mine." I wanted to tell him that felt like I was living in an after-school TV special, one of those cautionary tales about what can happen, if you're not careful.

While I was at the temple, Dad and the kids were out bowling and having pizza. Earlier, he had insisted I join them. "You have to come. It's only one night this week we see them," he'd said.

"No, I need to go see the rabbi." My mother had taken to waving enthusiastically when we pulled up in front of her house, like she expected me to leap out of the car and back into her life. She was the last person I needed to see right now.

Dad and I were talking as we headed home from the grocery store, the back seat of the car overflowing with $214 worth of food, toilet paper, and aluminum foil. There was going to be an aluminum foil shortage, according to Dad, so we spent half our money on the stuff—all sizes, all weights.

Dad tried another approach. "You don't really need to see the rabbi."

"Yes, I do. Divorce is hard on a teen. I have to see him so I don't get suicidal."

"Who said anything about suicidal?" he asked, sounding concerned. Maybe he really was worried that the only person still in his life on a regular basis might drop out. "You think about suicide?"

I paused, searching for the right words. What I thought about was more like suicide through inertia: letting the walls close in around me and doing nothing to stop them, letting them crush me and make me so small that I didn't exist anymore.

"Yeah. I do think about it." I expected the conversation to end there, but he surprised me.

"So do I." He took a breath. "In fact, I didn't go to Fatima's last night. I went to see the rabbi."

"But the cookies I made, the card, the photo?"

"They're in the trunk."

"We have to bring them to her right now!"

"Okay, okay," he said, actually slowing down and making an illegal U-turn. "So it's more important to you that Fatima gets your cookies than that your dear old dad stays alive?"

"I didn't say that. I mean, I didn't know you were even thinking about, you know, killing yourself."

"How would you?" He started to yell, and then stopped himself. "It's not like I'm gonna burden a kid with what this woman did to me."

That never stopped you before, I thought to myself.

At the beginning of our session, I had told the rabbi practically everything that had happened: the fighting and yelling before the divorce, the trips to the diner, the court scene, Dad criticizing my housekeeping and throwing pies at my head. Now all I could think of to say was, "You must think my dad and I are both crazy."

"No, I don't think that."

"But didn't he come to you, too, and tell you he has problems?"

"That's him. This is about you. If I ever have to choose, I will refer your father to someone else for help."

I was on the verge of telling him how I had messed up with Fatima, but just then we heard the voices of the youth group members echoing from the hallway that led to this one. We stood up in a formal way, our session over. He took a card out of his wallet and wrote something on the back.

"My home number," he said, handing the card to me. "Call if you have a bad night."

"You must think I'm a wreck."

"No, Deborah, I think you're doing remarkably well for someone in a wrecked life."

And that's when, despite the sound of platform shoes heading our way, I started to cry. He swung around and pressed my face into his shoulder, petting my hair. As soon as he did this, the voices that had been coming closer and closer to our hallway suddenly stopped and began to recede. While I cried, I got out the rest of the story. The rabbi held me tight, and after a while he said, "This was not something you did. Your dad was cheating on her, and she found out."

"But she only found out because of me," I mumbled into his shoulder.

"No, she knew already, but she wasn't sure," he said firmly.

I looked up at him with my mouth open. "How do you know?"

"I know," he said with such directness that I exhaled, cried a little more, and shook my head. "Deborah, believe me, she didn't hear about this the first time from you."

I stood there for a while, letting it all sink in. Then he showed me how to slip out of the building using the back entrance, sneak through the bushes, and come in the main entrance, walking into youth group like any other kid.

A few days later, I was working our booth at the auction with Eshe. She was leaning against the building, smoking a cigarette and telling me about her latest adventure with her boyfriend.

"You did it here, right up against the building?" I asked.

"No, around the corner, near the big pipe. We wanted a little privacy."

"Doesn't it hurt your back?" I imagined the indentations the bricks must have left in her tush. I wondered if sex felt like having something drilled into you, but I didn't ask Eshe that question. It was clear to me that she knew I was a virgin, but she didn't seem to hold that against me.

"No, it's fun. I like it better than giving him a b.j. in the car." She dropped her cigarette to the ground and I stepped on it. It was after three in the afternoon, a dead day. Eshe couldn't have stolen more than twenty dollars. Business was bad. Boy had been on his "sock-it-to-me" kick, singing "sock it to me, sock it to me" as fast and as loud

as possible every twenty minutes. Then he burst into the theme from
Dr. Zhivago, singing in a towering voice, "Someday my love, there will
be shirts to sell."

Dad had ignored us, leaving us alone at the stand for most of the day.
He had stopped in every hour or so in the morning, but we didn't see
him after lunch. When he returned at five-thirty, we loaded the truck
in silence. Eshe took me aside to tell me that she had almost enough
money saved for an apartment. "Deposit, first month's rent, and last
month's rent—that's what you gotta come up with. I'm staying with
that bitch until I have six month's rent together."

"What about your boyfriend? Could he help?"

"Him? I don't use him for money. I use him for sex." She laughed
and I had to smile, although I felt slightly embarrassed.

When it came time to pay Eshe, Dad said, "Girls, I'll treat you both
to a fried clam dinner at the shore for doing such a good job of running
the stand by yourselves." He smelled of beer but seemed very happy for
a change. Last night, he'd told me again that Fatima just needed more
time before he could marry her, and she would be my mom.

"Does that include beer?" Eshe asked. I had to admire the way she
never stopped pushing for a better bargain.

"You of age?"

"Hey, I didn't ask if you were gonna be my cop. I just wanted to
know if that included beer."

He thought for a moment. "Yeah, sure, why not? Hop in the truck."

Forty minutes later, we were seated at a little table with a candle
in the center. Dad turned to Eshe. "So, you seem to have a head for
business."

Eshe was playing with the nutcracker on the table. "For cracking
nuts. Doesn't this idea terrify you, Hank?"

Dad ignored her comment. "You look like someone who could
make it in the business world."

"True," she replied. "I like pushing stuff."

"So what are your plans after you graduate from high school?"

Eshe shrugged. I noticed she had a few freckles near her nose. "Get a job, don't get knocked up, don't become a drunk or drug addict, but have some fun. Avoid welfare, don't turn into a fat pig, and don't let anyone ride my ass. That's the plan. Kind of ambitious, but it works for me."

"What about college?"

"What about it?" she shot back. "You think I got the grades for that? Or the money?"

"What about your parents?"

"My parents," said Eshe, as she put a hard dinner roll between the teeth of the nutcracker and snapped it for dramatic effect, "don't give a rat's ass about me."

Our Caesar salads arrived, covered with giant croutons. I started eating mine, but Dad and Eshe just picked at theirs. "Deborah here, she has no sense of business," Dad said. "All she cares about is art. I'll have to shell out thousands for her to go to college, just so she can go make artistic donuts at the donut shop."

"Dad, I do photography, not art," I corrected him. "Eshe's a photographer, too."

"So you can take photographs of donuts in a donut shop," he shot back, ignoring my comment about Eshe and addressing her directly again. "But you have some potential. You could run a business once you learn the ropes."

I wondered if Dad knew she was ripping him off each week. Maybe he didn't care. Or maybe he was flirting with her. "I have a little proposition for you."

"Yeah, I'm listening." Eshe had stopped eating and was now staring at him intently.

"You commit to me, help me run the booth, be the manager, and I'll put you through college. Not anything too pricey, maybe community college. You could learn accounting, business planning, some of the other things you'd need, and then come to work for me in the city. I need an office manager who can keep books, keep everything moving—and I need someone who's in it for the long haul."

"But Dad, how can you have her keep books?" I burst out. "She's robbing you blind."

Dad and Eshe looked at me like I was from another planet. "No, she's not," he said.

"What the fuck you talking about?" Eshe said in a sweet, low voice. Then, as always, she upped the ante.

"Sounds decent, but where am I gonna live while I do this school thing? Or are you going to pay rent for my own apartment?"

"I'll make a deal with you," Dad said. The waitress put down platters of seafood, but even the sight of my favorite food couldn't take away that sharp feeling in my stomach, the sense of the world collapsing again. "You can move in with us. We have plenty of room."

I interrupted. "But what about Fatima and Theodore?"

"Plenty of room," Dad said, and kept right on talking numbers, timetables, what he expected. He'd look over her shoulder for the first few months, keep track of how she was doing. It was a big investment, and if she was serious she had better give it her all.

By the time I had managed to force down half my food, Dad and Eshe had discussed profit margins, marketing, the garment district, price markups, Eshe's moving date, and whether she could help me cook something decent if he bought all the groceries. I studied the large, fake fish mounted on walls draped with real fishing nets. If I came here with my camera early in the morning, when the light was even, surely I could find a way to turn those fish into a photo essay about what was wrong with my life today.

Chapter Nine

I sat at the kitchen table, trying to slice open a too-hard bagel with a huge knife without snagging my finger. Dad was reading the comics, almost finished with his bagel. It was exactly one week until school started, three days until Eshe moved in, one day until I met with the rabbi again, and—according to Dad—just a little bit longer until Fatima returned to our lives.

"Give her time," he said over and over again. "She needs this rest, and then she's moving in. We'll be a family."

"What will Eshe be?" I wondered aloud, pushing the knife down hard against the Melmac plate even though I knew it would leave a dent.

He shrugged. "A business investment. Don't take it personally. You're not suited to this, and I need someone."

I looked down. I was thinking of Fatima.

"That's the problem with you," Dad continued. "You take everything personally, as if the whole fucking world is set up around you."

I ignored him and focused on my fingernails, which looked worse than ever since I had been biting them lately. "I'm going to call Fatima," was all I could think, but he seemed to read my mind.

"Don't call her," he warned. "She needs a break."

One part of me was sure that she would come back if she could only hear my voice—at least, back to me. And I wasn't in the mood to listen to the other part of me, who knew better. I held off as long as Dad was around the house, but as soon as he left I picked up the phone. She probably wouldn't be home, with my luck, but I had to try anyway. To my surprise, she answered.

"Fatima," I started, "I miss you. Are you okay?"

She hesitated. "Who is this?"

"This is Deborah, you know, your surrogate daughter," I said, trying to joke so that she would laugh and tell me she was my surrogate mother. But she said nothing.

"I thought, since you're gonna come live here soon, it would be good to talk." She didn't say a word, so I stopped talking. The silence continued. I could hear her breathing into the phone.

Finally, she gave me something. "Deborah, I can't," she said, then added with a little more warmth, "I'm sorry," and hung up.

I stood there like some idiot in a bad movie, listening to the dial tone. Dad wouldn't be home for hours, and I had no idea what to make for dinner. Mom had stopped calling after I'd hung up on her a few weeks ago. "You're not even a real mother," I told her, right before I slammed down the phone in response to her statement, "I tried to be a good mother." It was odd, I realized now, that I didn't feel sad about our estrangement. There was only the strength of the wall between us, holding me up with ease.

I went into the living room and sat down in a folding chair. I didn't seem to know what to do about anything anymore. But I had to do something, anything—if I didn't, I couldn't stand it. The thunder kept coming like waves in my mind while I breathed heavily. Finally I stood up and marched out the front door. I don't remember the three-mile walk to the diner, only that when I arrived my sneakers were soaked and my cold socks chilled my feet. As I walked in the front door, I tried to act casual. Someone besides Fatima was hosting. She sat me at a small booth next to the revolving dessert case, which no longer seemed enticing but merely sickening. I asked for a cup of coffee, although I never drank the stuff. When it came, I dutifully poured in three packets of sugar and a bunch of cream and started sipping. It wasn't too bad.

On the other side of the room, a girl with blonde, stringy hair stared blankly across a table at the woman Eshe usually came in with. Her name was Jeanine, according to Eshe. "Yeah, she's my case manager, but mostly she just tries to calm everyone down. It sucks."

Then Fatima appeared in front of me, holding a pot of coffee. She leaned forward and refilled my cup, but said nothing. Her face was a map to nowhere.

"Fatima, sit with me, please," I said quietly.

She shook her head and started to move away.

"No, come back, it's okay," I told her, but she vanished through the kitchen door at the far end of the counter and didn't come out again, not even once, during the long hour I spent staring at that door and waiting, my coffee turning bitter and cold. By then it was late afternoon so I left a few dollars on the table and walked home. My toes blistered in my wet socks, my bare legs trembled in the unexpected cold as a front of fall weather swept in. Yet I couldn't stop myself; my body was too intent on returning to the mother ship to listen to any commands.

I arrived home tired and broken. Once inside I went to my room, took off my wet shoes and socks, and walked down to the kitchen. I stood in front of the dishwasher. Somehow, this hurt even more than when Fatima had her mental breakdown. Why was I so numb, and what would it take to bring me back to life? I could kill myself, I could pick up that knife again, my mind kept telling me. But that could hurt, and I'd probably do it all wrong. I could take a bunch of pills, but which ones? Every impulse in me said, "Do something, do something, do something quick!"

Lying on the counter was a notepad on which Dad had scrawled, "Defrost two tube steaks and clean bathrooms." I had performed neither of these tasks. But it was paper, and there was a pen nearby. Without thinking about whether this was the thing I really wanted to do, I picked up the pad and started writing a suicide note. The more I wrote, the more I felt like I was merely taking a picture that would be developed later. This note concerned another girl, the other part of me who was in such pain that her shadow hid me from myself. She was suffering so much that there was nothing anyone could do for her anymore. I couldn't even reach my hand out to touch her shaking shoulder.

I put down the pad and picked up the phone, but the panic inside made it hard to breathe, hard to remember if there was anyone I should call, anything to say. I dropped the receiver again, walked across the room to the TV and back to the kitchen counter. The news was on: first something about Ford and Dole, the team the Democrats needed to beat to regain the White House, and then a handsome woman in a tennis dress, knees bent, ready to pounce on the tennis ball. Renee Richards, who used to be a man, had won her first woman's tennis match today. Mom would probably be pissed off about this, how someone with the strength of a man was taking over her sport, even if she did look pretty much like a normal woman as she smacked the ball.

The more I tried to distract myself, the more I became aware that something was beating hard in me, battering me from the inside out, like it wasn't my own heart. Did I miss my mother? I couldn't tell what this feeling was, only that it was too much to hold inside my body. My mother didn't want me, my father didn't want me, Fatima didn't want me. I turned off the TV and paced the kitchen. Then I picked up the pad again and sat down in Dad's chair, the new easy chair he'd bought last week at a discount store in the city. He told me the chair was probably hot, but no one would look for stolen goods here. Sitting on the fake leather upholstery was a lot like sitting down on a cold lizard, but after a moment the upholstery warmed to my skin. I exhaled and started to read what I had written.

I wrote that I needed to kill myself because there was nothing to live for. I had ruined whatever chance I had at happiness. I had ruined this new family-to-be. I told Dad he probably wouldn't care that I was gone—it would make life easier for him. I felt myself shaking as I read the part about how Mom didn't love me. People might say that I should have waited to see how my life turned out, but I was too tired to go on.

After I finished reading the letter, I extended the recliner fully and placed the letter face up on my chest, with the pen resting on top of it. (Good thing I have such a flat chest that I can keep it there, I thought with grim satisfaction.) I must have fallen asleep, because I dreamed I was at the auction where Sergei tried to sell me paper. "You need all the paper you can get, girlie. Come get more." In the dream I was timid, smaller than usual. Boy was trying to get through a maze of racks and boxes stacked on wooden tables so he could help me. Then he turned into the rabbi, but when I looked again, it was Mr. Lexington. I looked closer and realized it was actually a man I didn't know. The hurt in me, unleashed a little bit more with each breath, would surely kill me eventually. Everything was broken. It might be a coward's way out, not to take pills or use a knife, but it was my way. I gulped for air, my chest trembling so much that the note shook, too, as if there were an earthquake beneath it.

The last thing I remembered hearing was Dad's voice, saying this whole thing was such a waste. I wasn't sure if he was really there, or if I was still dreaming.

When I woke up, there was a real man in front of me. He had worry lines all around his eyes and a little mustache. It was Dad, acting concerned and afraid. Behind him was the rabbi, right here in our house. The note was missing, and I realized that the rabbi was reading it. He put down the note, touched my arm, and asked me how I felt.

Then I realized that Dad was crying. I had never seen him cry before, and I was surprised by how much he looked like Roger. "I thought you were dead," he managed to say.

I wanted to say, "Next time, take my pulse," but it sounded too sarcastic. "I'm okay," I heard myself saying instead.

"What did you take?" the rabbi asked. He bent down and held my hand, his thumb on my wrist. He, at least, had the presence of mind to check my pulse.

"Nothing." I couldn't begin to explain why I put a suicide note on my chest and then fell asleep. "I thought about killing myself, but I just didn't know how."

The rabbi and Dad shared a little laugh, which was surprisingly good to hear. The rabbi, nodding reassuringly to my father, asked me if I wanted to take a walk and talk things out. Soon we were heading out the front door, my dad muttering something about work to do around the house.

The air had cooled off by then, and blue and purplish clouds stretched above us. I studied them intently. Everything was so calm and easy all of a sudden.

"Is the world just like you remembered it?" the rabbi asked, smiling.

"No, it's probably better."

By the time we had turned down the next block, I had told him about Fatima.

"Sounds like it was the last straw for you. Now what?"

"I don't know."

"Have you thought about how Fatima was a mother figure for you? Maybe now, without her, you might need to think about the loss of your real mother?"

I nodded without saying anything. New, delicate skin had somehow grown over my wounds while I slept, but if I said the wrong thing I would wind up in pain again. The breeze made me shiver, so we sat down on a railroad tie next to a garden of thorny bushes. He put his arm around me to warm me up.

"I'm just so afraid," I managed to say. I tried to recall the look on my mother's face as she lunged at me that day she found my diary.

"I know you're afraid, Deborah." We sat quietly for a while, watching a blue jay scream at a slinking orange tabby cat. The edge of the sky turned blue, as if someone had spilled the smallest drop of cobalt paint onto the wet line of the horizon. Without saying a word, the rabbi let me know that I didn't have to say or decide anything right now.

On the walk home, he asked me how I felt about the start of school. I told him it was something to do, at least. He pressed me about my extracurricular activities. "What about drama? Plays give you a second life. I used to be a thespian myself. It was groovy."

I shrugged. I was secretly afraid of standing up in front of people, and the idea of painting sets and collecting props seemed like just another kind of housework. Somehow, talking with the rabbi had made everything feel lighter, more ordinary. It was a gift I couldn't have imagined even a few minutes earlier.

The sky over the house was softly lit in orange when we returned, but the station wagon was missing from the driveway. Only the rabbi's bright yellow VW bug remained. The rabbi followed me into the kitchen. Dad was gone, too, but on the counter we found this note.

Dear Deborah,

You were right about Fatima. I just spoke with her, and she's never coming back. It's my fault, and your sadness and pain is my fault, too. You were wrong, however, to try to kill yourself. You should live, and you can live well on the insurance money. Once I'm out of the way, you can go back to the family, and they'll take good care of you. Take care, don't forget me, and remember that even though I'm not here, I still love you.
Love, Dad

We finished reading the note at the same time. The rabbi sighed—surely he was wondering about the odds of two suicide attempts in one family in one afternoon. For my part, I was back in hell again. I stood next to the rabbi, with no real idea of what I was doing. My new fragile skin was already ruined. If I didn't move quickly, take some kind of action, I would fall right back into the pain again.

"Let's go find him," I said, my voice rough and sketchy. The rabbi led me out to his little car.

We checked the diner, the bowling alley, and the auction, then drove to Fatima's. Dad's station wagon was parked in her driveway—intact and not dented in the least. Fatima opened the door quietly, looking not at all surprised to see us. She told us Dad was in the back yard, sitting in a lawn chair with a glass of water. He had arrived an hour ago, but she wouldn't open the door. He left and called her from a phone booth, then returned and banged on the windows. Finally, when she wouldn't respond, he climbed over the fence and took up residence in the lawn chair. Standing across from him behind the sliding glass door, she had watched him reach into his pocket and show her a handful of pills: the black ones he took for his ulcer, white ones she didn't recognize, and some yellow ones, too. Smiling, he stuffed all the pills into his mouth at once. She screamed and tried to unlock the patio door, but the lock was stuck. The pills were evidently stuck, too, because he started choking and ran for the hose. He hosed enough water into his mouth to make himself spit out most of the pills, swallowing only enough to leave him shaky and weak. By the time she got outside with the glass of water, he was no doubt embarrassed by his botched suicide attempt.

The rabbi asked Fatima to take me inside while he talked with Dad, who didn't even acknowledge our presence. He put a hand on Fatima's shoulder and added, "Take good care of her," as if I might just try killing myself all over again.

Fatima led me into the house and, still in her distant and professional hostess mode, asked me if I would like some tea and would I care to watch TV? We sat down on the couch side by side and watched *The Partridge Family*, with Shirley Jones and her gorgeous son David Cassidy arguing over curfew.

"I'm sixteen," David said, his wavy shag haircut hanging just right. "I need to make my way in the world."

"Not with those clothes," Shirley knowingly joked. Laugh track.

I thought about what I could say that might make her take us back. The topic of Theodore was out of the question, as was the auction—it would only remind her of that horrible day a few weeks ago.

"School starts soon," I heard myself say in my old, normal voice. "Do you want to go shopping with me and help me pick out some school clothes? You know how bad I am at this stuff."

I couldn't believe I was asking for her attention again, but I couldn't help myself. My father is sitting in a lawn chair in the back yard, still shaking, I thought. I have to do whatever it takes to get rid of the feeling that I've just been punched in the stomach.

"Your father will help you." Another punch, this one worse. She stared straight ahead at a vacuum cleaner commercial.

I could plead, but what good would that do? "It's good to see you again. I missed you," came out of my mouth instead. Shut up, shut the hell up, I told myself, but I didn't listen.

No response. Since I was so far behind already, what was there to lose by saying more?

"I really wish you and Dad would make up. I miss you so much. I miss your cooking and your jokes. You know, you two could go see a psychologist or something like Marriage Encounter. We could even all go together to get Theodore back. Or we could move to Greece—all of us. I mean, who wouldn't want to leave Jersey?" Now I found myself crying and laughing at the same time now.

She stood up and, without looking at me, walked out of the living room and into her bedroom, closing the door behind her. I collapsed onto the sofa, sobbing into the orange and brown tapestry while the Partridge family merrily sang. I hugged one of the corduroy pillows, pressing it into my chest as hard as I could.

As *Lost in Space* started, the rabbi and Dad entered the house, already joking together. We were going out, all of us, Dad said, to the bowling alley. The rabbi was our chaperone, I knew, but he was also, according to Dad, a good bowler. The rabbi briefly knocked on Fatima's bedroom door, asking her to join us. When she didn't answer, the rabbi jauntily said, "Come on, Hank, my game."

Twenty minutes later, I stood looking down a long wooden lane with my rabbi behind me, cheering me on. I had the ball in the palm of one hand, my fingers from the other hand across the top. I stepped forward, bent one knee as Dad had taught me, and threw the ball, careful to finish with my right hand palm up, reaching out. It should have been a strike—my pose was perfect, the ball flying out of my palm and dropping onto the lane, then speeding along a straight line with a small crook at the end. The only problem was that my straight line led the ball right into the gutter. Everything perfect, but I had forgotten to look at the pins.

The next night, Dad disappeared right after our dismal dinner of burnt pork chops and cheese doodles. He said he needed to run out for some paper towels and would be back soon. I was too absorbed in watching *Roots* on television and eating to notice his absence, but after the show ended he still wasn't home. My first thought was that he might try to kill himself again.

I called Fatima first. She wasn't home, which only made my heart race faster. I thought of calling the rabbi, but I was afraid we had relied on him too much lately. I dialed Lee, an old friend of Dad's who used to bowl with him before the divorce. After letting me go on and on about how I couldn't find Dad, how I was afraid he might be killing himself because he'd broken up with his girlfriend, Lee finally interrupted. "And what is this to me?"

"Find him, or help me find him," I pleaded. "I can't drive, and I don't know where he is."

"Like I said," Lee droned, "what is this to me?" He hung up.

There was no way I could call the enemy—my mother, his mother, all the other relatives—and I doubted that any of them would have helped me anyway. I was ready to call Boy and Big Boy, but they lived someplace in Delaware—I didn't even know the name of the town. I considered trying Liz, but I couldn't remember her last name. Instead I watched Johnny Carson without the sound, feeling my skin tremble and freeze up.

What now, what now, what now, my heartbeat asked. I hadn't tried to stop him. I hadn't flung myself spread-eagle across the hood of his car. I just watched him go out the door, more concerned about *Roots* and dessert than about having a dad, and now I was getting what I deserved.

I scanned the book shelf in the living room: *The Menus of the First Ladies, Judaica in the Desert, Your Erogenous Zones, Atlas of the Known World, Heidi.* None of them seemed even remotely appealing, so I kept watching the TV and dialing Fatima's number every ten minutes. I turned up the sound as Carson was asking his guest, a blonde with high cheekbones, what she liked best about a popular song.

"I like when it really talks to you," she replied. When she looked straight at the camera, straight at me, I jumped.

I rose from the new easy chair and sat in the folding chair instead. Little sounds were coming from the house that I couldn't identify. ("Just the house settling," Mom told me years ago, when we first moved in. "It will do this for a few years, and then it will settle." But it never settled.) As I half-listened to the creaky house, the blonde made jokes about her blip-blip.

"You bet your bootie," Carson said to her, and everyone laughed.

When I awoke at ten o'clock the next morning, there was still no Dad. I raced to his bedroom and discovered that he hadn't come home at all last night. I called the taxi service and found out he'd shown up for work at eight, but right now he was out getting a roll and coffee.

"Call back in ten minutes, hon," the dispatcher suggested, but I didn't call back. Instead, I fell asleep again in my own bed, my eyes burning from fatigue. I slept dreamlessly.

The next time I woke up, Dad was standing over me. It was 5:45 PM, and of course there was no dinner ready. He seemed oblivious to what I'd just been through. As if nothing had happened, he reminded me that temple youth group meeting was tonight and we had to leave in an hour.

"Where were you last night?" I yelled. "I was afraid you were trying to kill yourself. Every time I called some place you might be, you weren't there."

Looking suddenly sadder and older, he stammered, "I wasn't anywhere. I was sitting in the car all night."

"But you just went out for paper towels!" Despite the exasperation in my tone, I felt confused. I spent the whole night freaking out, and he had been sitting in the driveway the whole time?

"As soon as I got in the car, I realized all I wanted to do was drive into a building at a hundred miles an hour and end it all," he said quietly. "But I didn't. I stayed alive for you."

"For me?"

"The rabbi said to me, what do you love most? I couldn't answer, so he asked me, 'Well, what do you love?' and all I could think of were my children. All I could see was you in my mind. He told me to think of you, each time I wanted to kill myself."

I sat up straight, wide awake now as the late afternoon sunlight leaked in through a crack between the curtains. I didn't know what to say. "So what do we do now?"

"I don't know," he replied calmly. Then, casually, he asked me what I thought about pizza for dinner. I nodded and we walked downstairs together, discussing which pizzeria, Rudolph's or Mario's, could deliver a pie faster.

Twenty minutes later, we were downing a large pepperoni pizza on the patio table. Although we were both famished, Dad paused every few minutes to point out a bird I had never noticed before, darting through the trees on the hill. Behind us, the setting sun shone luxuriously. We watched gratefully as it bathed the yard in promise and orange, but our hands were trembling like the hands of people pulled from a burning house in the nick of time.

Part III

Chapter One

One unusually warm October morning, as we left the house for the bus stop, Eshe put her generous arm around me and led me across the neighbor's back yard. Instead of school, she said, we were going to the beach for the day. She had moved in just a month beforehand.

"How're we going to get there? And what about money?" I asked cautiously.

"Got it all taken care of. Just trust Aunt Eshe," she said.

We snuck through a dozen back yards, following the chain-link fences to Route 9 and cursing at the yappy little dogs nipping at our heels. I was wearing the blue tank top that Eshe had helped me find at the mall last week. After weeding out my closet, she had tapped Dad for the cash and a ride to the mall.

"You want your daughter to look like a seventh-grader?" she'd asked him, in a tone of incredulity. "She needs threads, and I can help pick out stuff that's gonna last."

Dad, of course, gave her anything she wanted. "I just need forty percent off the top," she told me, pocketing the money and doing a dance step like we'd seen Betty Ford do on TV with Tony Orlando. "See what a good businesswoman I'm turning into?"

She was turning me into something, too. Although the cool kids weren't really talking to me yet, a few occasionally nodded in my direction. Whenever Eshe spotted me in the lunch line, she'd yell out, "Hey, sweetpea, toss me a cigarette." She knew I didn't smoke, but I played along by pretending to look for cigarettes in the pockets of my jeans, while everyone laughed at my bit part in the Eshe show. It helped that some of Eshe's friends were in my art class with Ms. Sheplin. As she roamed the room in her low-cut granny dresses, she praised the "vivacious contours" of my charcoal drawings for everyone to hear.

We reached the highway, an edgy river of continuous traffic. "Now what?" I asked, beginning to get a little nervous. I had never even cut class before, let alone skipped a whole day of school.

"Now watch," Eshe told me. She stood lazily on the curb, looking bored, like a ride was the last thing in the world she needed. ("The look is essential," she whispered. "Look desperate, and you're dead in the water.") Then she casually stretched out her thumb and started singing Bruce Springsteen's "Tenth Avenue Freezeout" in a throaty voice. In no time at all, a businessman in a sports car pulled over. We opened the car door just in time to catch the final notes of "Tenth Avenue Freezeout" on the car radio.

"This is freaky!" she exclaimed. "I was just singing that song!"

"You like the Boss?" he asked, smiling up at her. It was a rhetorical question, of course—we lived five miles from the Boss's birthplace, and obviously were Jersey girls. Everyone I knew, even Dad, even Fatima, liked the Boss. It was like believing in God when you were falling apart—it was almost impossible not to.

"Where may I take you?" he asked in a flirtatious tone.

"The beach'll be fine."

She didn't bother to ask him where he was going. Instead, she leaned back so he could see her firm, muscular belly peeking out between her black tube top and skin-tight hip huggers. He turned up the volume on the radio, and I took refuge in the whaling of Bruce's voice, that crying out in great hunger or great pain. As Eshe sang along with the radio I found myself thinking about her mother, who looked almost like Eshe's twin but thinner, with a face full of lines and a fury that expressed itself best in her native language.

We had helped Eshe move her stuff one humid day, her mother following Dad and me back and forth to the truck, yelling and chain-smoking. When she saw Eshe climb into the passenger seat, her mother actually threw herself on the grass and began weeping. "Just drive," Eshe told Dad. "The faster, the better. She always gets like this before she goes really crazy."

As soon as Eshe settled in, Dad became more distant. He complained more than ever about my cooking and canceled our visits with the kids any chance he got. When I asked him how things were going with the taxi service, he would respond absently, "What? Oh, it's fine."

I rolled down the window and let in the smell of the sea. We were pulling over somewhere in Asbury Park. I expected the driver to let us out, but instead he was parking the car. ("He's a promoter for Bruce," Eshe explained as we got out of the car, "and he needed to go the Stone Pony anyway. Get this, he's going to get us tickets to see the Boss.") The promoter wore a little goatee and a three-piece black suit. His hair was obviously blow-dried. He gave Eshe a quick kiss on the cheek, as if they had just closed a business deal, and she shook his hand ceremoniously.

When we were a few steps away, I asked, "How do you know he wasn't just trying to get into your pants?"

"So what if he is? He isn't going to get any."

On a week day we had the wide boardwalk pretty much to ourselves, save for some old men playing checkers and a few fortune tellers who were windexing their booths. We wandered up and down for a while, stopping for fries and cokes and watching the pinball wizards, mostly out-of-work black guys in tight pants.

"That one," Eshe whispered, pointing to a guy in a sequined T-shirt, tattered and ripped at the shoulder, "has got the best ass in the place."

"Yeah, but he's a junkie," I pointed out.

"Hey, is it his fault his mama was bad to him? Besides, he's into boys. You can tell by the way he pulls back the lever to shoot those little silver balls."

We giggled our way through the arcade until we came out the other side. There was Mr. Promoter, waiting for us.

"Ladies," he said, "I was just at the Pony, and it seems the man I need to meet won't be in until this afternoon. So I'm yours all morning." He smiled, obviously pleased with himself, while Eshe raised an eyebrow.

"That's great, you know, but we're meeting our old men here," she said.

"There's yours right now," I said to Eshe, as we watched a huge Puerto Rican guy lumber up to the pinball machines. As if he had ESP, he swung around with a wolfish grin and called out "Baby!" to Eshe, then returned to his pinball.

With an elegant nod, Mr. Promoter added, "Ah, of course, but keep my card if you need me, and I'll be in touch about those tickets." He bowed and disappeared.

"Tickets, my ass," Eshe said. We sat down on the sand to watch the waves for a while, and she asked, "What do you want when you get out of here?"

"Out of where? Jersey?"

"Sure, everyone wants out of Jersey. You know, they did a study, and eighty percent of the people in this state said they would leave if they could. Is that Jersey or what? So what about you?"

"I don't know. I guess I want to go to college and study art, because that's what I'm good at. Maybe I can find a job afterwards in photojournalism, or advertising." I imagined myself working at a big newspaper in the city, rushing toward elevators and taking pictures of terrible accidents. I cringed.

"You don't want a husband, kids, a big house?"

"I can't tell." I lay down on the sand and stared at the sky. The sun hid behind a bank of clouds and the air was heavy but cool. "What do you want? Do you really want this business life with my dad?"

"Hey, I just want a way out, you know, and this might be the ticket."

"What about college?"

"What about it? I'm not into school, except for the chance to score some good lays."

"Oh," I answered. I wondered who she'd slept with besides her boyfriend, and what it was like. "You mean, with some of the guys at our school?"

"Believe me, it wasn't some of the girls! That's not me. Yeah, some seniors, some teachers."

"Teachers? Who?"

"You sure you really want to know?" When I nodded, she told me how the gym teacher—the one who'd suddenly quit teaching and moved out west—seduced her when she was a freshman. ("It's not like I was a virgin or anything.") He would meet her in the gym and then take her to his little office next to the boys' locker room.

"Who else?" I was frantically wondering about Mr. Lexington, but first she had to tell me about some English teacher who resigned and then got picked up by Eshe.

"I don't want complications, see, so with just one exception, I only sleep with the ones who aren't meant for teaching. Even old Eshe has some standards."

"Who's the exception?"

"Oh, I once had a little thing with Lexington, not full-blown sex, of course. Not that I would have resisted—he's a fox. We made out once behind some curtains. He was helping move some theater equipment and I was on detention that week, working as a slave for Mathers, that creepy theater teacher. It was cool."

My heart pounded so loudly I could hear it, but I pretended to be calm. Just the other day, Mr. Lexington had given me a wide smile when we passed in the hall, and then bent down to say he missed having me in class. I could smell his cologne for the rest of the day.

"He's that easy?" I asked casually, hoping she didn't know how much I liked him. Eshe's nose looked more upturned than usual, and off-center.

"Nah, he's not that easy. I just caught him off guard."

Over the next few hours we ate our way down the boardwalk, tried on Indian dresses, bought see-through peasant shirts, and held a contest to determine the most disgusting flavor of salt water taffy. Eventually we made our way back to the main drag and hitched a ride home. A college girl with long, straight blonde hair picked us up and got us back to Route 9, talking nonstop all the way about how Gerald Ford was a corporate tool and she hated his guts.

I started up the stairs as soon as we got home, but then I remembered it was Thursday, our evening to pick up Roger and Missy and go out for Chinese before bowling. Bowling, of course, meant Roger and Dad, while I entertained Missy, who was now capable of racing the length of the bowling alley. I usually bribed her with French fries while I read the two-year-old issues of *Glamour* that were always lying around. Missy liked to hold my hand, but she seemed like a stranger, certainly not my sister. Every week I invited Eshe to come with us, but she was never interested. ("I don't like spending time with someone else's brats, so don't take it personally," she told me.)

The evenings always ended with Dad driving us to Carvel for frozen custard. When we delivered the kids to Mom, there were always ice cream stains on the front of their shirts. "You can't even keep them clean for two hours!" she'd yell.

"You're lucky I even show up," he yelled back. "A lot of fathers don't care about their kids enough to babysit once a week."

"They're your kids! You're not babysitting. If you want to talk about time put into the children, let me tell you something." Then they were off to the races until Dad finally slammed his car door and rolled up the window. As we drove away, he always waved and smiled at my screaming mother.

I watched the action from the passenger seat of the car as if I were a stranger to both of them. Or I let myself fade into another reality, challenging myself to come up with ways to make an interesting photograph out of the exteriors of the look-alike townhouses. I imagined that the ideal shoot would take place at night, with the orange glow of the windows contrasting with the blue glow of the TVs in the living rooms.

Tonight, as I walked to the kitchen, I asked Dad the usual question: "Carryout here, or Plum Garden?"

"What?" He was looking through the mail.

"The kids. It's Thursday, isn't it?"

"Your mother called, and they have a doctor's appointment."

"In the evening?"

He was rushing toward the door, not even bothering to look over his shoulder as he muttered something about new clothes and picking up a bite on the way. Then my teenage father was out the door and off to the mall, the place I should have been going in his place. Instead, I was supposed to stay home, wash the dishes, and do laundry. A flash of anger shot through me, but I told myself to keep going, don't think about it, focus on the TV shows later tonight instead.

Eshe took off to meet her boyfriend, joking that no man could fence her in. I watched Mary Tyler Moore venting her exasperation with Rhoda, but my mind kept wandering to images of Eshe kissing Mr. Lexington. My body surged on their behalf and crashed on my own. I crossed my arms over my cold chest. That scene in the supply room—it could have been different. I could have caught him off guard, too, and started kissing him. But then what?

Close to midnight, as I was scooping cool whip into a cup of hot cocoa and getting ready for bed, Dad came in with his shopping bags. His old leisure suits were too tight and the polyester didn't age well, pilling at the elbows and knees. It turned out that leisure suits neither aged nor stretched well. He was thrilled, however, with his latest finds.

"Take a look at this," he said, pulling a reddish-brown suit from one bag and a dark blue one from the other. "They have span control, a new invention, and the saleslady thought these colors were especially slimming for me. I look as good in these as I did at my thinnest, so I ordered two more."

"This took you three hours to buy?"

"Oh, I got a bite, and because Linda was free, she joined me."

"Linda?"

"The saleslady. She's divorced too, and her good-for-nothing husband doesn't give her a dime, so she has to work. Great attitude though. I told her if she was ever interested in learning to be a dispatcher to give me a call."

"You're dating a saleslady?"

"No, not dating, just talking."

"What about Fatima?"

Hauling his treasures into the bedroom, he called out, "Live and let live."

"But weren't you practically engaged?"

"I'm over it," he said, returning. "That counseling with the rabbi really paid off." How could it work so easily for him, when it took me forever to feel and let go of anything? Just listening to him made me suddenly feel old and tired.

Then he remembered something and rushed back to the car. He returned with an Adidas shoebox. "Running sneakers," he explained. "It's the new thing, and with all the tension in my life, don't I need it." He put the shoes on and headed for the door, muttering something about getting in shape.

"You're going to run in the dark?"

"Why the hell not?" he asked. "Isn't this why we moved to the suburbs in the first place?"

I woke up much later when something crashed against my window. At first I was too scared to move, but then I realized it was just a little pebble hitting the glass. I cautiously pulled back the curtain. Eshe was standing in the grass below, looking up at me mournfully. I raised the sash and she whispered, "I forgot my key."

I snuck downstairs, trying to avoid making the stairs creak. The front door was too noisy, so I went to the sliding glass door in the kitchen. It opened with a swoosh, and a moment later she was inside. I was surprised to see she had been crying, black mascara rushing down her cheeks like finger paint.

"That bastard," was all she said. At first I thought she meant Dad, but after I followed her silently upstairs, she pulled me into her bedroom and closed the door.

"That bastard did this to me, and now he says, 'Get outta here.'" She fell onto the bed crying, curled up like a shrimp.

"Did what?" I asked, but I'd already guessed that she was pregnant again. She must have known it the day we skipped school. Why didn't she tell me? I felt guilty, as if I were somehow responsible, although I knew that was ridiculous.

"What do you think? He got me knocked up again, and this time he says, 'Pay for the abortion your own damn self. Get out of my life.' I'm the one stuck, and he flicks me off like a fucking mosquito."

"That bastard," I said. I put my arm around her, her face hot against my neck. I couldn't tell if she was hyperventilating or actually crying, so I just waited patiently, feeling like the old mother in a household of crazy kids. For a moment I imagined myself photographing the scene from the back of the room, so that only Eshe's forehead and hairline showed. Liz would respond to a picture like that, say it showed a lot of despair and energy. I held Eshe tighter, my friend, and she was crying so hard that her back shook and she didn't realize I was crying also.

When she was done, I went and got a blanket from my room and covered her up. I climbed into bed beside her, pressing my body against her back and wrapping myself around her. She held my hand against her stomach and I remembered how in health class they told us the baby was first the size of a dime, then a quarter. What was Eshe's baby worth?

Chapter Two

It was raining when the police came to pick up Eshe at the auction. We were so busy drinking hot cocoa under our massive yellow umbrellas that we didn't see the officers until they were standing right in front of us.

"Eshe Sadat?" one asked. He wore a little mustache and a police raincoat. The other officer, tall and beanpole lean, carried an official police umbrella.

"Yeah, what's it to you?" she snapped. I could tell she was scared, but I knew she wouldn't crack about the nail polish we had shoplifted at the drugstore unless they tortured her.

"We're here to transfer you to the juvenile detention facility for the county." The tall one took her arm and the short one did the talking. "We've received a court order for your transfer."

"A court order? What the fuck are you talking about?" She raised her voice, purposely trying to attract attention from the bystanders.

"We have a court order signed by Judge Deator Simon. You need to come with us at once."

Her eyes lit up. She screamed, "I'm not going anywhere with you motherfuckers!" and yanked her arm away from the cop. Boy heard the commotion and shot over to our booth, rain streaming from his cheeks and massive chin.

"What seems to be the problem here, Officer Barnard?" Boy asked, coyly reading from the tall policeman's nametag.

"There's no problem," the short one replied testily.

Eshe was backing away, toward Boy. "There's a huge fucking problem! They're trying to lock me up, and they won't even tell me why."

I grabbed Eshe's arm, ready to fight for her to stay with me. Boy put his long arm protectively around her waist. "Officers," he began, "you need to tell my client what charges you're presenting against her, and give us an opportunity to seek appropriate counsel."

"Look, mister," said the short officer. "This is a juvenile, and we have a court order. She doesn't get her rights read. She just comes with us."

"You need to tell her what crime she's committed."

"We have a court order, and that's enough." He turned to Eshe. "If you come with us, young lady, this will be easier for everyone."

Eshe didn't move. Boy had her right arm locked in a tight grip while I wrapped myself around her left arm. He was a good foot taller than the tall policeman. By now his father, who used to lift weights and still looked pretty strong, had appeared along with Sergei and a few of his boys. Dad was off somewhere, of course, missing his chance to be macho for Eshe.

"She's not going anywhere," Boy said firmly. Eshe was shaking a little. I couldn't tell if it was from the cold rain, or stark fear. The officers, looking like defeated soldiers trapped in the hostile land of the auction, looked at each other and shrugged. The little one said, "We don't need a scene here. We'll be back for you with reinforcements."

"But what if she runs?" asked the tall one.

"Correction. We'll be calling in reinforcements right now." As he whipped out his walkie-talkie, his sidekick snapped a handcuff onto Eshe's wrist and attached the other cuff to his own, linking them in a kind of prison matrimony. It happened so quickly that none of us saw it coming.

The men from the auction stepped in closer with grim faces, letting the cops know she wouldn't go without a fight. Eshe looked at me desperately. A minute ago, Boy could have lifted her above his head and run away. Now she was stuck. Boy seemed to know this, and although he whispered ideas back and forth with Big Boy, neither of them looked hopeful. We waited only a few minutes, but it felt longer. I held the umbrella over Eshe to keep her completely covered, even though it made all the water run down my back. Standing there, I knew that she was not just my only friend, but also my only hope for being a regular sixteen-year-old. Although she never said so, I knew she loved me, trusted me like she trusted no one else. If we could stay together, I would be okay, even if I did have a wacko life.

None of the passing customers dared to approach the solemn huddle of cops and scraggly-looking merchants surrounding two teenage girls. If I wasn't part of this, I would have taken panoramic shots: first the clouds, dark gray to medium gray, with no way of telling if the storm were blowing over or getting worse; then the men, completely soaked, with Eshe, beautiful and fragile, focused intently on the distance; and then the wet leaves stuck to the congregation of worn-out trucks near the booths. Watching Eshe's narrow back, I wanted to wrap her up in a blanket and let her wake up again later, in any moment but this one.

Finally, three more cops ambled our direction. Their leader had a huge gut hanging over his belt and rain running down his face like tears. He took the judge's order from the short cop, snorted, and said only, "Take her in." I tasted blood and realized how hard I had been biting my lip. My whole jaw was shaking. I wanted to kick and hit those cops so hard that they would lose focus and let me run away with Eshe.

"But sergeant," Boy began, "she at least has a right to know what this is about."

"What this is about? Youse really want to know what this is about? I'll tell you then—this girl is a runaway. Her poor mama, after crying her eyes out at home for months now, finally found her and wants her home. But this girl is dangerous, so the court decided to put her in the center for a while, do a little evaluation, cool her down."

"That fucking bitch is the dangerous one!" Eshe screamed. "And she knew where I was the whole time. This was her idea to get rid of me. You tell that bitch to let me the fuck alone!"

She paused, as if trying to remember something important, and hissed at me, "Call Jeanine." Then she launched into fight mode again, lunging at the cop attached to her by the handcuffs and biting his arm. I joined her, kicking the short guy and wrapping my arms more tightly around her waist. My body seemed to be moving at the same speed as hers, but none of my blows made any difference. The sergeant simply picked her up, lifting her right out of my arms, and flung her over his shoulder. The cop wearing the handcuff had to walk backwards as she thrashed and twisted, screaming "MOTHERFUCKER!" and raining blows on the sergeant's back. I ran after her with Boy, Sergei, and the other merchants right behind me. I heard myself howl "Eshe!" so loudly my throat burned. If this were a photo essay, I would show her with her feet over her head as the officers shoved her into the patrol car. The next shot would capture her face pressed against the window, her mouth open in a cry even more despairing than Springsteen's. Then she was gone, as the patrol car bumped slowly over the gravel to the main road and shot away into the distance.

"Those pigs, you can never trust them in this country," Sergei told his boys. But no words came to me. If I were a building, I would collapse. Instead, I sank down onto the muddy ground, shaking with a fury that made it hard to breathe.

Boy and Big Boy pulled me up, one on each side of me, and put their arms around me. I felt a little stronger as we walked back to our booths with our heads down. When we returned, a few professors were weaving through Boy's stand with bulging shopping bags. "Anything I can help you lift?" Boy bellowed.

"No, sir, we've looked all we need."

"Open those bags!" The young men looked stunned, trapped between their desire to run and their fear of what would happen if Boy caught up with them. They meekly opened the handles of their white "Donut-Heaven" bags while Big Boy surgically removed two or three sweaters from each.

About that time, Dad came strolling back. "What's happening? Where's Eshe?"

Boy and I told him the story, and in half an hour we had the stand closed and the truck packed. We raced down the freeway toward the Monmouth County Detention Facility, although the rain fell so heavily it was hard to see the pavement at times. I was too exhausted by then to do anything but lean against the cold window, dozing on and off.

Once we reached the white brick detention center, we drove along the borders of the giant lawn, parked the truck, and got out, the air around us weighty with humidity. Up close, the place didn't look quite so intimidating, merely stained and decrepit. The double glass doors led us to a half-circle white desk, where a woman with skin a little darker than Eshe's was reading *Glamour*.

"We're here for Eshe Sadat," Dad told her. She nodded and picked up the phone. I could smell something like vomit mixed with Lysol. Even the ceiling was a worn shade of green.

After making a few phone calls, she told us that Eshe, having just been admitted, could have no visitors until Monday. There was nothing for us to do but leave. We stopped at a nearby diner, old and shaped like caboose, and ordered mediocre hot beef sandwiches. We were both too tired to talk much. "Tomorrow," was all Dad said as he bit into his sandwich.

I told him everything I knew about Jeanine. As soon as we got home I went upstairs and collapsed on my bed, but I heard him downstairs making phone calls, tracking down Eshe's social worker.

Jeanine's office was located in an old warehouse along with all the other social service agencies for the county. That Monday was a school day and a work day, but we didn't care. We wandered down a long paneled hall with bad lighting and sat down next to Jeanine's green steel desk, which was piled with stacks of papers and folders. Amidst the chaos sat a group of plastic frogs with giant eyes and long lashes. Soon Jeanine appeared, backing into the room carrying a massive coffee mug that read "Have a nice day" on one side and "Have a $%##$@ day" on the other.

"Oh, there you are," she smiled. She had dimples, long black hair in a single braid, and the blackest eyes I'd ever seen.

Dad stood up and shook her hand. "I remember you from the chili feed."

It turned out that they had met at one of the Parents Without Partners events he sometimes attended with my brother and sister. (I usually missed the meetings because I spent those evenings tagging.) They discussed the upcoming apple cider party, then she leaned over, shook my hand, and said she was sorry about what happened to my friend. The shape of her face made me think she was from India, but there was no little red dot between her eyes. She wore a lot of pale pink lipstick and a bunch of silver rings on her fingers.

After listening to Dad for a few minutes, she nodded and picked up the phone. We heard murmuring and giggling, and then she hung up and said, "Let's go."

On the way, I whispered to Dad, "Indian, right?"

"Mexican. I bet you ten bucks." He smiled suspiciously.

"Wait, you know already. How do you know?"

"At the chili feed, they told me to introduce myself to that nice Mexican woman, said she was a real catch." He was smiling and strutting along in his span-control leisure suit and matching ankle boots.

It took us twenty minutes to get back to the detention center, and then a long spell in the waiting room while Jeanine spoke to various people. Finally, she called to us and led us in. We walked down a long white hall that smelled like fresh paint until we reached an enormous room full of metal bunk beds, each covered by a thin plastic mattress with no sheets and a dingy yellow blanket. Girls my age, but with stringier hair, were playing poker around a big round table. A young woman who looked just like Eshe, except for her short black hair, was dealing. A moment later, I realized it really was Eshe. When she saw us standing there, she threw the cards down and came over.

"Your hair!" I exclaimed.

"Yeah, those cocksuckers cut it off. They said I had lice, but this fat bitch just hated me. It took three nurses to hold me down, though."

Even with hardly any hair she still looked beautiful, like a delicate dark angel. The four of us strolled down the hall to a small room with a little folding table in the center. I sat next to Eshe, Jeanine across from her, Dad across from me. I wanted to put my arm around her, but I knew it wouldn't be cool.

"How you doing, Eshe Lou?" Jeanine asked, as if they were sharing a kind of private joke.

"How do you think I'm doing, locked up in this rat hole again?"

Jeanine nodded without looking up, and said, "Your mother accuses you of running away."

"But that's bullshit! You know that's bullshit. You even said it would be good for me to live at Deborah's house until Ma chilled out."

Jeanine continued, "And she accuses Hank, I mean Mr. Shapiro, of having sexual relations with you." Dad and Eshe both gasped at once.

"Who the fuck invents this stuff?" she demanded. Dad just looked pale, stupid, dumbstruck.

"I'm sure the judge will throw that one out," Jeanine said. She smiled at my father, as if it were the most preposterous claim in the world. "So there will be a court hearing on November 20. At that time the judge will decide if you should return home or stay at the center. He'll also decide whether criminal charges should be pressed against Mr. Shapiro."

Another court hearing. I suddenly felt nauseous.

"The good news is that your mother has no evidence for her claims," Jeanine continued. "With a little pressure or help, she may decide to drop the charges."

"What kind of help?" Dad asked.

"I can go visit her again and see what she really wants. I can emphasize the benefits for her, and for you, if you continue your business arrangement with Mr. Shapiro. But you'll just have to be patient, Eshe."

"Patient? You're telling me I have to stay in this piss hole for a month and then maybe, *maybe*, I can go back to my life? Or maybe get committed until I'm fucking eighteen? How the fuck do you expect me to stay fucking patient?"

Jeanine was obviously used to this kind of talk. She cocked her head to one side and said in a well-practiced voice, "I'm sorry there's not a better deal, Eshe. Fighting and causing trouble at the center will work against you. You know the drill: I write up a report, visit your mother, and wait for the system. Meanwhile, the better you behave, the better chance you have to convince the court that your mother is dangerous to you, and not vice versa."

The rest of the visit was dismal. We walked Eshe back to her room and I sat beside her on a bottom bunk while she stretched out and cursed her mother, the judge, the court system, and the police. "Fuck them all," she said in a hoarse voice.

I tried to ask her about the baby, but she ignored me at first. Then she grabbed my face in both her hands and whispered, "I have the money, and no one's gonna stop me. It won't be too late in a month."

Then, abruptly, she changed her tone. "You got your camera?"

"Yeah, of course, you know me."

"Liz would love this place," she said, raising her right eyebrow. She pointed as I took the shots, ending with a few of her lying on her bunk bed with an unlit cigarette in her mouth, her fragile face looking thinner and more tired, her long, muscular arms crossed over her chest.

"Take all you want," she said in a detached way, as if she were no longer paying any attention.

A week later, I walked into Karmic Clothes for the fall session of photography class. Mark, Abby, and Taz were already waiting in the back room. Taz had grown his hair long and bushy. Next to him, on the stool, was an old man eating a donut. ("Uncle Carl," Taz explained, raising his eyebrows as if this information were top secret.)

Liz floated back to join us, carrying a whole box of jelly donuts. "I'm going pure sugar on you," she said as she passed the box around.

My pocketbook was stuffed with photos of the detention center, but according to my father I wasn't supposed to tell anyone where Eshe was, for her own protection. So when Liz asked who had new shots to pass around, I shrugged. Mark passed me a small bundle of photos he'd taken at the beach: rocks beaten by waves, kids' broken pails and shovels lying under the boardwalk. Abby handed around pictures from her family's summer vacation at Rocky Mountain

National Park, which were unfortunately rather blurry because she had used the wrong lens. Taz had staged shots that made it look like vampires were attacking a little girl. Uncle Carl laughed at everything, delighted for no apparent reason.

"Okay," said Liz, "so it's not anyone's best work, but at least you're still taking pictures. Now Uncle Carl, this very old man," she added with a giggle, "is our guest speaker tonight. He's going to talk about portraits, how to really steal the goods. Actually, he's not *that* old. He's just done a lot of drugs."

She stole a look at him, and they burst out laughing together. "So let Uncle Carl talk, and me, I'm going back up front to work on the books. The freaking IRS is coming, and I think it was those Hassidic brothers next door who called them."

Carl smoothed a hand over his forehead. He had short white hair, almost a crew cut, and long tanned arms. "I'm not really her uncle," he confessed, "but I know how to get faces. Here's what you do: you don't ever ask anyone to pose. You get your subject involved in something else, and then you wait for the moment when their face changes. There's always that brief moment when someone realizes something, or changes what they're thinking. That's what you shoot."

"How do you know when it's going to happen?" asked Mark, leaning toward Carl intently.

"You don't." Carl leaned back. "You know, working for *National Geographic*, I did faces all over the world. It's all a matter of being completely aware of everything around you, so you can see it coming. Like that moment at a county fair when the judge bites into the pie that's going to take the blue ribbon. You watch, you wait, and then you move. Hesitation will kill you."

That evening, safely in my bedroom, I pulled the packet of detention center photos out of my purse. There was Eshe, lying in bed, staring straight at me. She was thinking about something very intently, or maybe thinking nothing at all. Then there were shots of a girl everyone called Sue, although she had a different name no one could pronounce. She held up her palms to the camera to show the crazy scars that ran in all directions from the center, like shattered stars. ("She thinks it's the stigmata," Eshe said, but then everyone laughed, even Sue.) There was a black girl braiding her hair, and Dad right behind her, sitting on the edge of an empty bed. He was leaning toward Jeanine as they talked, both laughing like they alone knew the punch line to a rare joke.

Looking at the photos, I realized I was alone again—"naturally," I added, taking a line from the song. But it wasn't as devastating this time as I thought it would be. Dad was out somewhere and tonight the house was relatively clean and quiet. All I needed to do was lean back and sleep until it was time to wake up again.

Chapter Three

Mark cued up the Beatles' "All the Lonely People" while Amy spoke about the lonely people in our communities, some you hardly saw and some you saw all the time. We were conducting yet another rehearsal of the service we were to lead at the temple in a few weeks' time. When it was my turn, I read my statement about reaching out to people in need, people usually invisible to us ("The invisible reading about the invisible," I thought). Then Mark started Fleetwood Mac's "Don't Stop Thinking about Tomorrow," at which point we were all supposed to dance. I dreaded this part the most, but I discovered I could hide my body from the waist down by staying behind the podium.

As I pretended to dance (which mostly consisted of tapping my right foot), I let myself think about my own tomorrow. I would go to college and live in a dorm with a roommate who received care packages every week from her suffocatingly loving mother. We'd stay up late at night listening to Fleetwood Mac and talking about boys. She would have a boyfriend who turned out to have a friend who would be just perfect for me. The boyfriend's friend would be tall with long hair and a flair for detailed pen and ink drawings. He'd be quiet and gentle, and tremble a little as he reached over to kiss me for the first time. Once in a while, I would meet Fatima downtown at a little café. By then she would be like an old friend, a mother figure, a big sister who bought me silk camisoles and flowers for my birthday. It would be our secret that we were still so close.

After youth group ended, it was time for my weekly conversation with the rabbi, but my anticipation faded as soon as Dad appeared. He walked over to the rabbi, shook his hand and said something I couldn't hear, then crossed over to me. "Deborah, we need to help some girls tonight." His dark brown eyes seemed glassy and small behind his aviator glasses.

"We need to do what? I have a meeting with the rabbi," I said, gesturing toward the door.

"Not anymore. We need to meet Jeanine in Marlboro so we can transfer some girls and keep them here."

"What are you talking about?"

The rabbi came over and put his arm around me, promising that we could meet on Thursday and reminding me to call if I needed him. He looked directly at me as he spoke, not acknowledging Dad, but Dad didn't seem to notice. As he pulled me toward the parking lot, he explained that the girls we were rescuing had been at the center for years. Now they had a chance at a better life, but they needed to lie low for a few days. We could hide them in the attic, and no one would know. I had to come along, he said, so it would look like he was just driving around with his daughter and a bunch of her friends.

I nodded as I climbed into the car. "But what are their names?"

"Angel and Tiffany, that's their names for as long as you know them."

"Why is Jeanine helping steal them? Can't she get fired over this?"

"Shut up!" he yelled. The intensity of his voice surprised me. "And don't tell anyone, not even the rabbi, do you hear me?"

Roger and Missy were supposed to come over tomorrow night, but I decided not to remind Dad of that inconvenient fact. I huddled down in the car seat and crossed my arms tightly over my chest. Screw you, I thought, and then wondered what would happen if I said it out loud. But I knew already what would happen, and how much it would hurt.

Dad drove like his usual maniac self—diving over medians, passing cars by using the shoulder or service lane, and generally going twice the speed limit—until we arrived in the parking lot behind a pizza parlor. The smell was intoxicating. Dad turned the headlights off, and both of us tried to act inconspicuous and nonchalant. A few minutes later, a white Volare pulled up alongside us. I could see Jeanine in the driver's seat, her hair hidden under a babushka scarf. She was wearing sunglasses, too, even though it was night. Two girls stepped out of her car, one my height and the other pretty short. Our car door opened as soon as Jeanine's closed, and the girls slid into our back seat.

"Hi, I'm Angel," said the short one. She had strawberry blonde hair, long, straight and parted in the middle. She looked like she belonged in an ad for Herbal Essence shampoo.

"And I'm Tiffany," said her companion, a girl with a nose so perky it looked scary.

Jeanine and my father nodded to each other, and she threw him a kiss before she gunned out of there. We took off, too, with Dad talking nonstop. "Girls, you can sleep in the extra bedrooms upstairs, but during the day you need to stay in the attic where no one can find you. Under no circumstances are you to go outside the house at all. In a few days I'll have a taxi take you to the city, where you'll catch a train to the airport in Washington."

They nodded as if they already knew exactly where they were going, but I didn't have a clue. This seemed even crazier than hiding Fatima's ex-husband from the INS.

"Where are you off to?" I ventured.

"Mexico. We're gonna live with Jeanine's aunt and sister, help take care of the aunt and help out with the family business."

"What's the business?"

When they laughed and replied, "Hot tamales," I looked at them incredulously. "Hey, we're not kidding," Angel insisted.

But they were kidding, according to Dad, who later told me that Jeanine's family ran a sheet rock company. Unless these girls got away, he said, they would be returned to their father, who was doing terrible things to them.

"Like what?" I asked.

"Sex. Now shut up." I had heard things like that could happen, but I didn't know anyone who said it had happened to them. No matter how bad Dad treated me at times, at least he never did that to me, I thought.

Dad pulled into the giant lot of a new drugstore so the girls could buy whatever they wanted, anything that would keep them from going stir-crazy in the attic for two days. They were thrilled. Each took a shopping cart and pushed it down the aisles with me trailing behind them. They filled their carts with magazines, boxes of cigarettes, nail polish, beef jerky, Hershey bars, cheap romance novels, licorice, greeting cards, stationery, scarves, lipstick, decks of cards, magic markers, crossword puzzle books, deodorant, tiny sample bottles of Charlie perfume, more nail polish, and toe clippers. Dad met us at the cash register and didn't even blink an eye at their haul. I felt a twinge of jealousy, remembering how Dad balked whenever I wanted to buy the Betty Crocker scalloped potatoes instead of the generic brand.

"Looks like you're gonna have one helluva slumber party," remarked the cashier.

"Yeah, it's gonna be great. Hey Angel, you got marshmallows?"

Angel tossed in a bag of chocolate covered marshmallows, bringing the bill to $214.69. Dad peeled some fifties off his wad of bills and handed them to the cashier.

"You're great," said Tiffany, "I only wish I'd known you sooner." Both girls snickered a little.

Dad drove home at a weary pace and let me usher the girls and their collection of bags into the house. It was almost ten-thirty by then, so I showed them to their rooms. Tiffany took Roger's room and Angel had Missy's. They thanked me, told me I had a cool father, and disappeared into Missy's room to paw through their stash, eat candy, and play cards. I asked if I could photograph them, but Dad overheard me and said absolutely not, because the authorities could use the pictures to prove that we had harbored delinquents.

"It's not like their pictures will be in the paper," I called after him, but he didn't hear me.

Tiffany looked up and said I should take lots of pictures. That was all I needed to hear. I took shots of each of them, using what I had just learned from Liz about adding depth of vision. I would make a small object, like a tube of lipstick, stand out in the center of the photograph, while the girls who had just applied it laughed in the background over their bags of loot. They started playing cards, not really noticing that I was there or asking if I wanted to join them. I didn't. They were living in a parallel universe, and I knew I wasn't supposed to cross the line between us. When I finally returned to my own room and drifted off to sleep, I could still hear one accusing the other of bluffing.

The next day the girls were poised for a great time, especially after Dad moved the TV into the attic, via a string of extension cords, to get them through the long day. I couldn't understand why he thought they were safe sleeping in the bedrooms at night, but needed to hide in the attic by day. Before they settled in, they helped themselves to piles of chips, crackers, cookies, a jug of juice, bottles of orange and cream soda, and a bag of apples. I told them I'd be home by three-thirty, and they told me all over again what an outasight father I had.

Once I got to school, I remembered all the homework I hadn't had time to do the night before. Fortunately, we had a substitute teacher in algebra class who sat with his feet propped on the desk, reading *People* magazine, which gave me time to concentrate on my French test. The test was on the conditional tense, and I was still mixing up *voudrais* and *voudrait*. "I would like," "I would have liked"—how on earth could I keep those two things straight?

At the end of the day I turned my mind to other things, taking a long detour down the hallway that passed by Mr. Lexington's office. When I glanced through his open door, I saw him sitting on his desk, talking in animated fashion to another teacher who smiled back at him. Not until I walked out the front door did I realize that the other teacher was Ms. Sheplin. I wondered if they ever talked about me. I imagined their dialogues would surely focus on my artistic abilities, and on maybe how smart I was, too.

I didn't remember the girls until I got home. I raced straight up to the attic. Surely they were going out of their minds after being crammed up there all day, surrounded by pink fiberglass batting. I flung open the attic door and called to them, but they weren't there. The TV was missing, too, along with all the stuff Dad bought them at the drugstore. I rushed downstairs to find the clock radio gone along with the little stereo Dad bought me after Mom moved out. I went straight to the potbelly stove where we stored our emergency cash, usually $100 or so, and it was missing, too.

I plopped down on the floor, feeling as emptied out as if they had stolen a part of me. They had tricked us, used us, taken off, taken everything they could. But how could they carry it all? They must have had boyfriends or something, people on the outside.

When Dad came home, he found me asleep on the kitchen floor. Before he had a chance to panic, I sat up, suddenly wide awake.

"Good, you're okay, now where're the girls?" He had a bucket of Chicken Holiday in one hand and a grocery bag with different side dishes and desserts in the other. I rose from the floor, perched on a stool, and told him everything. We agreed that we both felt like shit.

"Maybe I should be lying down on the floor, too," he said.

I expected him to call Jeanine right away, but instead he spread his wares out on the counter. Sitting side by side on the stools, we ate the delicious food and joked about what idiots we were, what suckers, how easy it had been for them to rip us off.

"I can't believe I fell for it," he said, handing me a drumstick. "And you, too. You believed them."

"I don't know what I believed," I said, dishing out more fries. "I mean, they seemed pretty slimy, Dad. Think of how much money they spent at the drugstore." I could see he was embarrassed about being so gullible, so I tried my best not to rub it in. "Of course, you had no way of knowing."

He shook his head. "People like us shouldn't have kids."

I started to laugh right along with him, but then remembered that I didn't actually have any kids. His kids, the ones he was supposed to be picking up at this very moment, probably would agree with him, though. He remembered what time it was at the very same moment I did.

"God damn it," he yelled, lunging for the phone. Within minutes he was yelling at Mom as usual, telling her she didn't know shit about the pressures of his life. If he was caught late in the city some nights, working so he could make her alimony payments, she better just shut up and accept it. Only after he slammed down the phone did it occur to me that I was not a negligent parent, but one of his kids, too.

Chapter Four

On the morning of Eshe's court hearing, Dad woke me up to tell me we weren't going to the courthouse after all. Jeanine had called, and the parties had reached a settlement.

"What does that mean?" I asked. I rose up on one elbow, wearing an oversized New York Mets t-shirt I got at the auction.

"Just that we reached a settlement." He started to walk away, but I flung myself out of bed.

"You mean you paid her mother off? You paid money for Eshe?" It didn't make any sense to me that he would need to pay off Eshe's mom, especially since he was innocent of her fabricated charges.

"Something like that," he said in a low voice, without turning around to face me. When he reached the bottom of the stairs, he yelled up at me to make a good dinner tonight to welcome Eshe back home.

"When is she coming home?"

"Right now."

"Wait, I'm coming with you." He looked pissed off at being held up, but he waited for me to get dressed.

"What do you think Eshe will want to do when she gets home?"

"Who the hell can tell?" he said. "She might just want to relax, rest up. I don't think those girls get a lot of sleep. Some of them are real messes, keep the others up all night." I noticed that his voice seemed happier than usual, more relaxed.

"And Eshe?"

"She's just a jewel in the rough." We both turned quiet, thinking about Eshe.

"Oh, and one other thing," Dad added casually. "When you see Jeanine, it's your fault the girls ran off."

"What do you mean? The other night, you said it was no one's fault."

He stared straight ahead, the veins in his neck bulging a little. I knew if I said another word, he would yell at me, but at that moment I didn't care. "Dad, it's not fair to blame it on me just because you've got a thing for Jeanine."

His right hand suddenly shot out, smacking hard against my cheek and making it burn. He put his hand back on the wheel without even taking his eyes off the road. I slid over against the window and put my hand on my face, felt the heat in my cheek. It didn't hurt that much, now that the sting was fading.

Very low, I said, "But I need to go to school." I was careful to stay close enough to the window so he couldn't reach me again. But this time he simply ignored me, speeding up to pass a driver who was going less than twenty miles per hour over the speed limit.

The receptionist at the front desk had never heard of Eshe Sadat. It took ten minutes before she found a social worker who did know something. As she came charging toward us, she blurted out, "I'm sorry."

We stared at her as if she were speaking another language. "Miss Sadat left last night, estimated time of departure 2:45 AM," she continued. "No one knows where she went. It was a runaway situation."

I froze, unable to take my eyes off the white and red print of her shirtdress, cut from the same polyester as the pants we sold. The print was all wrong for her body, making her look like a large rectangle on stick legs. Her red hair was teased up to form another head that towered above her real one.

"She must have gotten scared, because of the court thing," I said. When Dad remained silent, I turned and looked him in the eye. "Why didn't you tell her that you had a deal, that everything would be okay?" He couldn't hit me this time, not with this woman watching.

He was already deflated. "I didn't want to get her hopes up," he said in a low voice. "How can we find her?"

"Search me," said the social worker, suddenly looking more distracted than concerned. "But if you find her let us know, so we can readmit her and check her out properly."

"Why would you have to do that?" I wondered out loud, but she was already halfway down the hall. We both sighed, trying not to look at each other.

"Let's go," Dad said, but from the look on his face I knew he didn't mean the car. We marched straight to the office of the detention center director. Mr. Leonard wasn't in, according to his secretary, but Dad ignored her. He flung the office door open, ready to demand a resolution. As it turned out, Mr. Leonard really was out. The secretary, apparently accustomed to such outbursts, just shook her head and went back to filing.

For a moment Dad stopped in his tracks, then he politely asked to use the phone in the director's paneled office. She waved us in without looking up. Dad pulled a piece of paper out of his wallet and dialed. I studied the photographs of young children that decorated the walls— children barely five years old, holding strings attached to bouquets of red and yellow balloons, children who had nothing in common with the kids who lived here.

"Jeanine?" I heard Dad's voice now, speaking into the phone. "Yeah, she's gone. Oh, you knew already?"

"Ask her what we can do," I whispered urgently. "Ask her where Eshe might go."

He waved at me to be quiet. "Yes, of course," he said to Jeanine. Then he leaned toward me and whispered, "The boyfriend is gone too, probably out of the state by now."

He listened for a while longer, then sighed. "What you gonna do?" he exclaimed, and then he laughed at whatever Jeanine said in reply.

"Ask her where out-of-state they might go first! Maybe we can hire a detective."

He ignored me and turned away. "So I was wondering about this Parents Without Partners thing on Saturday night," he said smoothly. "I hear it's adult-only this time, a cocktail party. Or maybe you'd rather do something else."

"Dad, you're asking her out? We need to find Eshe!" My face still felt hot where his hand had struck me.

He was already in another world, stepping as far away from me as the phone cord would allow. I stared at the wall again, where a framed diploma, lined with gold, certified Cecil Leonard as a leader for "Teen Terrific Training." I racked my brains, trying to remember if Eshe had ever mentioned any friends in other states. Then it hit me that we would never find Eshe if she didn't want to be found. She was smart—and she probably was hundreds of miles from here already.

As I walked to the car, my hands in my pockets, that old sickening feeling was back in my stomach. Having Eshe in my life had been too good to be true, I told myself. Not that she ever paid that much attention to me, but when I was with her I was almost one of the cool kids—still a little too quiet, but generally okay. She was like a television drama with me cast in a supporting role. Without her story playing across my screen, I was dark and empty.

On the way home I leaned my head against the window again, a cold window this time, with high cool clouds and a sharp wind just beyond my reach. Then I felt someone touch my hand. It was Dad, mumbling, "Sorry, honey." I jerked my hand away, an involuntary reaction.

Chapter Five

Parents Without Partners celebrated Thanksgiving at Jeanine's small bungalow, which was sandwiched between an apartment building and a bar in Red Bank. The living room furniture pressed up against the walls with painted seascapes and framed photographs of dead relatives filling up whatever space the furniture didn't. Little end tables were crammed into every corner and lined up next to the worn yellow couch, while a multitude of folding chairs prepared to welcome the stray partner-less parents. As I looked around, I realized that the scene was virtually impossible to photograph. Too many objects competed for the attention of the camera, with no real center to hold the image together. Plus the lighting was all wrong: too dark in one half of the room, while the other half was far too bright with all the lamps huddled together near the couch and a single chair.

"Please, make yourselves at home," Jeanine said, appearing at the foot of the stairs to welcome us. "Mrs. P will be out in a second, and you can meet her. Meanwhile, Sal!" She turned and shouted the name loudly up the staircase. "Sal, come down and meet Hank and his daughter, Deborah."

Before I had time to wonder who Mrs. P was, a small boy with dark shiny skin, luminous brown eyes, and black hair zoomed into the room. He buried his small face in his mother's hip.

"This is Sal, my son," she explained. "Sal, say hello, then show Deborah the house." He looked more like he came from India than from a mother raised in Mexico.

Sal craned his neck to look up at me, mumbled hello, and then extended his hand. I took it and he led me off to the kitchen, which felt more like the inside of a carpeted space ship. Jeanine had lined up on her counters every kitchen appliance that had ever existed, all gleaming as if they were brand new. The oven was on and the whole room smelled like turkey. Next we visited the bathroom, mostly decorated in yellow with little ducks on the bath mat and towels. Jeanine's small bedroom was overwhelmed by a giant bed laden with file folders and big stacks of paper. More stacks sat on the night table and the chest of drawers. We trotted upstairs to Sal's room, which seemed far more airy with its bunk bed, small desk, and chest of drawers floating on a big sea of off-white carpet. All his toys were shoved under the bed and into the closet, as he showed me with a grin. I grinned back.

As we left his room, he pointed toward a closed door and whispered, "Mrs. P, we don't go in there." The door opened momentarily, however, and a small woman emerged. Her reddish hair was teased into a sixties-style bouffant, and her lined face was adorned with what my mother called "beauty marks." I assumed that she must be Jeanine's mother, but there was nothing in her complexion or green eyes to indicate that she was related to either of these two. She looked right past me and started down the stairs, as if she were a servant reporting for duty.

As soon as she was out of earshot, I asked Sal who she was.

"She cooks everything." Sal's voice was simultaneously lilting and rough, a little like Missy's, but somehow darker.

"Where did you find her? Is she a housekeeper or something?"

"No, she's just someone my mom got. She used to live next door."

As he led me around, I couldn't help thinking how different Thanksgiving was with Mom. She never had the food ready on time, and she usually sent Dad out to the store in a hurry to get something she forgot. Nana and Pop came most years, sometimes Mimi, too, although she usually spent the holiday in the city with Uncle Leo's beautiful family. Our house was filled with an unpleasant blend of chaos, burnt rolls, and arguments in the kitchen. Nana would insist on dusting the figurines in the dining room even after Mom told her to stop, and Pop would tell me his latest long and boring joke about a priest who wandered into a nudist colony.

When we came back downstairs, a dozen middle-aged women were gathered around the piano. One wiped her eyes and pressed her hand against her heart as a bald gentleman flawlessly rendered "Moon River." Open boxes of chocolates called from the end tables, garnering repeated cries of "Oooh, I really shouldn't" from the delighted women. To my surprise, Dad was actually the best-looking and least disgusting man at the party. Sal took one look around the room and slipped back up the stairs—headed, I imagined, for the small table in his room where he was building a space station out of Legos.

I pulled out my camera and leaned back to remove the lens cap. Here was a perfect opportunity to capture this huddle of women on film, their faces powdery from too much makeup, hair glimmering with the sheen of hairspray. I started snapping pictures from different angles, but I found the best one by squatting down next to the piano player. From there, the women looked just like a pack of coyotes howling at a nonexistent moon.

A lady in a tight beige polyester dress with puffy see-through sleeves put her arm around me as I stood up. "You, you're the lucky one," she said as she offered me a heart-shaped box of chocolates. (No doubt purchased months ago when it was on a sale, I thought, as I bit into a stale caramel.) "You have your youth. You have your looks. You have your whole life ahead of you."

"So did we once," sighed an enormous woman in a green and white plaid muumuu. (Size 52, I judged, based on the width of her hips.) "But look what happens when you get on in life, cookie. We just have to accept who we are."

An older woman wearing a neat bun and a maroon pants suit tapped my hand. "Don't listen to them," she whispered. "And don't get bitter like them. Keep your faith, that's what's kept me going." After delivering her message, she sat down genteelly in a folding chair with a white lapdog, its coat so long that I was uncertain as to whether or not it actually had eyes. Strangely enough, none of the women seemed to notice the camera hanging from my neck, or mentioned the photographs that I had taken.

I pictured my mother and Geraldine sitting in one corner of the room, raising their eyebrows and nodding at me in a knowing way. They would notice every amusing detail in this room so that we could laugh over it later. But why, I wondered, was I even thinking of my mother right now?

Soon Jeanine signaled for me to join her in the kitchen. She looked happy and relaxed, not at all what I expected after Dad had returned home late last night, explaining that he'd been working with his lawyer to help Jeanine.

"Help her with what?" I had asked.

"Are you always this dense?" he asked, picking up the cold lamb chop I had broiled for him hours earlier. "Her job is in danger, and her license, too. All because of those girls." He shot me a stern look to remind me that these troubles were all my fault.

Amidst the Parents Without Partners crowd, however, Jeanine shone like a star, offering hospitality with grace and control. In the kitchen, I watched Mrs. P lift the turkey out of the oven and place it on a hot pad. Dad aimed an electric knife at the perfectly-browned skin, (a new trick for him since my mother always did the carving at home), joking that holding the knife was like grasping a tennis racket. The counter brimmed with platters of vegetables, cheese and crackers, jello molds shaped like various fish, cakes, cookies, and a basket of various breads. The range was going full-force under a bevy of shiny pots. If I could lean back just a little, I thought, I could fit the stove and table into a single photograph that would show more than just the sum of the food.

"Mrs. P," Jeanine said casually, "this is the girl I was telling you about, the little Jewish girl, Deborah."

Mrs. P. seemed as taken aback by this introduction as I was. We both looked away before we looked at each other. She merely nodded at me and went back to tending the food.

"Okay, at least you met," Jeanine said with a smile, herding me back toward the living room, "Go keep those women from ruining their dinners with all that candy."

I walked away fast. Jeanine seemed nice enough, but there was something about her that scared me, something I couldn't trust. Last week, when I told the rabbi Dad was dating her, he immediately asked if I was burnt-out yet on all these mother surrogates.

"What do you mean?" I asked.

"First you had your mom, then Fatima, then Eshe."

"Eshe was my age, just a friend."

He nodded. "I know. I just mean that you keep pinning your hopes on women who dash them to the floor." I immediately pictured a glass shattering as it hit a stone floor.

"They do?" I stopped and thought for a minute. "No, with Eshe, that was Dad's fault. And with Fatima too. With my mom...."

"Deborah," he said gently. The sound of my name kept me from continuing. "Take a breath, take your time. Don't give your heart away too soon. These are tricky times, and it's hard to know who's staying and who's going."

His words left me with a hollow feeling. There was no one I could trust, he seemed to be saying, except for people like him and Liz, people I only saw occasionally. I certainly didn't live with anyone I could trust, not even myself.

Later that night, I helped Jeanine carry the plates to the kitchen counter, where Mrs. P scraped them meticulously and muttered to herself about the waste of food. I asked if she wanted me to load the empty plates into the dishwasher.

Mrs. P looked up at me like I was speaking a foreign language. "Or if you want, I could sweep." I knew I was trying too hard, but did the rabbi really mean I shouldn't try at all, just wait and see?

Mrs. P didn't answer. Jeanine, who heard me, quietly told me that Mrs. P had her own ways of keeping the kitchen and liked to do everything herself. I turned to face the window, which still held a little light before sunset. I should try to talk with Jeanine, I thought, but what would I say? I decided to ask her if she wanted to go for a walk, but before I could get the words out, she had asked me first.

The outside air chilled my face instantly, but that was okay after the stuffy kitchen. Jeanine wore a dark wool coat with wooden toggles that seemed a little large for her, as if she had bought it cheap at the auction. Her braid was tangled in a red and white scarf that looked like something the Cat in the Hat would wear.

"That auction is the place for bargains," she told me, as if she'd read my mind. "I've been getting all my clothes there, Sal's too, for years."

I wanted desperately to ask what happened to Angel and Tiffany, and whether she was going to lose her job over them. It seemed more diplomatic, however, to ask first about Mrs. P.

"Oh, she's had a hard life," Jeanine replied vaguely. "Once you grow on her, then she's fine."

"You know her from next door?"

"I know her from the supermarket. Then one day I got a letter of hers by mistake, so I went next door to give it to her. Sal was just a baby then, and my husband was still alive, but not for long." Jeanine paused for a moment. "Anyway, Mrs. P answered the door, crying. Her husband had died only a few days before. She had no family, no friends really, and not much to live on."

As Jeanine continued her story, I tried to picture tears coming from the solemn woman who orchestrated all those kitchen appliances. Jeanine started making weekly visits to Mrs. P, letting her know about job training programs and other social services. Mrs. P, however, wouldn't take anything that came from the government. ("She was just one of those types," Jeanine said.) Instead, Jeanine asked Mrs. P to watch Sal while she was at work.

"I tell you, she was a godsend. I had no childcare, and my husband was on the road four days a week." Jeanine soon discovered that Mrs. P was a great cook. Since she had no time to make anything more elaborate than toast, she hired Mrs. P to come over every Monday and cook a week's worth of meals.

After Jeanine's husband died, it seemed like only a short leap from Mrs. P doing all the cooking and childcare to Mrs. P moving in. The only difficulty was Mrs. P's abundance of furniture. "What can you do?" Jeanine asked, laughing. "Mrs. P loves her things."

When I asked Jeanine how her husband died, she shrugged off the question. "He was a truck driver, right?" I pressed, remembering something Dad had said over dinner.

"Yeah, and it pissed off the neighbors to high heaven to see his big rig parked in our drive," she answered, sounding a little amused.

I decided it was time to change topics. "What about Eshe? You were close to her for a long time, right?"

"I was assigned to her when she was in fifth grade. She was a handful from way back when, and her mother has a lot of problems. Some immigrants never adjust."

"But aren't you worried about Eshe now? What should we do to help her?" What I really wanted to say was, "How could you give up on her so fast? Why aren't you looking for her?"

Jeanine laughed, but this time it was a bitter laugh. "Eshe made her bed. She knew what running away would do. But hey, let's not talk about her. I spent way too many years on that one already."

We walked past an old man on a ladder, stringing red and white Christmas lights across the top of his garage as his wife called out from the driveway, "No, a little higher." A dog barked in a high pitch. The wind blew. I decided the moment had come to ask about Jeanine's job.

"I hear things aren't so good at your job lately," I ventured. "Are you going to be okay?"

"Me? I'm always fine, because I learned a long time ago that in this work you can't get too attached to the kids. I lose at least one a month. Maybe it's drugs, pregnancy, running away—or sometimes they die. You know, I've had enough. I've been trying to help girls like this for over two decades. It's like your father says: 'You can't save the world.'"

"But your job?"

"There is no job anymore," she said, cutting me off. "Besides, I'll like doing the taxis. It'll be a relief to just give people a ride, and when I go home for the day, I'm done." She rubbed her hands together and dropped them.

"It wasn't my fault those girls left. Did you know that?" I asked anxiously. Then, after her words had a chance to sink in, I added, "Wait, you're going to start working at the taxi service? In the city?"

"Didn't your father tell you?" She spoke casually, as if these plans had been in the making for a very long time.

I shook my head, trying desperately to think of something to say that would make me sound like a good girl, not like the kind of girl who had cost Jeanine her job. All the while, another part of me wanted to ask her why she was suddenly working for Dad.

"I don't care anymore," she continued. "You know, I've been trying to reach girls like Eshe for years. I do and do for them, and what do they do? They run away, steal, lie. Hell, some of them have probably even killed. I've had it, and I'm ready to move on."

Jeanine fell silent, lost in her own thoughts. I looked around at the colorless lawns, the full living colors of summer reduced to stark black and white. I didn't understand how Jeanine could just give up who she was, what she did.

As we rounded the corner toward her house, she asked, in a little girl voice that I didn't know she had, "You want to know about my husband? He killed himself. In a motel in Iowa. He took sleeping pills."

"Why did he do that?"

"I don't know. He was always sad, that man. He was from India, and he missed his country, but he might have been sad there, too. He just had a sad soul."

She paused, as if considering what else to say, "That's why I like your dad so much. He doesn't need help." I didn't contradict her, even after she added, "You guys are in good shape."

I flinched. That felt more like fiction, or a wish. Did this mean she would be with Dad all the time now, her life disappearing into his? If so, what did that mean for me? Jeanine was easy enough to like, but there was something distant about her. She was like someone who, no matter how often you took her photograph, always held something back.

"How can the birds go on singing?" Boy sang out. Sergei, who was selling sweaters hand over fist, echoed the word "singing" at the end of every line. It was a bad duet, made even worse by the extra lyrics Boy invented, like "How can the fish go on flinging?" and "Don't they know it's the end of the world? It ended when you didn't buy sportswear."

Thanksgiving weekend was the single biggest sales day at the auction. Dad and I were manning the booth alone, selling so much stuff that neither of us had taken a break for hours. Sergei's girlfriend occasionally tottered over on high heels, cleavage spilling out of her sweater, to hand me a hot cocoa or a chocolate bar. It appeared that Sergei kept a stash of Kit Kats under his folding chair and the girlfriend thought he was getting too fat.

"Too fat for what, darling?" he asked, seeming puzzled that his appearance would even matter to her.

Although it was only two o'clock, I felt more exhausted than I usually did at closing time. Coming back from the truck with another stack of shirts, I spotted Jeanine. She was charming Boy with a rendition of Barry Manilow's "Mandy." I had to admit that she had a good voice, its timbre loud, clear, and low. Mrs. P was holding Sal's hand and staring at the clothing in disgust. Suddenly what we were doing didn't feel like a social service, but more like playing in the mud.

Dad took Mrs. P by the hand and introduced her to Sergei. "See, you're from Poland, and he's from somewhere right around there, too," he announced excitedly. "So you can speak to each other!"

Mrs. P raised her eyebrows in a subtle way that convinced me I might actually like her someday. Sergei, who was actually from Yugoslavia, disdained Poles and ignored any woman over twenty-five. He shook his head and looked at Mrs. P as if she were a sweater that had fallen into the mud. He said hello in Serbo-Croat, and she answered in Polish. Having done their duty, they turned their backs on each other. Oblivious to the whole interaction, Dad boasted to Jeanine about how he had introduced them.

That night we went over to Jeanine's place, where Mrs. P served us a wonderful meal of beef stew. I sat next to Jeanine on the sofa, watching a TV movie about a housewife who develops a drinking habit, then turns to drugs and prostitution—all in between shuttling her kids to football games.

"Looks like her life is ruined," said Jeanine.

"Yeah, but she didn't mean for it to be."

"You make your own bed in this world," she said, passing me the chocolate-covered peanuts.

She said the same thing about Eshe, I remembered, or maybe she meant all of us. "You grew up in Mexico, right?" I asked.

She nodded. "Cuernavaca. Nice city, but not for me."

"Why did you want to leave?"

Jeanine took a long sip of her Tab. "You know, I grew up in a big family. If I stayed, I could have worked in the family business, but that wasn't for me, either. I had ambition. Besides, I needed to leave."

"Why?"

She gave me a curious look, and then called out to my father, who was reading the paper in the other room, "You want another soda, Hank?" When she turned back to me, she gestured toward the kitchen. She seemed suddenly nervous, or maybe just sad.

"You know," Jeanine said, steadying her voice, "you guys should try to be family to each other. Especially with what she's been through."

I realized she must be talking about Mrs. P, who had never said more than two words to me. "Well, I never had anyone die like that," I began apologetically, feeling a little nervous about discussing the dead husband thing. "I don't know what it's really like."

"No, I mean the camps. You know she's one of your survivors?"

"Which camps?" I asked, but I was slowly beginning to put the pieces together.

"I don't know, but she was in more than one. That is, after she hid in a barn with her first husband for a year or something. No kids, thank heavens. I don't know how people got over losing their kids that way."

It struck me as a strange comment, considering that Jeanine lost kids all the time at her job. "And he, the first husband, he didn't make it?" I wondered.

"Nah, no one else in her whole family survived."

I had never met a Holocaust survivor before, let alone had one cook for me. In junior high, they made us read *The Diary of Anne Frank* and showed us newsreels of piles of dead bodies and naked crowds herded into showers. At Hebrew School, we always talked about how noble the survivors were, how grateful they were for simple things like a sunset or fresh bread.

"It doesn't seem like she's all that glad to be here. I mean, I always thought people who survived the camps would be happy to be alive."

Jeanine laughed as she reached for the chocolate-covered peanuts again. "Those are just the good-ending stories, like Anne Frank."

"But Anne Frank died. How is that a good ending?"

Jeanine shrugged. "Everyone thinks she's great, right?"

Chapter Six

Mom was not amused when Dad said he wanted the kids for Christmas. In response, he yelled into the phone, "They're my kids, and they can do one goddamn Christmas in their lives!"

She must have yelled back for a long time. He waited tensely, then screamed, "Well, then there'll be two less pain-in-the-ass Jews in the world, and I can dance at their big church weddings!"

I opened the fridge to get out some juice for breakfast, but as I headed upstairs for a shower Dad followed me into the foyer with the phone. "Your precious mother, she wants to talk with you."

Just then the doorbell rang and Dad let Jeanine in, kissing her quickly on the cheek. It was a Friday morning and a teacher in-service day, meaning no school for me. Dad had decided I should accompany him and Jeanine to a hearing in Trenton. The two of them lingered nearby, looking at the piles of pink and orange polyester slacks on the living room floor, as I took the receiver from his hand.

"Yeah," I said, to let Mom know I was there. Although I had my back to Jeanine, I knew she was watching me.

"Deborah! It's just so good to hear you," Mom exclaimed, although I'd barely said a word.

I held the receiver to my ear, but neither of us spoke for a long time. I wondered if people all over the world did this, calling each other up, holding the phone, and saying nothing. This is my mother, I told myself, a little surprised at how little I felt, as if I had never known her. At the same time, the silence we shared seemed like a kind of secret language that didn't translate into my life.

"Don't you miss your mother?" the rabbi asked nearly every time we met. He seemed to think that if he kept asking I would crack, start crying, and say, "Yes, yes, I need my mother," but I never did.

Now, in the silence, the old sinking feeling that something was broken beyond repair flooded over me. Finally I managed to get out the words, "I've gotta go," just as she started to say, "I was wondering—"

This time, there was something about her voice, the way it cracked a little, that ripped into me. Maybe the rabbi was right.

"I was wondering if you might want to have lunch today. I hear you kids have the day off," she continued.

"No, I'm busy."

"Some other time?" she asked, her voice strained. I could feel Dad watching me, standing next to Jeanine.

"No."

Then her voice broke. I heard her gulp, but she wasn't finished yet. "Haven't you punished me enough for whatever I did wrong? Whatever it is, I'm sorry," she yelled, trying to cover up her tears.

"You're not my mother anymore."

I said it quickly, in a robotic voice, so that I didn't leave her a chance to reply. Then I carried the receiver, attached to its long cord, all the way back to the kitchen and hung it up. I could imagine exactly how Mom looked at the other end. She would hold the phone for just a second, maybe cry a little, and then punch in the number for the other Bev or Geraldine so they could talk about me.

"That's the kind of mess we have," I heard Dad explain to Jeanine, but I dashed upstairs before I could hear what he said next.

Ten minutes later, Dad stood in the doorway of my room. "So why am I going with you again?" I asked, stuffing my feet into a pair of loafers I had found at the auction. I liked how much older they made my feet look.

"It's a preliminary hearing with the social work people. I told you," he hissed.

"But why should I go?"

"What? You want to go live with your mother instead?" His eyebrows shot up, outraged.

"No, I was just wondering."

"Look, Manicotti said you could help Jeanine if this case ever went to court. You could say she kept you from being homeless when your mother threw you out, that she worked hard to reunite you with your father."

"What are you talking about? That's not what happened at all." Then I added, in a mocking voice, "It's not like that hearing would happen to be today, would it?"

"Shut the fuck up!" he yelled, slamming his hand against the wall so hard that the room shook.

"Hank?" Jeanine called from downstairs. "We need to get a move on it."

Dad leaned into me, his face so close that I thought he was going to spit on me. "I don't care if you're a selfish little bitch. Jeanine has done enough for girls like you, and if you can help her, you're going to help her. I don't want to hear another goddamn word about it." He took a breath, "And if you don't do what I tell you—without any problems for Jeanine—you can just go back to your mother."

Going back to my mother would mean that my life was really over. Yet when I asked myself why, I couldn't think of a good answer, only that it was wrong. So were things here with Dad, but at least he was a known entity, and better than being on the street. Maybe suicide would be an option, too, if I weren't such a coward. I imagined explaining all this to the rabbi, who would put his arm around me. I knew what he would say next: "Tell me again why you won't live with your mother." But I never could explain.

I had challenged Dad, and I knew exactly where it was going to land me. I had gotten used to living inside the part of me that swallowed everything without question. But that me was at war with the other part of me, the pissed-off girl who sometimes jumped out and screwed up my life. Now I followed Dad meekly out to the car and pressed myself into the backseat corner of the little Datsun. The thought of living with my mother was suffocating, as if I were threatened with being enclosed in a small closet for hours. But that image brought to mind the darkroom in the hall closet, which somehow seemed like the opposite of that enclosed feeling—a place where what I saw took on texture and a million shades between black and white. I could still smell the toner on my fingers from last night's session with the developer. It was a smell that seemed to say "home" every bit as much as Jean Nate perfume once did.

I opened my bag and started sorting through my new photos, looking for places where I might add some more contrast. There was Boy's wide face staring away from me, probably watching to see if a professor was swiping shirts. His eyes were sharp and his cheekbones surprisingly high. Sergei, on the other hand, looked right at me as he gestured for me to sit on his lap. Drowsiness crept over me as I stared at the images, and I vaguely remembered that people sleep too much when they're depressed.

When I woke up some time later, Jeanine was still chirping happily to Dad in the front seat.

"What time is it?" I asked.

"She's awake," Dad said to Jeanine.

She turned to me and smiled. "So you're up. Hey, this shouldn't take long, and then you know what we're gonna do? We're going to the aquarium. You ever been to the aquarium? I always wanted to go but couldn't—too much work, too much running around," she continued. "But we're here, the fish are here. I told your dad it would be a nice thing, a way to make a day out of it."

What rushed into my mind was the day that Dad and Fatima took me to the garment district, then brought me home late to the cold knishes. "I have photography class this afternoon," I said.

Jeanine shrugged and said we had plenty of time. I should relax and enjoy—and besides, the hearing wouldn't last long.

She was wrong about the hearing, of course. I waited on a long, cool wooden bench in the hallway next to Dad while she was inside, hidden behind the imposing wooden doors of the hearing room. Jeanine had told us it would look better if she came alone, making it seem like this job was the only thing between her and living in the alley, which only made me more confused about why I was there. Dad tapped his foot as we waited, occasionally getting up to pace. I held my bag close to my side and debated whether I should look at the photos again. I decided to wait until later, since I didn't want Dad criticizing them.

"Look," Dad said, more gently. "These three aren't the first girls."

"What do you mean 'three'?"

"The two girls we helped, and Eshe of course."

"They're blaming her for Eshe?"

"They checked the phone records. Eshe called Jeanine from a phone booth after she ran away, which doesn't look good for Jeanine."

Why didn't Eshe call me? I wondered, "There were others before?"

"Jeanine's helped a few here and there. Some are in Mexico, I think, and one even went on to college eventually. It's not Jeanine that's the problem. It's the system."

"Then why doesn't Jeanine try to fix the system?"

He shook his head. "That just shows how naïve you are."

We passed the next forty minutes drinking sodas, splitting a pack of candy, and watching women in dark suits and clicking heels emerge from one set of large doors only to disappear behind another set. I finally got bored enough that I pulled out my package of photos, keeping my back toward Dad.

"What do you have there?"

"Nothing, just my pictures."

"Lemme see."

I handed him a shot of Big Boy sitting on top of a pile of messed-up sweaters, swinging his legs and laughing so hard that you could see his fillings. He looked like a giant kid. Dad laughed when he saw it.

"What else you got?"

I handed him pictures of Boy, Sergei, and an old woman from Pakistan named Nora, who sold scarves and needed dentures. There were a few wide-angle shots of our stand that showed the tables laden with piles of pants, and Dad in profile arguing with a customer over what kind of deal he could give her. He stared at himself for a long time. Then he nodded, said it was a good shot, and he needed to get thin like that again, although I was greatly relieved he had gained so much weight so he no longer wore those pastel-colored leisure suits.

"You know, you're not half bad at this. I bet you could get a job with a newspaper or something, make a living that way."

"But I want to go to college."

He shrugged. "So go to college. You could major in, what's it called? Photojournalism. Newspapers like people with degrees." It was the first time he'd spoken to me about college, despite the fact that I was a junior and needed to start applying to schools in the fall. The idea of leaving home, living in a dorm with amusing but sometimes inconsiderate roommates, made me light up inside. I knew I would love everything about it, especially being away from home. I wondered how far I could go.

Dad reached out his hands for more photos, so I gingerly handed him the two pictures of Fatima. In one, she held her starfish hat on her head with both hands and smiled at the camera like Marilyn Monroe. In the other she leaned against a table, half turned away from the camera, smoking a cigarette while talking with a large woman. I didn't pull any shots of Eshe out of the folder—I wanted to keep her for myself, an old harbor of a friend.

"Why don't you have any of Jeanine?" Dad asked. He barely glanced at Fatima, as if she were of no interest to him.

At that moment the hearing room door opened and Jeanine walked out with her union representative. A gangly man with a too-short pinstripe suit and a baby face, he shook his head, muttering something low to Jeanine about "the bastards."

"Can't win 'em all" was all Jeanine said. Then she looked at Dad, who was already standing. She looked sad, and I realized that, when she wasn't talking or laughing, her face became almost heart-shaped. As the union rep walked away, she shrugged. "You know what? I'm through. What do I want with a license anyway?" She didn't look at me at all. I could tell she really wanted to keep her license.

"Don't worry, hon, we can still sue them."

"Nah," she said. "Enough is enough. I'm done with this crap. I'm ready to start my new life. Let's go home."

She and Dad kissed, then walked arm in arm toward the exit as I trailed behind. As I took a step toward the revolving door, with Dad and Jeanine already on the other side, I heard a man say, "You need anything from me, babe? A shine on those nice loafers?"

I turned to see a small black man lounging in the shoeshine chair. He had his hands folded behind his head, and he was smiling sweetly at me.

"No, I'm fine."

"You sure about that, babe?"

I nodded, but he and I both knew that I wasn't fine. As I walked down the courthouse steps, I pulled out my camera and framed the corner of a pavilion with a man sitting on the curb, holding out a paper cup for change. He must have been Dad's age, but his face looked at least twenty years older. Then I turned and took a few shots of Dad and Jeanine, his long arm around her shoulder. She was so small next to him that she seemed like a child.

Jeanine stayed quiet during the ride home. We never made it to the aquarium, but we did get back in time to drop me off for the "Shooting the World" class, where I went from Jeanine's sorrow to Liz's bear claw pastries and fast talk about motion blur photography. "The crazy part is to balance that blur with focus so that it all looks crisp. You get me on this?"

She handed us a five-by-seven print that showed a child being spun around by two people, one on each side, holding her hands. She was wearing a little white dress, blonde hair shooting out behind her, her neck arched, face ecstatic. She could not have been older than three or four, but in her face I could already see her as a teenager. She would be simple and beautiful, with a wide forehead and deep-set eyes. As I stared at the photo, I realized that I wasn't jealous of her beautiful future—I was jealous of those invisible hands lifting her off the ground.

When class was over, Dad was late picking me up. Liz and I stood at the big windows, staring out. She was uncharacteristically quiet. "Liz, I didn't show you the new pictures I had."

She smiled, turned toward me, and put out her hand.

"They're of Eshe in the juvenile delinquent place, and I'm not supposed to show people."

Liz took the photos and leafed through them as she nodded. "This is her, who she really is," she said, pointing to a shot of Eshe's back. Eshe was turned just a little toward the camera, her hands on the table near the cards. "She's just a scared little girl."

I felt suddenly embarrassed. Was that what I was, too? Dad's horn honked, so I grabbed the pictures and slipped out before Liz could say anything else. When I was almost to the car, though, she called out, "Those pictures are gutsy, like you. Keep being gutsy."

I turned back and nodded, amazed.

The house was filled with candlelight and Christmas stockings hung on the bookshelves, our names carefully embroidered on them by Mrs. P, despite the fact that she was Jewish. A tiny silver tree seemed overpowered by the pile of gold and bronze wrapped gifts decorated with garish red bows. I felt like I was in the middle of one of those Currier and Ives cards depicting a living room on Christmas Eve.

Tonight was the kids' debut with Mrs. P, however. She nodded at Roger and Missy as they were introduced, yawned, and then went into the kitchen to get dinner ready. It seemed like the more people showed up who were related to my dad, the more Mrs. P kept out of sight.

Mrs. P wanted us to open the presents without her, Jeanine explained; although Mrs. P liked putting together beautiful events, she didn't enjoy being at them. Jeanine told all us kids, even me, to sit in a semi-circle around the tree, the way they always did it. Dad handed out the gifts he had bought with Jeanine's help. Then she said, "Ready? Set? Go!" and everyone tore off the wrapping paper.

Sal kept saying, "Cool!" in his little voice as he opened his Nerf basketball and Legos fireman set. Missy opened her gift, a Barbie wearing a bikini, and then a plastic dish set much like the dishes I used at home. She giggled as I helped her free the dishes from their cardboard holders. Roger tried to act like he was fine with his own

Legos fireman set (although I knew it bothered him, since he was twice the age of Sal) and a book on tracking animals. All the time he was saying "thank you," he held tightly onto the book he'd brought along with him.

I carefully lifted out my gifts: a glass Christmas tree full of bath oil beads and an oversized night shirt advertising the new King Kong movie. Not so bad, I told myself, as I leaned over to give Jeanine something I had found for her at the auction. It was a ceramic statue of a man and woman dancing in a garden, while a little music box played the theme from *Love Story*. Watching her open it, I was afraid that it was a stupid thing to give a grownup. But she said she loved this kind of stuff, and set it on a high shelf. I could tell she really did love it from the way she smiled and winked at me. Dad gleamed like the tree himself. I had already given him his Hanukkah gift (a new bowling bag) so I didn't bother giving him anything now, but Sal handed him a small wrapped package. Inside was a silver pocket watch with a gleaming tractor-trailer engraved on the back. Inscribed underneath were the words, "To Sam, for 15 years of righteous driving."

Jeanine looked worried and signaled to Dad that this wasn't the right gift. "Sal," she said, before Dad could embarrass himself, "this is your dad's. You need to keep this one, okay?"

"Okay," he said, but he looked disappointed as Dad handed back the watch. Still, there was something in the exchange of all these gifts that seemed to merge our families, and I felt a mixture of dread and hope. Missy started crying and Dad told me to take care of her, so I lifted her onto my lap and helped her stack the silly Melmac plates.

"Hon, come outside with me. I have something to show you," Dad told Jeanine.

"You think I'm going out in that cold with you? You got another thing coming, mister," she teased.

But she followed him to the door, telling us kids to sit tight. Roger settled back on the couch with his *Pride and Prejudice*. "What happened to the Brontë sisters?" I asked him.

He shrugged. "Finished them."

"So what are you reading now?"

"Isn't it obvious?" he asked, going back to his book. His voice had dropped in the last few months and now he sounded like Dad, only a nicer version of him.

"You going to read all of Jane Austen?"

He nodded without even looking up. Sal pressed his head against my leg, seeming just a little sad, but then he remembered something and ran upstairs. I took *Pride and Prejudice* from Roger so I could look at it for a minute. When I opened the cover, I saw the inscription "To my best boy, love, Mom." It hurt, just like when Dad slapped me.

Roger shrugged and said casually, "Mom gave me a whole set of these books for Hanukkah this year." What would it be like to have someone know you well enough to give you books that you loved, someone I used to know? The pain was so fierce for a second that, before I realized it, I had chewed my pinkie until it was raw. What did I want with her anyway? My chest involuntarily shivered.

Sal came back downstairs a minute later and showed me a tiny bottle with a ship inside it. It bore a small plaque that read, "Greetings from Ocean Grove, N.J." He bounced in his chair, ready to give Dad this treasure in place of the last one. When Dad and Jeanine came back inside, their faces red—either from the cold or from laughing, it was hard to tell which—Sal lit up and rushed over to Dad.

"Okay, son, you can give him that," said Jeanine, shaking her head and raising her considerable eyebrows as she directed us to the dining room table.

The table was set with a red velvet tablecloth and covered with platters of turkey, mashed potatoes, tamales, three kinds of salsa to put on the tamales, and a five-color vegetable medley. At each place setting sat a small basket of three different home-baked breads, plus a crystal fruit cup layered with red and green fruit. During dinner, I tried to make conversation with Mrs. P about how great the food was, how beautiful the table looked, and how nice her dark red dress looked next to those green beans. She occasionally nodded, if only to let me know that she wasn't deaf. She was a woman who made herself look much older than she was, I realized as I studied her face, carefully avoiding eye contact. She had smooth skin, the kind that would shine in the right kind of picture, and if she would just use some conditioner the frizz in her gray hair would die down. If she smiled, she would be a completely different woman.

I ate the food, all of it good, but I had an odd feeling inside. Dad had been more evasive than usual, not talking to me much and spending hours on the phone late at night with Jeanine unless he was out on a date somewhere. He seemed happy in a way that made me wonder if happiness was just a rushing blur. Jeanine was nice to me, but in the same way she was nice to everyone. Her niceness was like a smooth surface: maybe you could place your things on it, but when you came back to get them, they might have disappeared.

After the German chocolate cake, and before Mrs. P had a chance to clear the plates, Dad cleared his throat. "Kids, Mrs. P," he began. "We have something to tell you."

They hardly know each other, I thought. How can they be thinking of marriage so fast? It must be something else. I imagined describing this scene to the rabbi later as he rolled his eyes and said something like, "Oy, that father of yours."

Dad was fumbling with Jeanine's left hand under the table—he didn't have to say anything more. Jeanine's eyes sparkled as brightly as the green silky top she wore. She raised her left hand and showed us a diamond ring. The smile on her face was so wide that it made her squint.

"We're getting married!" she announced.

I glanced at Roger and Missy, my allies. Missy seemed confused, as if Dad had said, "We're going to the ice rink instead of the roller rink." Sal, next to me, started giggling. Roger immediately went back to his book. His strategy, in all things involving our parents, entailed simply refusing to absorb any of the impact. I was suddenly jealous of what he could do.

Then Mrs. P grabbed Dad's dessert plate and slammed it onto the pile of other plates so hard that they all broke. She swept out of the room with the shattered plates as Jeanine whispered something to Dad before following her to the kitchen. Sal, Missy, and Roger went straight upstairs to Sal's room but Dad and I lingered in the living room, trying to hear what was happening on the other side of the wall. Jeanine murmured something, but Mrs. P remained silent, still slamming lids and plates.

Finally, I heard Mrs. P speak a sentence—yell it, actually—in a trembling voice: "You said you would never marry again!"

I couldn't see how this would possibly matter. I heard Jeanine assuring her that she would still be needed, still be part of the family, only now the family was bigger. Then Jeanine said something about us being Jewish and Mrs. P yelled back, "No, not real Jews!" and then the biggest crash of all happened. Whatever I felt was eclipsed by her rage, and to be honest, it was a great relief. There was no chance of me doing anything that might get me in trouble.

When Dad and I rushed into the kitchen, we found Mrs. P bent over a stack of broken plates, her hand bleeding into the leftover mashed potatoes. "Here, let me," Jeanine was saying. "You go fix your hand." Mrs. P, however, was determined to do the dishes, and she pushed Jeanine's hand away. Dad tried to squat down and help, but Jeanine only hissed, "Get out of here!" with a fury worse than the worst of Dad's rages. We backed out of the kitchen, shaken both by the sight of Jeanine's anger and by all the blood spilled on the off-white kitchen carpeting.

We didn't know what else to do, so Dad picked up a TV guide. "So what's on tonight, hon?" he asked gingerly.

"*Starsky and Hutch*,' and then a special on deep sea diving."

"You like that Jacques Cousteau guy, don't you?"

It was true, but not because I was fascinated by Cousteau's discoveries. I loved his French accent, the way he talked right to the camera, and how he kept surfacing again and again. At that moment, he somehow felt more related to me than anyone in my own family.

Chapter Seven

We were in a forest at night, walking down a path. There was enough light to see the path, probably from the moon or stars. After a long walk we came out of the forest and there, in a big field, lay our future.

"What do you see now?" the rabbi asked the members of the temple youth group, as we lay all around him on the carpeting in the darkened room. I saw the ocean. But when I looked around for what would come next, it surprised me so much I almost gasped out loud.

Our topic that evening was the future, and the rabbi had just led us through something called a visualization. He was sitting very still, although I could hear him breathing beside me. I tried to focus my mind back on the ocean scene.

Just an hour earlier the rabbi had told me, "You should be furious." We had been talking about Dad calling me a slut when I asked him for a ride to youth group. Yet somehow I didn't feel furious, or anything loud and edgy. Could anger be soft and meek, so much so that it made it hard to stay awake? "You're repressing your feelings," Mr. Lexington would say, although I hardly saw Mr. Lexington anymore, and when I did, I couldn't help but think about him making out with Eshe. Liz would say, "Fuck 'em if they can't take a joke," even if there wasn't a joke involved.

I tried to breathe through my stomach, the way the rabbi had told us to do, and wondered how long we were going to lie here in this dark room. I started to fall asleep, but then an unexpected image woke me up: Mom lying on her couch, her feet up, wearing her pink fluffy slippers, the ones I gave her a few years ago, when I still had a mother. I wondered what the other people in my life were doing. I imagined Fatima at the diner, seating a large party of teenagers who had just come from the winter formal. I saw Eshe—where?—maybe in a trailer park, living with some guy she met on the road. He would be good to her, even insist that she get her GRE so she could go to college someday like me, but she wouldn't believe him. I saw Boy driving an empty truck on the New Jersey turnpike, heading south to Baltimore to get another load of the irregular sports shirts that he hated. Maybe he was singing, but probably not.

Then I started seeing places, mostly through the lens of a camera—places far away and yet at the same time familiar, if I only looked at them long enough. I imagined the pictures joined together like those panoramas of the Grand Canyon Liz once showed us, each image linked to the other, tumbling down a long chain of postcards. At the end of the chain was the one sight I dreaded most.

The rabbi turned on the lights, making us blink, and asked who wanted to start.

"I see mosquitoes, and they're all over me," said Jon. Abby and Sam giggled.

"Yeah, and wild dogs, they're attacking us," said Abby.

"Ack! It's the ax murderer," Randy said, and everyone either laughed or yelled, "Shut up!"

The rabbi rolled his eyes and waited. He glanced at Amy and Mark, the two people who usually sobered up first. Amy picked up on his cue.

"I saw a house, like in a housing development, only it was in the field," she said. "And I was living there with my husband, who was tall with red hair. I was pregnant and kind of scared, but my future self seemed pretty excited. I walked into the new room for the baby and it was this beautiful shade of yellow, like butterscotch pudding, and it felt so good being in that room."

"That's amazing how much you saw," said Abby. She'd mostly seen herself gaining and then losing weight, breaking up with guys and meeting new boyfriends, changing jobs a lot. "I guess it means I don't know what I want," she concluded nervously.

My turn was next. "I didn't see any one place, but I saw myself with my camera, taking photos. First of the ocean, up close, and then from a lighthouse near those black rocks I read about, up in Maine. Then I was in the mountains, standing in a big field and looking at snow-covered peaks like the ones Abby took pictures of."

"Those pictures sucked," Abby interjected.

"I thought they were good. Anyway, I saw myself photographing trees, rivers, lakes, weird rock formations."

"Did you see any people?" Mark asked, suddenly interested.

"No," I answered, "not exactly."

But I couldn't go on, couldn't tell them that the last thing I'd seen was my mother, sitting on a rock and looking at the ocean with her back to me, and how I wanted to fall into her lap, wanted to run away. I burst into tears so abruptly that even the rabbi was taken aback. Mark put his hand on my shoulder, and I felt warmth from him pouring through me. I took a breath and stopped crying, and said that was all.

Later that evening, after everyone else had left, I asked the rabbi, "Will I always be alone?"

"I'm a rabbi, not a fortune teller," he laughed, dipping the mint teabag into his mug. "But you want to know a secret? I think you'll be fine."

We were sitting in his office, the new carpet scent almost overpowering. I looked at him and waited. "You're smart. You have enough courage to get through, and I think you'll find a way, probably one we can't imagine right now." He looked into my eyes, but it all felt like too much to take in, although I didn't know why. "So what else did you see?"

I was afraid that saying something now would make me cry again. "You know."

"Your mother?"

"Sitting on a rock. She wasn't looking at me."

"Maybe you weren't looking at her."

This thought was too painful, too much for my mind to hold. I changed the subject. "Yeah, well, there'll be enough people not looking at me at the wedding. A ton of people are coming."

"Oy, the wedding!" he said. He shook his head.

I was relieved that he'd gone along with my topic change. "It's too fast, isn't it?"

"It's not unusual, though, for divorced men like your dad to remarry right away," he said, leaning back. "You remember that I told you this happens often."

"I don't know. I mean, everything is going to change, but with Eshe gone, maybe it'll be good for me to have something new happening. It's just all coming so fast—first Fatima gone, then Eshe, and now this whole family moving in."

"So you haven't let yourself feel it yet?"

"I don't know how to feel it," I told him. This was the most honest thing I had said in days—days spent shopping with Jeanine for wedding outfits for the family, helping her address invitations, nodding wisely when she said she thought simple yellow roses were enough.

I wondered what was wrong with me that I didn't think about Fatima much any more, except on the mornings when the school bus drove down Taylor Mills Road, past the turnoff to her house. As soon as the turnoff disappeared my mind clicked over to something else, just like it did on those mornings when I woke up wondering what my mother was doing now. Was it different than what we were doing a year ago, when she still lived here?

A few days later, I was waiting around at Liz's store after photography class, feigning interest in the new Faded Glory jeans so that no one could tell I was worried that Dad might forget to pick me up like he had last week. In class, Liz had described the techniques of double exposure photography: you needed to line up, from memory, whatever you shot first with what you were shooting next—either that, or "just take a pot shot." Her pun had made us both laugh hard. I was thinking that I might rewind a roll of photos I'd taken at the auction and shoot new images in the cluster of woods behind our house, contrasting Boy with the small saplings. Then I noticed that Liz had walked to the other side of the display table and was looking at me, in a curious way.

"What?" I asked.

"I was just thinking," she said, checking to make sure the jeans were folded neatly and shuffling them so that the smaller sizes were on top, "that you have serious talent as a photographer."

"No, I don't. I know I need to learn a lot more about being precise and all that. My technique sucks."

"Two things you got wrong," she said, her eyes turning even more green with a light that surprised me. "One, you never argue with a compliment, especially one about your artistry. Accept it. Artists get enough of a hassle. Two, there's nothing wrong with your technique. What you need to do is stop watching and start feeling. That's how you go from getting the good shots to the great ones. Just because you're holding a camera between you and the world doesn't mean you don't live in the world."

I slid my hands between two pairs of jeans, wondering what I was doing wrong that I couldn't even feel what I was supposed to feel. The denim was cool and smooth around my fingers. Was I some kind of robot watching my own life? When I looked back up at Liz, she was still watching me.

"You know, I used to be like you, only not so quiet—but that was just a cover. Okay, maybe I wasn't so well-behaved. I wasn't a good girl like you."

"I'm not a good girl."

"You absolutely are a good girl. If they had 'good girl' listed in the dictionary, you would be there, wearing oven mitts or something." I was hurt and she saw it, so she hastened to add: "What I mean is that there are a million ways to zone out on your own life, to blow your attendance record. I did a lot of acid and had sex with every Tom, Dick, and Harry, not to mention the occasional Lucy and Ethel.

"But you had your photography during that time, right?" I asked, picturing photography as some kind of large and infallible life boat.

"No, this was before photography. But it was photography that made me change. You know how? Someone gave me a picture of me, and in that picture I looked so fucking sad that I didn't know who that girl was. Or maybe I should say I didn't know the girl looking at the picture. You know what I mean?"

I remembered a self-portrait I'd taken with the help of the bathroom mirror, a shot I hadn't shared with the class. I had been shocked by how narrow and sad my face looked, like someone caught by surprise in her pain. Maybe, I thought, I could double-expose that self-portrait against a storefront or highway and see what that revealed. Then I remembered that Liz was still talking to me. I looked up and nodded, but I'd missed out on most of whatever she'd just said.

"Just promise me that you'll think about it, *oui?*" She winked, then noticed the look on my face. "Think about going out with me on a little photography mission into the city."

This time I smiled. "Absolutely. I would love to."

She smiled back. A moment later, we both noticed Dad standing in the threshold, holding the glass door ajar.

"Whaddya doing in here, you idiot? I've been outside for ten minutes waiting." He yelled as if Liz weren't even there, as if we weren't in a public place of business. I couldn't believe he would call me "idiot" right in front of Liz, even though he said it like it was supposed to be a joke.

"Hello, Mr. Shapiro!" Liz yelled back, in her cheerful, over-the-top way. "You know, there's no idiots here. Slobs maybe, but that's mostly me, losers at times, but that sure doesn't include your daughter. No idiots. Just geniuses."

Dad ignored her as I picked up my bag and headed for the car. "Goodbye, Mr. Shapiro," she yelled, with exaggerated friendliness. Then, in a quieter voice directed at me, she said, "Think about what I said."

Chapter Eight

The wedding was set for Valentine's Day, which happened to fall on a Saturday that year. The rabbi would preside rather than Jeanine's priest, who wanted no part of a ceremony involving a partner who was divorced. I would take pictures as my gift to them. Jeanine seemed pleased, but Dad insisted, "I want color film! I don't want my wedding"—gazing at Jeanine—"to the love of my life to be in black and white." After the wedding, Jeanine, Mrs. P, and Sal would move in with us. Mrs. P would take Roger's room, one of the larger bedrooms upstairs. As a special consolation, Dad was building her a private bathroom in the adjoining attic space.

I was looking forward to taking tons of photos, some for them, and many for me. I figured I would call my next photo essay "How My Life is Falling Apart Again," or something spiffy like that. It would make Liz smile, maybe even crack up the rabbi. I would buy a lot of film and carry it with me for quick reloading. Deep down, though, I knew that I really just wanted to take photos so that no one could see my face, a good enough reason, I thought. "Whatever gets you through," the rabbi had advised me the other day.

"Whatever it takes," Dad said, echoing the rabbi as he prepared to drive me to temple on a Friday night. Our youth group was finally performing the "All the Lonely People" service, but I didn't know if Dad even remembered. Ever since the engagement he'd stayed busy on the phone with Jeanine, going over plans for the house and job prospects for her in the city so they could be together.

"You know what she said?" he kept repeating, a little amused with himself. "She said, 'Don't expect me to let you out of my sight much.'" He chuckled. "What a woman!"

Seated in a folding chair, I was transferring all my things—house keys, cloth wallet from Pakistan, lip balm I never used, bobby pins, a few very small tampons (carefully hidden in my palm as I moved them), butterscotch candies, rolls of extra film, a big envelope of photos—from my old purse into a new macramé pocketbook with heavy metal rings. I was trying to figure out the best way to fill up each of the new purse's many compartments.

"This will be good for you, Deborah," Dad continued, looking up at me from the other folding chair near the window where he'd been reading the paper. "You need a mother—all girls need mothers. It's too bad your own mother is mentally ill."

I stared at him. He had always said that she was crazy, bonkers, cockamamie, off her rocker, a total bitch, controlling, and selfish, but he had never used that term before. It sounded so clinical and removed, as if he didn't even know her.

"Yes, that's what she is. I'm pretty sure—not that I'm a shrink or anything—that she's what they call 'borderline.' That's someone almost delusional, someone who purposely destroys any environment she's in because of her"—his voice softened as he looked directly at me—"illness."

"Where are you getting this? I mean, yeah, she's got problems, big problems, but—"

"Jeanine is an expert at people, and she says it is a classic case." He looked down at his nails, as if he were checking to see that they were all still there, and repeated the part about the "classic case." I had never heard that word "borderline" before, even in sociology class. I wondered if it was something real, or something people made up to describe people they didn't understand.

I looked at the clock, but we still had a minute or two before we had to leave. I asked him if Jeanine was upset about losing her license.

He looked surprised. "Jeanine? Nah, she's fine. She has a can-do attitude, and that's what makes a difference between winners and losers in this world."

"But isn't she upset about not being able to be a social worker anymore?"

"Jeanine isn't one of these crybabies, like your mother," he said, spouting another term he had picked up from Jeanine. "She said to me, 'Hank, I was a good social worker for twenty-two years, and now I'm ready to move on. I'm not gonna give those bastards the satisfaction of me losing an ounce of sleep over this.'"

"She's not even a little sad or anything?"

"You don't know *my* Jeanine," he said, emphasizing the "my" as if he had known her for thirty years, not three months. "You know the biggest difference between her and your mom, besides your mom being borderline? Jeanine is an adult. Things happen, you move on, you make something with your life. Not like your mom, who cries boo-hoo to lawyers all the time about how much money I'm hiding from her."

I placed the freshly loaded pocketbook on my lap, the old bag drooping forlornly on the floor. "But you haven't been hiding anything from her, have you?" I asked.

"Not that she knows about," he said, raising his eyebrows. "Besides, Jeanine says it's all a matter of keeping my assets safe. That's why I'm putting the business in her name, and half the house, too."

"But what if it doesn't work out with you and Jeanine? I mean, look at Fatima."

He rose quickly, biting his tongue, his eyes suddenly ignited. "You of all people aren't going to blow this for me, not after all I do for you. You don't like that? I tell you what, then, you go and live with your mother."

The rabbi had explained to me that Dad's anger wasn't my fault. Knowing that fact, however, did little to keep that scared wall inside me from shaking every time he got like this. "No, I didn't mean that you and Jeanine couldn't make it or anything. I just wanted…" I realized I was talking to him as if he were an unruly child.

"To see if you could get my money?" He shook his head in disgust and started toward the kitchen, but not before adding, "It's like I was telling Jeanine, let's just send her back to her mother's. But no, she says we need to give you another chance, that you might be useful to this family, as if that's possible." He waved his hands for extra drama, although none was needed.

As if on cue, Jeanine, Mrs. P, and Sal rang the doorbell. I rushed to greet them, eager to prove I was useful. Jeanine and Dad kissed quickly as everyone came inside. Mrs. P walked past me without a word, but seemed pleased by the size of the rooms. She frowned at the gold wallpaper in the hallway (picked out by my mother) and at the Mediterranean design in the dining room, picked out by my father many years ago. Sal ran into the kitchen to look around, then zoomed upstairs. I saw Mrs. P studying the lawn furniture, which didn't seem to impress her, but I could tell she saw that the place had the potential to accommodate all the furniture she owned, with some breathing room.

"I was telling Mrs. P how much she would love this place," said Jeanine, "and then I thought we should just come see it."

Mrs. P opened the closet door, exposing my darkroom. She looked puzzled and a little angry.

"It's where I develop pictures," I explained, "and Dad said I could keep it. We can get a really good coat rack for people to use."

"What about galoshes?" She sounded more upset than I expected.

"We can figure something out," I shrugged, but she crossed her arms over her chest, this one detail seemingly enough to ruin the whole house for her.

I told Jeanine we had to leave immediately for the service, although Dad was trying to wave me off like it didn't matter. I needed him to hear what I had put together tonight, to see other people reading the words that I wrote, to see a world in which I was considered "very talented" and "a really together person" by the rabbi and the youth group. I was so nervous that he wouldn't let me go that I almost decided to slip out and run the three miles on my own.

"Service? What kind of service?" Jeanine asked, seeming delighted at a chance to reunite Mrs. P with her native religion. Soon it was decided that all five of us would go. Mrs. P, hearing this, seemed to recoil, but after the plate-smashing episode she probably didn't want to make a scene. She grunted at me and stuffed her hands in her pockets.

When we got to the temple, the parking lot was glowing with cars and well-dressed people. I held out my hand to help Mrs. P out of the back seat, where she had been sandwiched between Sal and me. She walked with her head down, as if she were being dragged into a shopping mall she didn't want to visit, yet she didn't look all that different from the grandparents streaming across the freshly paved lot.

I left them to find their own seats and rushed to the youth group room. Everyone smelled good and was giggling a lot. Mark, wearing new khakis and a ponytail just like the rabbi's, rushed over and gave me a kiss on the cheek. Sam said I looked great and told me I should wear skirts more often. ("I'll say," Mark chimed in.) "Five minutes to show time!" the rabbi called into the room, then winked at me before heading to the sanctuary. He looked different in his black robe, much more rabbi-like than he did a few days earlier when we had talked.

We filed into the sanctuary behind the rabbi and stood on the bema. The crowd hushed. The divider walls at the back of the temple were open tonight to make room for six more rows of chairs, all of which were full. As the rabbi talked, I counted seats. On each side of the aisle were eighteen rows, twelve chairs in each row, filled with parents, grandparents, aging uncles from Long Island, and antsy cousins from Brooklyn. I felt scared to be standing level with the Torah. Then the music started and John Lennon's melancholy voice filled the sanctuary. We stood there like statues for the first verse and chorus. Then Jon, sitting in the back beside the eight-track tape player, faded the music down a little.

"To be alone," said Mark.

"Isolated," added Amy.

"Betrayed," echoed Abby.

"Forgotten," I said.

"Invisible," Randy added.

The line of words continued. As we read from our scripts, I looked out over the audience. I could see Dad whispering to Jeanine, but she, at least, was watching and trying to listen. He wound his long arm around her, so proud to have his fiancée out in public. Mrs. P sat solemnly next to Sal as if waiting for a root canal to begin. I saw some neighbors—the same ones who had refused to speak to us after the divorce—all dressed up, perfumed and beaming at us. Then I saw my mother, a small figure in the third row from the back, sitting next to Geraldine, no kids with them, her shoulders hunched up. She was wearing a pink blouse I had never seen before, and her hair was longer, swept up, teased a little so it was big. It made her face look child-sized. Was it a borderline face, I wondered?

I swallowed hard, wondering how I would I get through the evening. How could she do this to me? No contact since May, and now here she was. Then I started worrying about her bumping into Jeanine, about

Dad and Mom seeing each other. Mom watched me exclusively, so I had no choice but to look in every other direction. I couldn't look at Dad, or she would see where I was looking and look that way, too.

Abby, sitting next to me, nudged my elbow. "What's wrong?"

"My mom's here," I whispered back. My cue came, and I rose to the podium to read what I had written:

> People from all walks of life face isolation and loneliness all the time. Maybe they're lonely because of economic conditions, family breakdowns, religious differences, age, disability, or race. But they share the invisible link of being lonely. A link that, if realized, could help them connect with each other and find more companionship and friendship. All the lonely people, as the Beatles call them, are all around us. Open your eyes. Open your hearts. Remember that in all our lives, we will each face seasons of loneliness, too. So in all seasons, we should reach out to people who need our help.

This short speech immediately segued into the Schechyanu, a prayer for the seasons. The cantor, a short man with a voice big as a Cadillac, led the congregation in the singing. I was seated by the time he began, with various youth group members reaching over to shake my hand just like the adults did whenever anyone said anything aloud on the bema. Now I wanted to run home. The adrenaline had kicked in to such a degree that I was sure I could do it, too.

The service ended with Mark reading something he wrote about the difference between being alone and lonely, and how we all need to learn to be alone. "Like two solitudes bordering each other," he said, explaining this line was written by someone named Rilke, a German poet. ("Germans, that'll go over well," Abby said during rehearsal.) I barely heard him, because now I was increasingly terrified about having to go out after the service for the oneg, where everyone ate rugalah cookies and drank bad coffee.

After the applause faded, we filed back into the little room behind the sanctuary. Once the door closed us in, we all started hugging each other and saying, "That was great! We are so cool." I was very quiet, so a few of the girls put their arms around me. Soon everyone had gathered around. "Don't make me go out there," I managed to say in a cracking, crying voice. My mouth was making funny shapes the way it does whenever I cry and I felt embarrassed, but I couldn't help it. Everyone kept hugging me and telling me it was okay. I was smothered in perfume and aftershave.

Then Abby proposed a plan. I would not be left alone for a moment. Everyone would take a turn accompanying me while the other kids greeted their own families. When I got to Mom I would nod and move on without saying anything to her.

"Or," suggested Mark, "we could sneak out, and I could drive you home right now."

I liked Mark's plan better. "But what will I tell them?"

"Nothing," said Amy, jumping in. "We'll find your dad and say you weren't feeling well. You know, men always think women have female problems. And we'll say someone who was leaving gave you a lift."

Mark's car, a yellow Dodge Dart with a black strip down the side, smelled like incense. He drove in a relaxed way, turning every so often to flash his brilliant smile at me. From time to time I would tell him "turn here," but he drove as if he already knew the way. When we pulled into the drive, it felt like I was in another world. Snow was starting to fall in big, wide flakes. Mark grinned, his brown eyes shining. In the moment before I opened the door, I realized that I had come to a stopping place, a clearing in the craziness where I was finally safe. I felt the same way I did the first time I saw a waterfall in the mountains, when I was eight years old.

"So this is it," he said.

"Yeah, thanks for driving me."

Then he did what I knew he would do, although I still didn't believe it was possible. He bent over and kissed me on the lips, slowly. It was so soft and quiet. When he straightened up, he smiled again.

"Okay, see you Thursday," I managed to say.

"I hope so," he answered, and I walked off into a sweet place all my own. Everything at home was changing so quickly, but at least there was this for me. I was astonished that something good was happening, at last.

Chapter Nine

The guests arrived all at once, a small explosion of people in dress-up clothes climbing carefully out of station wagons, pickup trucks, old Lincolns, and beat-up Volkswagens. Boy looked taller and more dramatic than ever in his navy blue suit. Big Boy wore a silver western-style suit, with the small blonde, as usual, on his arm. There were a few round-faced people from India—some of Jeanine's late husband's relatives, I thought—who sat politely on the couch and padded chairs transported from Jeanine's house only the day before. Meanwhile, Jeanine's Mexican relatives were busy in the kitchen, calling loudly to each other in Spanish. Having them there made the house seem new and bright, as if we had just moved in.

Dad was accompanied by Missy, decked out in a new pink dress, and Roger wearing the suit Mom bought for his upcoming Bar Mitzvah. Missy ran to me with her arms up, and as I lifted her I was surprised by how heavy she'd gotten. She quickly wiggled down and followed Sal, who was dressed in a miniature light blue leisure suit, upstairs to his new room. Roger walked by me with a nod, as if today were nothing out of the ordinary. He had a book under one arm, and obviously planned to devote more attention to Jane Austen than to his father getting remarried in the house where our mother once lived.

Dad seemed pleased that Mom had dressed the children well, and he was even carrying a little gift from her.

"Be careful, it might be a bomb," I warned.

"Actually, it's for you."

I took the small package and ran upstairs to the bathroom. Ripping off the paper, I found a card inside with a dancing frog and a note that read, "I'm so proud of you, love, Mom." The gift was a journal, cloth-covered, with a pink and white floral design. The pages were blank, which seemed somehow appropriate since it came from my mother. Yet even the phrase "my mother" suddenly struck me as false. I rushed into my room and threw the journal under the bed, burying it with all the dead stuffed animals from my past. I stopped: why would she send me a journal after what had happened to my last journal? I pulled it out again, ready to throw it in the trash, but instead I put it back in the closet.

On my way back downstairs, the rabbi waved and smiled like we shared a secret, and Boy greeted me with "English Leather, that's what true gentlemen wear." We went into the kitchen together to behold the trays of food layered one on top of the other in the refrigerator. Several Puerto Rican drivers and a Syrian from the taxi service poured in. They were taller than the other guests, dressed all in leather, and seemed oddly amused to be here. One of them tossed a small tape measure up and down in his hand before signaling to the others, heading over to a wall, and measuring it.

I slipped out the sliding glass door into the back yard, but when I walked around the house and in again through the front door I ran into the Parents Without Partners crowd. Six women and the bald piano player were removing their coats, commenting on the pretty gold wallpaper and saying how lucky Jeanine was to get a good one. "And if this doesn't work out, Hank," said the bald man, placing his hand on Dad's shoulder, "you know where they are." The women burst out laughing, and I seized my chance to run back upstairs.

In my room, with the door closed, I retrieved the journal. I flipped through the blank pages and thought about the message this gift was intended to deliver—that maybe she was sorry for taking my journal to court, maybe she was crazy but not so mentally ill she couldn't watch me perform with the youth group, that she still wanted to be my mother. I slipped the journal under my bed again and started to walk out, and then I went back and hid it under my pillow. I had no idea what I was doing, what I was feeling. I picked up my camera, letting my fingers load it with film and adjust the settings as if I were really one person, not several people who couldn't seem to find each other.

I descended to the landing and started to aim my camera at people, like I was supposed to be doing. Mrs. P stood woodenly next to Roger, who kept his hands in his pockets, while Missy and Sal fidgeted at their feet but stayed put. Dad and Jeanine faced the rabbi, who uncharacteristically wore a suit but still kept his hair in its long ponytail. Lou from the taxi service, wearing only a fraction of the gold chains he usually wore, stood beside Dad as his best man. Jeanine's coworker, Lena, stood next to Jeanine in a loud orange dress. Jeanine had asked Mrs. P to be in the wedding party, but she had refused.

After I snapped some pictures of the wedding party from the stairs, I maneuvered into the living room so I could get a few shots of Dad and Jeanine's faces. Dad, thankfully, wasn't dressed in a leisure suit for once, but wore a three-piece, pin-striped gangster suit with a red carnation in his pocket. Jeanine wore a red nylon dress that made her look a little like Gladys Knight. I focused the frame close around their faces and pressed the shutter, then adjusted the camera to get a wider angle.

After the prayers, the rabbi asked, "Do you, Jeanine Guadalupe Martinez Govindarajan, take this man, Harold 'Hank' Bernard Shapiro, to be your lawfully wedded husband?"

"So she'll be Jeanine Guadalupe Martinez Govindarajan Shapiro?" whispered one of the taxi drivers with a slight grin. I caught that moment on film, too.

When Dad's turn came he sneezed twice—a high-pitched sneeze like a yippy dog, which made everyone laugh. Mrs. P was not laughing, however, and she pressed her hands together so tightly I could see the veins in her neck. I tried to take a few more pictures of Dad and Jeanine, but by then I was out of film. By the time I got the new roll loaded, they were already married—no glass wrapped in a linen napkin to step on, just the rabbi shaking their hands. Dad and Jeanine kissed unceremoniously and turned toward the crowd. I pointed and snapped the shutter in every direction: first Dad, then back to Jeanine, then both of them folded up inside a spilling crescent of people congratulating them with hugs and sly jokes. It occurred to me, as I framed Dad smiling at Jeanine while she hugged a taxi worker, that one wrong move now meant I was out on the street or back with my mother.

"Bravo! Bravo!" Boy yelled. Without missing a beat, he poured out a version of the Carpenters' "Close to You" in his perfect baritone as the newlyweds smiled and hugged people.

I slipped upstairs to the bedroom, only to bump into Mrs. P coming out the door of her adjoining room. She glared at me. "This is not right."

She had never said a complete sentence to me before. In her dark blue dress, obviously several decades old, she looked like someone who had turned up at the wrong funeral, but at least she was talking to me.

"The wedding? Yeah, I don't know."

"No," she said forcefully. "This is not Jewish life. Not that ceremony. Not what you did at shul with all those kids."

"What do you mean?" I asked. "We're Jewish. This is what we do. I know it's not like what the conservatives or orthodox do, but –"

"No, you are not Jewish," she interrupted. "You do it right, or you don't do it at all." She pushed the bathroom door closed so fast I didn't have time to answer. I felt like I had done something terribly wrong, but what else was new?

Downstairs, the party was in full swing and strange music from India flooded the living room. Jeanine's ex-father-in-law, a lanky man who spoke only scattered English, stood in the midst of the crowd singing in Tamil. He was linked arm-in-arm with Boy, who made up some Tamilese-sounding words as they went along. Jeanine's mother, who had flown in from Texas that morning, filled up the couch. She wore a red velour tent dress, and had her white-flecked black hair in two gorgeous braids, wrapping Heidi-style around her head.

"Come here, baby," she said to me, "come sit." So I sat next to her. "You are my new granddaughter, *no?* And you are a good girl, I can see that, a good girl."

She put her arm around me; I could feel her warm body pressed against my side. "You are the granddaughter I always wanted. Everyone else gives me boys."

"Oh, yeah, but you knew them since they were born."

"No, that is not my meaning. You are *my* granddaughter, just as if I held you as a baby and held you all your life." She smelled like cinnamon, cayenne, and perfume all at once, but somehow the combination worked on her. I smiled and took her hand, which was soft and small. She whispered, "*Eres mi nieta.*"

Despite my strict orders to the contrary, I felt tears leaking out of my eyes and knew it was too late—she could see it all. I tried to make them stop by looking away from her and saying, "Thank you," but she only leaned over to kiss my cheek. "Do you want a plate of food?" I finally managed to ask.

"No, child, I have eaten while I cooked. You eat, you're so thin,"—she beamed at me—"and such a beauty." She kissed me again as I extracted myself from the couch. I looked back at her briefly as I headed toward the kitchen. She was still smiling so broadly that she squinted, the same way Jeanine smiled at Dad. Something I couldn't name rattled inside me, as if I held onto a wishing well into which this new grandmother had dropped a coin. I had forgotten how to have relatives, but I hoped I could remember soon.

I filled up a plate with fried samosas, enchiladas, turkey breast, yogurt sauce, tortilla chips, beef curry, chicken tandoori, and a slab of flat bread. I sat down near Boy, who had a plate twice as full as mine. Lou winked at me from across the room, while the Syrian woman with the glittering green eye shadow elbowed him and teased, "What you doing, winking at a girl?" A few minutes later the rabbi, who was carrying a Tupperware drink container and shaking hands on his way out, slipped over to me to say goodbye.

"You can stay and eat with us," I offered, but he muttered that he had a whole container of homemade carrot juice already and just needed to get home. He seemed bemused by the array of guests and told me we'd have a lot to talk about on Thursday.

Boy shot to his feet, shook the rabbi's hand vigorously, and told him, "You Jews really know how to marry people! And bury people. I think the Hebrews understand how to deal with grief better than anyone."

"Well, you know how it is, we're 'the chosen people,'" the rabbi said jokingly, but Boy didn't take it as a joke.

"You are the chosen ones, and don't I know it! If there's such a thing as reincarnation, I'm coming back as a Hebrew, one of those Hasidic ones, too. I think I'd look dashing with those curly sideburns."

After the rabbi departed, Boy and I went back to our food.

"How long do you give it?" I asked him.

"Oh, the marriage? Let me calculate: about five years for her to mold him into the man she needs him to be, about five more years for him to notice, and another ten years for him to go back and forth in his mind about leaving her. Then for the rest of their lives, because by the time he gets tired of her he'll be too old to do anything about it, unless he goes the route my dad went, but to be honest, I don't think your dad has my dad's Kennedy-esque charisma."

I was shocked by his precise detail, but I liked it anyway. "What about other women? You know, he can't really seem to be—"

"Faithful? Don't worry about that. Jeanine is the kind of woman who'll make him faithful. She'll be by his side every minute, and she'll throw him enough curves that he won't have time to get bored."

"Oh." I wanted to know more from this man who saw all of life at the auction, where all of life was there to be seen. "So why didn't it work out with Fatima?"

"Why? It's simple. She trusted him."

"And Jeanine doesn't?"

"Not as far as she can throw him. And let me tell you something, she's got everything under control."

"But what about Mrs. P? I mean, she runs the house."

"Precisely. So who doesn't have to? That'll give her more time to be glued to your dad. In the end, it'll be a good thing for him."

"If you're so good at predicting futures, tell me mine."

Boy stopped eating, leaned back, and studied me earnestly. "You're not such an easy read, but what I see is this: you'll go through another year of hell and then you'll fly, go to college, get a degree, and meet some guy. You'll get a job teaching photography to a professor's crippled child or something, get married, wait a while to have kids, and then have two. You'll be happy, happier than you can imagine, and much happier than those of us you're leaving behind."

Boy's eyes were red, and I wondered why they turned that color. "Well, it sounds nice, but what about you? You said you wanted to become a lawyer, so when will you go to college? Next year? The year after?"

"Me? No, babe, that's just a pipe dream. I'm signed up long term for the rags-on-the-road life."

"It doesn't have to be that way. You could go to school, take classes during the week, and then work weekends. You could make it work."

He shook his head and repeated, "No, I can't be a lawyer."

"Yes, you can! Why do you say you can't?"

"Who's gonna run to western Pennsylvania to the factory? Who's gonna go down to D.C. to get the specials? My dad's too old, and I need to keep helping my sister. This is my life. Maybe in my Hasidic Hebrew life, I'll become a lawyer." He laughed at himself. "A Hasidic attorney with a fat wife and twelve little Hebrew kids, all with those curlicues hanging around their faces."

"You could take night classes. If your dream is to be a lawyer, you should do it now," I insisted. "You shouldn't let anything stop you."

"You," he said, in a deeper voice, "don't know how to read people." He smiled and shook his big head. "Once a working class bum, always a working class bum. There's the Bolshevik, and there's the bourgeoisie. That's the rule. You watch your whole life, and you're gonna only see a handful of exceptions."

"Why can't you be the exception? You're strong enough. You can do anything!"

"Now you're reading yourself." He rose to his feet and stuck out an elbow. There was some kind of bad polka music playing in the living room. "Shall we?"

I had danced the polka years and years ago with my grandfather, but with Boy it came back faster than I thought possible. Every time I got ready to leap, he just lifted me and tossed me around to the next step. First came the "Beer Barrel Polka," and then another called the "Dream Street Polka." We flew around the living room, now empty of furniture except for one couch reserved for the elderly, who moved their arms and legs in time to the music. Every time a dance ended, the whole roomful of my new relatives applauded us.

"Such a beauty, she can fly," exclaimed my new grandmother.

Chapter Ten

The next morning I was still in bed when I heard voices, laughter, and people walking in all directions, doors opening and closing. Before the party ended, Dad and Jeanine had left for the Airport Hilton in order to catch an early flight to the Bahamas for their honeymoon. I had stayed up late trying to find something to do—sweep the kitchen floor, load the dishwasher, clean the bathroom—that Mrs. P wouldn't automatically re-do just to prove me wrong. My house was suddenly filled with another family that didn't seem to need me, and I wanted to prove this feeling wrong.

I was still exhausted, but I threw on some clothes and ran downstairs. The crowd from the taxi service was back, hauling in ladders, paint cans, brushes, and all kinds of tools. And, of course, their trademark little cups of Greek coffee accompanied them as they moved around the house.

"Hey, Deb, what's happening, girl?" Lou yelled to me from atop a ladder. He was dressed in painter white except for the checkered woolen cap on his head.

"You tell me, Lou. What's going on?"

One of the new drivers, Elaine, and Tammy, the night dispatcher who had lizard men tattooed all over her arms, laughed. "You mean this is a surprise for you, too?" They explained that Jeanine and Mrs. P had met with them last week and laid out a plan for painting most of the downstairs rooms ("Gotta get that hideous gold paper off the wall," said Lou, who felt only humans should wear gold) and Mrs. P's room upstairs. About half a dozen people from the taxi service were here to prep and paint. Lou explained that Jamal had taken over dispatch while the new guys from Saudi Arabia and Pakistan worked the taxis today.

Tammy wrapped her gum in a little piece of paper and tossed it in the trash. "Same pay for us, and no lousy customers."

"And hey, we're safe out here in the 'burbs. No Pakistanis to attack us in the subway," joked one of the Pakistani drivers, which ignited Lou's crazy laugh.

"What's this about attacks in the subway?" I hoped I could distract them enough so that no one would notice my face, which surely gave away how I was feeling. This was my house, and here they were taking it over without anyone even bothering to warn me.

"You didn't hear?" asked Lou. "This Paki tried to hold someone up with a water gun. You better wear plastic to protect yourself, 'cause you never know where you'll find another Paki with a little pink water pistol." He rolled his eyes. "Your dad was on the floor, on the floor I tell you, over that one, little Debby." It was hard for me to picture Dad laughing that hard over anything, especially lately, and harder to think of myself as Debby.

When I walked into the kitchen, Mrs. P was taking a huge coffeecake out of the oven. I overheard one of the guys joking from the other room about sleeping in the boss's bed tonight. "You want something?" Mrs. P asked me.

"I just, um, I'll make myself some toast."

She crossed in front of me to open the breadbox that she had brought over from Jeanine's old house. She pulled out a loaf of bread and placed two slices in the toaster. Embarrassed, I headed to the refrigerator to look for some juice. Halfway there, I turned back to face her. "You know, I can make my own toast."

"So?" she answered. How dare she come in here and talk to me like I was a little kid?

"I did all the cooking here before you came," I said sharply.

Before I could say more, she cut me off. "I heard." Then she turned her back on me and walked away.

Out in the foyer, I could hear the taxi people high-fiving Sal and calling "My man!" to him as they prepared to turn this house of mine into a house for someone else. My stomach hurt, my head ached, my face burned. I hated them, all of them. I pushed my way quickly out of the kitchen and out to the street, where I could walk and photograph normal houses, ones where people didn't just show up and take over.

That night, after Mrs. P went to bed, I slipped down to the kitchen to investigate. New appliances inhabited the corner where our two counters met: a KitchenAid mixer, a four-slice toaster in gleaming sterling, a blender with a bottom wider than most blenders, four matching canisters in almost the same shade of mustard as the crock pot beside them. This small army of appliances would obviously have a hand in feeding me, probably better than I'd ever eaten in my life, yet at the same time it felt like the enemy. I pictured myself breaking each one, but even the idea of dropping the crock-pot and watching it turn into pieces couldn't comfort me. I could haul everything outside, hide it in the thicket of pussy willows. Just thinking about it made me stand up straighter. But anything like that would bring down my father's anger on me, and then where would I go?

Panic rose up inside me, a shakiness that made my throat hurt and my stomach tremble. Defeated, I walked back to my bedroom, the one part of the house that was staying the way it had always been. Even before I reached the phone I was pulling the rabbi's number out of my pocketbook.

A day later, across plates of eggplant parmesan at the diner, I described it all for the rabbi: the shiny yellow kitchen, the baby-blue dining room, the bathrooms done up in shades of peach or off-white.

"So how does it make you feel to have your house taken over by pastels?"

Just sitting there with him brought a certain lightness to my body, as if I could finally breathe again. I replied, "Well, it's not actually my house, not technically."

The rabbi rolled his eyes and swirled his herbal teabag, part of the stash he always carried with him, in a little pot of hot water. "And how's it going with the new brother?"

"It's not like he's actually a brother to me—it's more like he's just a little kid who lives there. He's pretty easy to get along with, though. He mostly plays with other kids on the block. You wouldn't believe how popular he is. But I do have to explain all the time to Mrs. P where he is, and who the other kids' parents are, so she doesn't worry."

I didn't tell the rabbi that I usually made up the facts for Mrs. P's benefit. I would describe one parent as a lawyer and the other as a cooking contest winner, until I saw the sharp crescents of her thick eyebrows relax.

"It's like Sal is more Mrs. P's kid than Jeanine's, if you know what I mean." I paused for a moment, and then added, "Each time they paint another room, I feel a little like I'm in reserve development—you know, like a photo that's put in the water and then loses its image."

"So you're turning into a ghost?" he asked. His blue eyes were tinged with green and gold, and some concern, too.

"The worst part is the darkroom." I took a deep breath. I didn't lead off with this story, because as soon as I found out what was happening to the darkroom I'd started crying and couldn't stop.

The rabbi leaned in closer, and I told him about Tony pulling me aside and telling me I needed to clear my equipment out of the closet, or he would toss it—Mrs. P's orders. "Tony looked so sorry for me."

I didn't mention my flood of tears or that Tony actually hugged me and said, "You're a good girl. I'm sorry people are so bad." While I sobbed, he helped me carry everything to my room, telling me over and over that I was good girl, it would work out, don't worry, don't cry.

"They made you get rid of the darkroom? This woman, this overly privileged housekeeper with a bad attitude, gets to call the shots—and you're not upset?" the rabbi exclaimed.

"Well, she is a Holocaust survivor," I said. It was a line I repeated often to myself. "And I was already planning to move the darkroom into my own closet. It's just that the closet doors have slats, so it isn't dark enough."

"No excuse," he said, shaking his head. "Just because someone has seen the worst of mankind doesn't mean they get to inflict pain on someone else. We don't need the oppressed in this world becoming the oppressors." A few months ago, he'd given a talk on this very subject to the youth group.

"I am upset," I said. I felt my face getting hot. "But what do you expect me to do about it? If I complain to my dad, he'll send me to Mom's."

The rabbi wiped his hands on a napkin before speaking. "And what, I keep asking you, would be so bad about that?"

"I just can't. You've got to believe me."

"You still haven't told me why, no matter how much we talk about this."

"I don't know exactly." Out of nowhere, shame flushed through me. "There's something about my mom, the way she would get depressed out of the blue and just pull away from us all. I'm so tired of being the one who does that to her."

"What are you talking about?" he asked, staring at me in disbelief. "You don't make her sad, Deborah. You're her daughter. If anything, you give her new life, some hope for the future. You know the story of the exodus, right?"

"Yeah, Moses, Pharaoh, the Red Sea."

"Do you know what I get from that story? That hardening our heart to anyone—like Pharaoh did to Moses—is the path of suffering. This life is about breaking your heart open so it can't become hard."

But couldn't he see that my life was already broken open? The only thing holding the broken pieces together in the same shoebox were the people like the rabbi—all the people I would lose if I moved to another town to live with Mom. Couldn't he see that only he, Liz, and the youth group made me feel like I belonged, even if the price of belonging was having to watch everything I said at home?

Something smacked hard into the window beside our booth. Instinctively the rabbi and I rushed outside, where cold, miniature pellets of ice stung our faces. He lifted up a small, reddish-brown bird.

"A junco," he said. "They usually know better than to fly into windows."

"Will it live?" I asked, but I already knew the answer.

Chapter Eleven

Boy sang "Unforgettable," telling everyone he was a reincarnation of Nat King Cole, while Big Boy held a cup of hot coffee in his leather-gloved hands and leaned against our truck. Ever since Dad and Jeanine got back from their honeymoon, two weeks earlier, they had spent most of their time in the city. I hardly saw them except on Saturdays, when Dad usually set me up in the stand and disappeared for a few hours. Jeanine would come in the afternoon, take whatever money I'd made, and remind me that Dad would be back to help me pack up in a few hours.

Today sales were exceptionally slow because the forecasters kept saying a big winter storm was on its way. I had Boy watch the booth while I called Dad to ask if we should close up early.

"It's just like the last storm that should have come," he snorted, "and what did we get? Two lousy inches and a little wind? Those weather guys, I tell you."

I looked at the sky and pleaded, "But Dad –"

"It's fine. If it starts snowing, just pack up what you can, go to the tavern, and wait for me. I should be back by three."

I sat on the corner of a table, swinging my legs to keep warm and drinking coffee—something I'd discovered I really liked, as long as I added three packets of sugar. I thought back to that afternoon in the kitchen, a few days ago, when I'd told Dad about the darkroom.

"Don't start with me," he had said.

"But my darkroom, it's important to me."

"It's just a little girl's hobby," he replied, turning to the fridge. "Besides"—the words came out casually, over his shoulder—"it wasn't her idea to get rid of it. It was mine."

Just thinking about those words made me slam my hand down onto the corner of the clothing table so hard that my wrist hurt. At the time I'd yelled at him, "But it was mine. I gave up everything, and you couldn't let me have this?"

"You didn't give up a thing. You just keep getting and getting, and I've had it," he yelled back. "You know, I'm ready to send you back to your mother's. I would right now, if Jeanine didn't think it was a bad idea. You think you mean anything to me?"

I knew the answer even before he walked away, shaking his head.

When I tried a few days later to speak to Jeanine about the darkroom, she only said, "That's between you and your father. Don't bring me in."

"But it's your house too." As I pleaded with her, it dawned on me that it wasn't really my house at all anymore.

She yawned and waved me off. I followed her. "Jeanine, I really need your help."

"I'm done with the help business," she said, slamming the bedroom door behind her—except now it was her and Dad's bedroom door.

The door stared me in the face, as if to say I was an idiot for even trying. I kicked it hard and ran upstairs.

"Lost in space?" Boy asked, towering over me.

I looked up into Boy's face with the feathery snow lilting down around him. "Guess so."

286

"We better make ourselves scarce, little traveler," he said. "The wind is coming."

"The wind is coming, my son," Big Boy echoed, smiling a little as he started to pack boxes. He turned toward me and called out, "Yes, it's coming, little daughter, for you too. Where's your dad?"

When I shrugged, Big Boy looked down and shook his head. I started packing up, but within minutes that light snow had turned into the gusty kind that smacked me in the face every time I tried to get away from it. I felt a light panic rising up my legs.

"It's a Nor'easter," Boy called out, one ear glued to his transistor radio.

"Close?"

"Close."

As the wind picked up, the snow got heavier. In between closing his own boxes and tossing them into the truck, Boy rushed over to help me. We worked together, holding the boxes open and piling in the pants—neatly at first, but once the rain mixed with the snow and our cheeks started to ache from the cold, he followed my lead and smashed the clothes in haphazardly. A rack fell over but when I ran to lift it back up, Boy was there in a flash. It toppled over again, and this time some of the blouses hit the frozen mud.

"Let's get it straight to the truck," he yelled over the wind. I reached into my pocket for the key that unlocked the padlock on the back doors of the truck, but I found only money, money, and more money. I searched through every pocket in a growing panic. I even checked the cab of the truck, which Dad always left unlocked, but there was no key there, either.

By that time Boy, Big Boy, and Sergei had already steadied three of my racks against the wall with a table. When I told them I had no key, Big Boy fetched sheets of plastic and silver duct tape. My parka was soaked and Boy's cheeks bright red as the four of us worked together, throwing our weight against the clothing so that Big Boy could secure the plastic around the racks. Then I went and retrieved sixteen boxes from the stand and stuffed them into the cab as Sergei, whose own stand was already packed, handed me box after box. I feared the clothes were ruined, but I reassured myself that nothing ruins polyester.

I kept looking around as we packed, expecting to see Dad show up any minute. How could he not notice the weather? When Boy and Big Boy finished their own loading, I went over to help. "Take care of yourself," Boy said, kissing my cold cheek after I pushed the doors of their truck closed. "We gotta hit the road quick, get ahead of this storm." As they drove off, both he and his father threw me kisses.

I rushed over to the tavern, relieved that the big heater on the ceiling blasted warm air on me in a way that exaggerated the tantalizing smell of burgers and fries. I piled my coat and purse on a wooden table in the corner and tried the pay phone. No answer at home, so I sat down, ordered a corned beef sandwich and pored over a little newspaper that was mostly full of classified ads. Apartments for $120 a month—that's what Eshe wanted. I wondered where she was. There were some jobs at the Dairy Queen and McDonald's, some at the mall. I could get a job and live in a $120-a-month apartment. I would need something to get me around, of course, and I'd need to learn to drive. I found an ad right away for a red Volkswagen, "beat up but runs good, $400."

I had almost $250 in savings, although I had no idea how to drive. What would it take for me to live on my own? A year of saving? Could I really find a whole new life from these want ads? My fingers burned, my face burned, and I was so tired by the time the food arrived that I could hardly convince myself to eat it. Yet the appeal of moving out on my own was enough to wake me up a little. I imagined renting a tiny apartment in Englishtown, taking a different bus to school, and coming home to make myself toast and hot chocolate. I could still see the rabbi. I could probably work out a way to get myself to Liz's class every week—maybe catch a ride with Mark, although I hadn't seen him in a while because I'd missed the last class.

The other tables at the tavern now seemed grubby and dark, with only a few clusters of lingering diners. I tried calling Dad again but still got no answer, so I sat back down and finished the last of the fries. What next? Finally, I called a taxi. Half an hour later, I walked into the empty house. I checked the kitchen to see if there was a note for me, but found nothing. I plopped down on a kitchen stool, too sad and exhausted to move, and looked over the unfamiliar clean counters, the newly painted walls, and the gleaming stainless steel sink. Still, without Mrs. P here, the house seemed a little more like the house I had lived in for so many years.

Liz always said that when you were depressed, the only way out was to do something, anything. ("Even if it's the most screwed-up thing in the world, it's better than inertia," she had told the class.) So I took a hot bath that made my body ache as the burning hot water touched my ice-cold skin. Before climbing into bed in my thickest granny gown, I lit my favorite white candle, the one that smelled like rain. I was shaking, freezing, burning, raging. I was on fire and so far away from anyone that I couldn't imagine how another human being—even the rabbi, even Mark—could possibly help me.

Yet at the same time the flame of my candle seemed to tell me that all I needed to do was to watch it. As long as I was watching that steady flame, I was okay. And watching it made me imagine a woman a bit like me but older—an older version of myself, perhaps—climbing into bed behind me. She would put her arms around me and hold me against her warm, stable body. We would fall asleep together this way, just like I fell asleep spooning with Eshe months ago. But she wouldn't disappear like all the other women in my life. She would be far too substantial to be swept away by any kind of bad weather. Although I could not see her face, I knew she wouldn't be Fatima or Jeanine, but someone more like me twenty years from now.

The next morning was a Sunday, when no one went into the city. I walked into the kitchen and found Dad reading the paper and eating two gigantic Belgian waffles. Mrs. P was washing the breakfast dishes and glaring at my father for taking so long. I took a plate from the cabinet and helped myself to a waffle. Mrs. P ignored me.

I sat opposite Dad and waited a moment, but he didn't look up. I demanded, "Where were you? Do you have any idea what I went through yesterday?"

He waved his hand at me as if shaking off a fly, and kept reading.

"Dad, do you hear me? The truck is still there, and all the racks, too. Everyone could be ruined."

He turned a page and saw nothing interesting, then picked up the comics instead. "It's all taken care of, so don't bother me."

"What do you mean, all taken care of?"

He exhaled and rolled his eyes. "The truck is in the drive. If you had bothered to look, you would know that. Mrs. P, got any more?"

She nodded and walked over with a large waffle at the end of a long fork. She dropped the waffle on his plate and looked briefly at me. Although she didn't smile, she didn't frown either. I nodded, and she brought me another waffle.

I pressed Dad for an explanation, but all he said was that he and Jeanine stopped at the stand on their way home and finished packing the truck while Sal and Mrs. P waited in the car. Then he drove the truck back to the house. "But it doesn't matter anymore, so let me read the paper."

"What are you talking about? Didn't the clothes get ruined?"

He slammed down the comics and shouted at me, "I said to leave me alone! We're selling everything from the auction, and what we can't sell we'll dump at the Salvation Army. The auction is over."

Jeanine came in just then to refresh her cup of coffee. She nodded in my direction and asked, "Ready, Hank?"

"Where are you going?"

Dad shrugged and tossed the comics on the table in disgust. "We're going to the city."

"But it's a Sunday. Why are you leaving now? Besides, what about Roger and Missy?"

"We're leaving because we have work to do on the new business," said Jeanine.

"Anyway, we just saw them at the wedding," Dad added, as if the wedding had taken place yesterday instead of weeks ago.

"What new business?"

I followed them out to the car, and Jeanine rolled down her window to patiently explain her new idea to use taxis to deliver food to people around the city.

"So the taxis will deliver the food in between picking up people?"

"Yeah, it's a natural. We have thirteen restaurants signed up already. When the guys pick up someone from the airport, they'll hand him a menu and say something like, 'You must really want to just relax in your room, watch some TV and get a hot meal.' They'll tell the passengers how they can deliver whatever they want: Chinese, Italian, American, whatever."

"Let's go already," said Dad. "I'm exhausted."

I persisted. "Well, what if they want food from a restaurant that's not on the way from one of the airports?"

"Not a problem," Jeanine said. "We can drive anywhere, and we make more taxi fare in that case, too. Everyone wins." Her face was gleaming as she waved to me and rolled up her window. I watched the car back out of the driveway with Dad looking over his shoulder the whole time.

Not long after they left, I was carrying my plate to the sink when Mrs. P turned to grab it out of my hands, and then promptly dropped it. Instinctively I looked down, expecting her to yell at me as if it were all my fault. I was so busy thinking of excuses that it took me a while to realize that she wasn't concerned about me at all. Her face was frozen as she held tightly to the sink with her other hand, and then her knees started to buckle.

I leapt toward her and put my hands on either side of her waist, steadying her as I lowered her to the floor. Her legs sprawled and her head drooped to the left. I leaned her limp body against the cabinet and rushed to the door, calling after Dad and Jeanine in the vain hope that they were still within earshot. Then I laid her down as gently as possible. Her face was turned to one side, her neck twisted in a funny way. I jumped up to call an ambulance and then knelt down next to Mrs. P as she lay there, perfectly still.

As I listened to the phone ring I kept hearing the words *you killed her* even though I knew that wasn't true. Strangely enough, it didn't feel scary to be with a dead body, but was she really dead? A woman's voice at the other end of the phone asked me to speak slowly, say my address, explain exactly what happened. With the phone cord stretched to capacity, I told her everything I could. I pressed my thumb to Mrs. P's wrist. Yes, there was a pulse. Yes, she was still breathing. I could even see her chest rise and fall slowly—she was alive. Relief shook me into speaking faster, although I was still afraid I might throw up.

The woman on the phone kept talking to me until the paramedics raced into the house. Then I finally hung up the phone and stood back, watching them tap her cheeks and take her blood pressure. They pulled her out from the wall and into a reclining position, then moved her onto the stretcher.

"Who will be coming with her?" one of the paramedics asked. I realized that there was no one but me. I called the mother of Sal's friend, explained that Mrs. P was going to the hospital, and asked if Sal could stay there a while longer. Then I followed the stretcher outside, picking up my pocketbook along the way.

During the short ride to the hospital, I sat on a plastic-cushioned bench next to a paramedic who had Mrs. P hooked up to an oxygen tank, with the little mask covering half her face. I smoothed her skirt down so that her thighs wouldn't show. "It's probably a stroke and, from the looks of it, not a bad one," said the paramedic. He was so tall that he had to hunch over to ride in the back of the ambulance with me. "We're not supposed to say anything until the doctors confirm it, but your grandma is going to be okay."

"She's not my grandma," I said, but he didn't hear me. He went on about his own grandparents and how important it was to have them in your life while you were growing up, and how his grandfather, in particular, was like his real father.

Once we arrived at the hospital, I asked to use a phone. No one answered at the taxi service, so I stood leaning on the admissions counter.

"You eighteen?" asked a short Haitian woman with tired eyes.

"No, sorry."

"Too bad. Is there anyone else who can fill out this paperwork?" She waved a clipboard with a thick sheaf of papers.

I shook my head. "Can I use your phone again?"

She set the phone on the counter for me to use. First I called the rabbi, but there was no answer. Who now? Then it occurred to me to try Karmic Clothes, but the store wasn't open yet. I asked for a phone book and found Liz, right there, under Stevenson, Elizabeth. Such an ordinary name for a force of nature. She answered right away.

"I know this is going to sound weird," I began hesitantly.

"Deborah! What is it, hon?"

"I haven't told you much about my family."

"Your pictures sure have. What's wrong, baby?"

"Well, you know that my dad got remarried, and his wife has this housekeeper, more like a friend, but not a friendly friend, who came with her. She's a Holocaust survivor and she does all the cooking and cleaning. But today –" I spilled out the whole story, and Liz told me to hang tight, she would be right there.

Ten minutes later, she burst through the emergency room doors. As soon as I saw her, I ran to her and started crying. "Oh, sweetheart," she said, holding me tight, "isn't life just like this?" but I couldn't stop crying.

A little while later, I finally reached Dad. I told him Mrs. P almost died but all he said was, "Fine, we'll be right there," like I was merely calling for a taxi. Liz and I waited in the small cafeteria, where we ordered instant mashed potatoes and large hot chocolates.

"You can't make stuff like this up," Liz told me. "But you'll make your way out of it."

"I know," I said, although I didn't share her confidence. "I'm so sorry I had to call you. You probably had other plans."

"Just to sit around in a hospital cafeteria eating mashed potatoes. You know, they're so bad they're good." She paused and looked at me. "Deborah, you gotta get out of that house."

"I know," I said again, then rushed to change the subject.

We met Jeanine on our way back, running down the hallway and crying so hard that her mascara was running, too. She grabbed my shoulders and demanded, "Is she all right? Is she?"

I had never seen Jeanine like this before, like she really cared deeply about something. Dad looked uncomfortable but he managed to nod at Liz, remembering he knew her. "Did you drive them here?"

"Hank, of course not," Jeanine interjected. "They would have taken the ambulance, right?" When I nodded, Jeanine grabbed me and hugged me, then got ahold of herself and pulled back. "Your daughter knows the right thing to do. You call an ambulance—that's what you did, right?" I nodded again and she seemed to calm down, her face returning to that smooth surface.

I tried to introduce Liz to Jeanine, but Jeanine was too busy filling out papers and demanding information on Mrs. P's condition from anyone in authority who would listen. Dad sank into a chair and started reading an old fishing magazine, although he had never fished in his life as far as I knew. Liz nudged me. "Let's get dessert."

We returned to the refuge of the cafeteria, securing chocolate pudding cups for us and apple turnovers for Dad and Jeanine. "Pudding was made for this kind of day," Liz informed me. "Now, tell me more about this Mrs. P."

"I don't know much about her, except that she was in the war and she seems to hate me. She doesn't like Dad either, but she makes the best desserts every night. You would die, Liz."

"I would. You know how I am with sweets. So it's weirder than all fuck in your house?"

"Kinda." I smiled and she smiled back.

"Well, time to take pictures, isn't it?"

"That's what I've been doing all along."

In the elevator, heading back to the emergency room, Liz asked me something I didn't expect. "He ever beat you?"

"My dad?" I thought for a moment. "Sometimes, but it's mostly just a kick or a push. He usually just threatens to throw me out of the house and make me live with Mom again."

"Would that be so bad?" she asked, as the elevator came to a halt.

"Yeah," I answered quickly.

"I know what you mean, hon. My mom was a bitch on acid." Liz looked suddenly sad. "I cut ties with her a long time ago. I thought we would get back together, but it never happened."

She paused before she continued. "I was overseas when she died, and I didn't find out for months. Even then it was from a cousin I met in Amsterdam, who told me while we were smoking weed. It made me feel like such a shit. You know, if there's any chance you can fix things with your mother, you should. You have no idea how this is going to hurt like all hell when you grow up."

It took another hour before a completely bald doctor with deep-set eyes appeared in the waiting room. He was so dramatic-looking that Liz nudged me and whispered, "Good subject." He said Mrs. P had had a minor stroke, nothing serious, and she needed to sleep now. She was conscious but not talking yet, although she had excellent responses to the tests and could move her eyes, fingers, and toes.

Jeanine was so relieved that she burst out crying and fled down the hall. As Dad rushed after her, Liz and I slipped into the room where Mrs. P lay sleeping. "Whoever you are, may you come back to us the best you can be," Liz intoned. She waved both arms dramatically and threw her hands out in front of her, as if she were casting a spell. We both started laughing so hard that we had to slip out of the room again before Dad and Jeanine returned.

Chapter Twelve

Once Mrs. P came home from the hospital, Jeanine and Dad stayed home every night with Sal. No one seemed to mind when I said I wanted to spend the night at the temple for the youth group lock-in. Jeanine thought it would be good for me, and even Mrs. P nodded her approval. Ever since her hospital stay she had treated me like family, although she was still distant with Dad. Even Jeanine noticed the change. As she dropped me off at the temple she said, "Mrs. P, you just need to let her warm up to you, and you did that."

I thought about adding that I was also the one who got her to the hospital after her stroke, maybe even saved her life. But instead I simply agreed with Jeanine and climbed out of the car with my sleeping bag and little red carryall. Inside the social hall, I put my things on the bema. I looked across the massive room and saw that the first person there was Mark, leaning on a table and watching me.

"How are you?" he asked.

"I don't really know. It's been kinda crazy lately."

He put his arm around me. "I like you. Tell me about it."

"Oh, I guess it's not that bad. You know that Mrs. P I told you about? She had a stroke, and actually she's a little nicer to me now."

"And your dad, is he being any better?"

Just the night before, when Jeanine was out, Dad had yelled at me for being inconsiderate and a drain on his money. Then there was our big fight this morning, when Dad kicked me and said he wished he didn't have any children. "He's been a little distant lately," I said. I didn't know how to explain to Mark the kind of craziness that was my dad.

"You got your driver's license yet?"

"No. I keep meaning to learn, but it's been insane ever since the wedding."

He squeezed my shoulder as we scooted onto one of the tabletops and sat down cross-legged. "I'll teach you. I bet I can teach you to drive in two weeks, three weeks tops."

"You must be a good teacher."

"Or maybe you'll just turn out to be a naturally good driver."

"How can you tell?"

"Well," he said with a smile, "you got here without falling over."

I smiled back at him. "It really would be neat to learn to drive, but I don't know if my dad would go for it."

"If he loves you, wouldn't he want you to have all the accouterments of adulthood, like a driver's license?"

"I don't know if he loves me." The words startled me, even as they came out of my mouth. "Well, I don't know if he loves anyone, really, least of all me." He loves Jeanine, I thought, and he acted like he loved Fatima. Yet both women happened so quickly—was that really love?

"It could be that he really does love you, but he just doesn't know how to say it. You know, my mother's an alcoholic and she's kinda like that, too."

"I don't think so." I looked at Mark, wondering why I didn't know about his mother before now. Then it struck me how ludicrous it was that we were talking about love, and I smiled. Mark smiled too, and soon we were laughing.

"Okay, so I take it back. Maybe he doesn't know how to love."

"Or he just doesn't love me."

"No, you got it wrong, girl," he said, putting his hand on my shoulder. "You're infinitely lovable."

My heart raced and I ran after it, trying to find something to say. "Thanks. So are you. I mean, how are you lately?"

"I'm good. My mom's drying out at the detox center, so it's quiet right now at home. Jim, this kid who lives down the block, has been over a lot lately helping me work on Lucy—you know, my car."

"Oh, is something wrong with Lucy?"

"Something's always wrong with Lucy. But this week—I really mean it, I can pick you up and teach you to drive."

Just then Abby, Amy, the rabbi, and Jon burst into the room. "Hey, someone's here," Abby yelled, turning up the dimmer switch on the lights. "What are you guys doing, making out?"

To my surprise, Mark didn't stiffen up at that remark. We both smiled and shrugged, feeling a little idiotic, maybe, but somehow it was okay.

The rabbi planned to sleep in his office on a little Japanese bed (a futon, he called it) while we spent the night in the sanctuary in our sleeping bags. Originally we had planned to sleep in the youth group room, but it was so small that some of the parents feared it would lead to sex.

"That room is so small the only sex we could have is an orgy," Amy joked.

Orgies had no more appeal for us than smashed saltines, and the idea of everyone naked in a small space made us squeamish. The rabbi said he trusted us, but we needed to make sure we didn't do anything that would upset our parents. What the parents didn't realize was that the large, spacious sanctuary had hard, uncomfortable floors. The only carpeted area was the very small bema.

"Yeah, it's like God's living room," said Jon.

Before we settled down for the night on the bema, we had another rap session with the rabbi. The topic for tonight was what we wanted most out of life. Samantha, her long red hair hanging over half her face, started off. "I want my dad to get a new job, one that doesn't keep him away from us all the time. I feel like I don't know him." Jon wanted better grades so he could become a doctor and help people, especially children who got hurt in accidents. "I know, I'm just a football player, but I'm not an imbecile," he said, and we all laughed. Amy wanted to go on a trip around the world. Abby wanted to be ten pounds thinner. When everyone stared at her, she said, "You want honesty? Well, this is what I think about all the time, and this is what I really want." Mark, of course, wanted his mother to get better, and I wanted someplace else to live.

It was a quick round of answers, but the rabbi had a follow-up question up his sleeve. "Now, why do you want this? And before you answer, I want you all to write for ten minutes."

We scrambled for notebooks, pens, and pencils, and started to write. I leaned against one side of the tripod podium with Mark and Amy on the other sides. We joked that as long as we all sat very still, no one would fall over. As we wrote, the rabbi sat cross-legged, watching us. When time was up and we came back to the circle, he turned to me. "You go first, Deborah."

"But I hate going first." Everyone laughed a little.

"Exactly," said Abby, "that's why you have to do it." Her green eye shadow glittered when she blinked.

I started reading out loud what I'd written about Dad, who whispered insults whenever Jeanine was out of earshot. It surprised me that I didn't feel anything, as if it were a story I was making up, even when I got to the words, "I wish you weren't my daughter." I described how I had to sneak downstairs if I wanted get out of the house and sit cross-legged behind the daffodils, watching the clouds race over the moon. When I came to the morning when he kicked me in the back of the thigh, I could still feel the bruise, large as a grapefruit, as I read. ("Just a tap," he'd told me as I got up off the floor. "And if you make a big deal of this, you'll be sorry.") Yet a few hours later, while I was loading the dishwasher, he walked into the kitchen and said warmly, "Hon, great job helping out."

I stopped reading and realized that everyone was staring at me. Emily, a quiet girl with a pockmarked face who had recently joined the group, was even crying a little. Mark put his arm around me again and leaned into me. I couldn't understand why it seemed so sad to them—just a tap, I thought.

There was a long silence before the rabbi said, "Thank you," and smiled at me. Mark picked up his paper and read about how his mother started drinking when he was six. Tears started running down his face, and in a minute I was crying, too. I looked around the room and saw that everyone was in tears because Mark was crying. He told us about coming home to find his mother sleeping in her own vomit, and how he cooked dinner every night for his father.

I was relieved that Abby was next. She was so shallow that I expected her to give everyone a break from the crying. Instead, she told us how she hated her body, hated herself. Every time she looked in the mirror she saw how fat she was and realized that no one would love her, ever. Ever since she ballooned up to a size seven, her life had been hell. She tried eating nothing until dinner, but then she'd pig out and have to make herself throw up in the bathroom. It was easy, just stick a finger down your throat. But now she was doing this after every meal and it was making her stomach hurt all the time, although she admitted that it was kind of pleasant to throw up ice cream. The worst part was that she still wasn't getting thinner, even when she cut every apple into thirty pieces to make it last longer.

The rabbi nodded as tears and green mascara ran down her beautiful crystal face. "We *will* talk later," he said gently.

It was past midnight when the session ended. We had cried off and on for two hours, and now the only thing left was the hugging. I put my arms around Abby and told her that she wasn't fat—maybe a little bony, actually. She laughed. I saw Mark hug Emily, so I went over and hugged Amy. When he hugged Jon, I hugged Sam right next to him. Finally Mark grabbed me, held on for a long time and cried a few tears on my shoulder. "I really like you," he whispered.

"I really like you, too," I whispered back. The moment was like an island, surrounded by tranquil water and floating far away from the rest of my crazy life. I felt the warmth of his body, the weight of it, against mine. So good.

That night, we put our sleeping bags side by side on the edge of the bema. "Don't fall off," I warned Mark, since he was on the edge.

"Oh, my problem is I might fall in, to you."

When the lights went out, he nuzzled his bag against mine. We lay facing each other, our knees almost touching through the two layers of flannel—his sleeping bag and mine. He reached out his hand and stroked the side of my face. We couldn't see each other, but in the dark we traced each other's features with our fingertips. This is what it must feel like to have a home that isn't just a house. We fell asleep that way.

The next morning I walked into the house smiling. Nothing could shatter this happiness, I thought, nothing could touch this feeling, just like nothing could take my photography away from me. Dad was sitting in the kitchen, eating a cake from the box, a cake someone had brought for Mrs. P. I was going to comment, but I didn't say anything.

"Jeanine out?"

"Shopping." He looked up from the paper. "You didn't go to the temple last night."

"Of course I did. Call the rabbi if you don't believe me."

"That rabbi is in cahoots with you. Probably letting you sneak off with some boy, and I know what boys are like."

"Look, I was there! You can call Abby's parents, or Jon's. Call all of them and you'll find out I'm not lying. I never lie to you." Well, almost never, I rationalized.

"Just like your mother," he said in a mocking tone as he stood up, still holding his fork. "And that's where you should go—back to your mother, so you can learn to lie well enough to get married."

"Believe what you want," I said, and turned my back on him to go upstairs.

The fork got me in the back of the calf, leaving a small puncture wound on the body that, moments before, had felt perfect.

Chapter Thirteen

Despite the lingering smell of stale milk cartons, our high school art show lit up the cafeteria. The lunch tables held sculptures and drawings and the walls were covered with photography and paintings. I followed Jeanine, Dad, and Sal around the room in a state of dread. Mrs. P was still weak from the hospital and told me she wanted to stay home and read, but she said it nicely, almost smiling.

As soon as Mark spotted me, he raced over to stand at my side. I introduced him to Dad.

"Now, what are your intentions, young man?" A joke, of course, but it didn't come out as a joke.

Mark answered without missing a beat, "to be her friend and get to know her better."

Jeanine, who had been staring cross-eyed at an abstract painting behind him, raised her eyebrows as if to say, "Good boy."

The school year was ending—and everything else, too, it seemed. Our last day of the auction was this Saturday, and the rabbi had told me he would be looking for another position in the fall, although he wouldn't tell me why. He said there were some details of adult life I didn't yet need to know.

As we rounded the pottery table I saw Mark's photographs: a shot of the sun rising over a puddle in the middle of a highway, vivid and crisp-edged, and a picture of his father, his face caught in the moment it changed from hope to despair. Next to the photographs was a line drawing of Patty Hearst with a gun in her arm and a beret on her head. The caption read, "Patty was right."

Dad joked that the man in Mark's photo didn't look so happy with his son at that moment. Mark shrugged. He whispered to me that his father was helping nurse his mom through another detox, so he couldn't be there.

We walked on, Jeanine cooing over some paintings of owls.

"I like owls, too," I told her.

"They stay up late. They think they're so smart," said Dad.

Then, at last, we came to my photographs—seven of them, which was a record according to Mark. All the ones chosen were from the Englishtown Auction, and they were strung together in a photo essay entitled "A Man Named Boy." I had given Boy his own eight-by-ten prints last week; in return, he'd sent me a postcard of the Eiffel Tower with a message written in large capital letters with a black marker. He said no one had ever understood him so well before.

"This is so beautiful, Deborah," Mark said, touching the center of my back lightly. "You have so much talent."

"Talent for all sorts of things but what's useful," Dad snapped, but Jeanine shoved him lightly with her elbow. My own elbow boasted a fresh bruise where he had grabbed my arm two nights earlier.

Now someone else took my arm, and I heard a familiar voice. It was Mr. Lexington. "I see you're well represented here, Deborah. In fact, we could even say you're the belle of the ball when it comes to this art show."

"Hey, I'd go with that," Ms. Sheplin chimed in with her Boston accent. She had her arm linked through Mr. Lexington's. So they were a couple—I briefly wondered what had happened to the woman I'd seen him with at the dance.

The room was now so crowded with people that I could no longer see Dad, Mark, or Jeanine, so I went on talking with the teachers. "I try," I said.

"I think you do more than try, my dear," said Mr. Lexington. "Darla here has been telling me that you'd be a shoo-in at a good art school."

Ms. Sheplin beamed beside him. I noticed that, instead of the hippie granny dresses she usually wore, today she had on a low-cut tube top under an open gauzy shirt, a good look. She turned to Mr. Lexington and asked, "Isn't there a wonderful art program near your new school in the city?"

"You're leaving?" I exclaimed.

"Duty calls, young miss. I've accepted a new teaching assignment at an all-girls' school in the city, right in midtown."

"New York?"

"What other city is there?" asked Ms. Sheplin. They both laughed at her joke even though neither was a native New Yorker.

"Finally! I had to plow through miles of hormones just to get to you," said Liz, coming up behind me. "This place is overwhelming with sex, sweat, and bad vibes." She wore a black, low-cut shimmery top and carried a paper cup of juice.

She exchanged smiles with Ms. Sheplin and Mr. Lexington as I introduced everyone. Before I could say more, Mark sidled up to me with Styrofoam cups of very red punch and a look of exasperation on his face. "Your dad," was all he said.

My teachers were swept away into someone else's conversation, so we rejoined Dad. He was edging into the hallway where I had two mixed media paintings, both abstract.

"Oh, there you are," he said. "This place is a zoo, and Jeanine and I need to do some work tonight, so let's go."

"Dad, you know Liz," I said, but he merely nodded and looked away. Liz and I rolled our eyes at each other, and she said she'd see me in class. I knew exactly what she was thinking: he'd spent over an hour with her in a hospital waiting room, and now he couldn't even say hello.

I followed Dad and told him, "On the way out, let's look at my other photos, but don't look for meaning. These are abstract." On one I had painted circles on top of overlapping circles, using a photograph taken while I was looking down at a stream. The other one I called my "ugly painting," with everything thrown together to make the ugliest picture possible. It was brown poured on black, on green, the colors both vibrant and smeared. I thought of it as looking straight down into mud at night in the rain. Although it was so dark, with many layers of color piled on color, it reminded me of what it was like to climb up out of pain. It was hard to tell that originally it had been a photo of a highway. I loved this painting, and felt very protective of it.

Mark stood with me for a long time, holding my hand. He seemed moved by the painting and kissed me on the cheek.

"No making out in front of the dad," said Dad in a pinched voice, trying to sound funny and, at the same time, as if he actually cared who I was.

On our last day at the auction we sold everything for a dollar apiece and then, at the very end, for fifty cents apiece. We sold it all, even the boxes for a dime each, and Sergei bought our racks. In the end, there was only the empty truck. Boy walked me to the passenger door. "I'm going to miss you, puppy girl."

"Why 'puppy girl'?"

"Because you'll never lose your innocence. But I tell you, if I were ever to marry, you're the kind of girl I'd get down on my knees for." He bent down and kissed me on each cheek, slowly, and then cast himself into yet another role. "Oh, Natasha, we must part, but nothing, not the Red Army, nor the Bolsheviks, will ever keep us apart."

Big Boy walked over, shaking his head. "Six hours, and I've only got a hundred bucks to show. This is no way to live, girlie." Over the past few months flea markets had sprung up all over the East Coast, which meant that the buses from upstate New York, Long Island, Pennsylvania, and Washington, D.C., had stopped coming.

"Don't you think it'll come back? I mean, it's almost summer, and things always slow down right before summer, right?"

"You're a sweet girl," Big Boy said, kissing the top of my head. "But everything in life comes to an end." He started to walk away, then turned back, took my hand, and kissed it like he did with all his lady friends. His charm suddenly reminded me of Mr. Lexington and of the rumor, passed along to me by Abby, that he was changing schools because he was caught making out with a student.

The next day, Liz picked me up at nine. She was supposed to arrive at eight, but said she had trouble extracting herself from Carl's loving and very heavy arms. She brought coffee for me (she'd taken the liberty of dumping in three packets of sugar and two creams, just like her own) and, of course, a bagel with cream cheese. I slipped into the car and we started giggling.

"As soon as we get on the bus, it starts, you got it?"

I tapped my camera and told her I had packed ten rolls of film.

"Maybe that'll be enough," she said, winking and taking a giant bite out of what was left of her bagel.

We parked at the gas station on Route 9. While we waited for the bus, we circled the building with our cameras on our chests and film in our pocketbooks. She immediately pointed out a bird perched on the telephone wire, right above a sign that read, "Kiss the Cook If You Love Our Food." I took my shot from an angle that exaggerated the word "Food" and focused on the pigeon, as if it were the food. I tried to bring out the graininess of the sign's fading frame as well as the peeling paint. When I looked up, Liz was signaling that the bus was coming.

During the ride into the city, we surreptitiously photographed the old man sleeping in the seat across the aisle, snapping a whole cluster of pictures as he snored away, oblivious. Liz whispered that the blurred background would stand out more distinctly if I tilted my camera like hers and adjusted the F-stop. Then she surveyed the rest of the passengers and declared the bus a dead zone, so we relaxed in our seats. The scenery outside my window dotted itself endlessly with deli gas stations, parking lots, and errant car dealerships.

"I want you to know that you've got it," she said out of the blue.

I gave her an inquiring look, not wanting to beg for praise but at the same time craving it. "I don't know."

"Well, I do know. You have an eye, a natural sense of design, and a passion for this. Can you imagine where you could be a decade or two from now?"

I couldn't, of course, so she told me. "You'll be living in a city, I think, a friendly one that isn't so dog-eat-dog—maybe one of those Midwestern cities, which I hear have at least some good food. I think you'll pick Minneapolis, because I like the sound of that word. It sounds like Indianapolis, doesn't it? But everyone I ever met from Indiana was boring-ass crazy, so don't go there. Go with Minneapolis."

"Isn't it cold there?"

"Yeah, but I bet the summers are great. Besides, you'll have long underwear and a boyfriend, a cute one. You'll have a great apartment and a good view out of the bedroom window."

"A view of the river. There's big rivers up there, right?"

"Yeah, the Mississippi River, and you'll work at a museum teaching kids photography. You'll have your own business and new shows opening all the time at little art galleries—the kind that serve real hors d'oeuvres, not just those disgusting pigs-in-a-blanket. You'll have some great friends and you'll travel a lot, taking pictures. You might even be thinking about marriage and kids, because you would be a great mother."

My mind went cold. "No, I wouldn't."

"Baby, you don't know the half of it. You're headed for a great life. All you need to do now is hang the fuck on. It's all coming."

Chapter Fourteen

Mark and I were lying on our separate beds, seven miles apart, talking on the phone. Over the past month we had gone out for two movies, pizza, and a meal at the diner. Mostly we went driving, Mark in the passenger seat, showing me how to move the car from drive into reverse and how to direct it smoothly along the crescent-shaped streets of my housing development. Cul-de-sacs were especially fun.

We had kissed often, lately using our tongues, as we leaned hard against each other in my driveway. Then I would get out of the car, waving at him like an idiot and walking backwards into the house.

"So tell me about your first time," he said.

"Well, I had my clothes on, and I never exactly said no, so it wasn't like it was rape or anything."

"Is that what it felt like?"

"Yes."

"Then that's what it was."

Dad always said he knew what boys wanted, how boys thought. Yet Mark kept surprising me.

The first time happened for him in a bedroom at his uncle's house, during a cousin's Bar Mitzvah party. A pushy girl led him, all of thirteen and a little drunk, into the darkened room. "I kept feeling like

I was doing it wrong, not that she let me actually do anything. She just kinda undressed me and moved everything around until it happened. It was weird never seeing where I was, or what the room looked like. I mean, it felt good, but I couldn't wait to get out of there."

We talked about how we wanted to have sex when the time was right, about how it shouldn't happen in a car or in a rushed place. After what he'd been through with his mother and what I'd been through with the divorce, we deserved to do this in a truly special way.

"It will be perfect. Dad won't be back until Thursday, and I can make you lunch. You like beef stroganoff?"

"Yeah, but what about protection?"

"I can get some rubbers."

We both got quiet.

"But only if you're ready, Deborah. I don't want to rush you."

"No, it's okay, I'm ready."

"You're already there, girl," he said. "How about doing it next Saturday, right after you get your license?"

"It?"

"I know, it's weird to say it like that." We both laughed, just as Dad opened the door to my bedroom and peered in.

"What do you think you're doing?" he barked. Jeanine had mentioned that he hadn't been able to sleep well lately.

I whispered into the phone, "My dad's here, gotta go." Before I could hang up, though, Mark said, "Just put the phone down. I want to hear this," so I placed the receiver on the pillow.

"I'm just talking, looking at want ads for jobs," I said, pointing to the open newspaper by my feet. "Why, what's wrong?"

"Nothing's wrong." He turned my desk chair to face the bed and sat down, asking defiantly, "Can't a dad talk to his daughter once in a while?" He was hovering over me like a junkyard dog that smelled an intruder without being able to see him.

"Sure, but what do you want to talk about?"

He glanced around the room quickly, trying to take in its contents. My bookshelves were piled with stacks of photographs, contact sheets, and supplies from the darkroom, all crowded up against the Madame Alexandra Cinderella doll that Mom had given me years ago.

"I don't want to talk about anything. I'm not the one with the problem."

I suddenly felt scared, wondering if he might throw something at me. "Don't you want to talk to Jeanine? She's your wife."

"She's my *second* wife," he answered, his voice tinged with anger. "You know what that means? That means I have to support two cockamamie families, and now we have a second business that's eating up our profits and keeping me working even crazier hours. Your mother just called, and you know what? She doesn't want the kids to come over to the house anymore, because she says we ignore them—like it's somehow my job to keep them entertained."

I had no idea what he was talking about. We hadn't seen the kids in weeks because he was always working. I was beginning to suspect that Jeanine didn't want them around, either.

"And what do you do? Talk on the phone with your boyfriend? Make plans to ruin your life?" He stood up. "You know what I was doing at your age? I was working two jobs. I was driving a lousy cab, and I was carrying groceries for rich old ladies at the supermarket, friends of my mother, and where is she now?" He looked puzzled for a moment. "I could have done something else, maybe written books, mysteries. That's what I wanted to do."

Then he caught himself and his expression changed. "But I worked day and night, still do. You think I like that? Oh, who cares what you think, you're just another ball and chain around my neck, making me sick."

I tried following the rabbi's suggestion to think of a diversion when he got like this. "Wouldn't you rather talk to Jeanine or"—now my mind was racing—"get something to eat in the kitchen? Mrs. P made brownies tonight, the ones you really like."

I had watched her stir the batter while we had our first real conversation. She had told me that these brownies were her husband's favorites, and that she missed him even more than she missed her parents. I wanted to ask her more, but I left for photography class before the brownies were done.

Dad squinted, drawing his eyebrows together. "The ones with the big chocolate chips in them?" I nodded. As he left he said, "Thanks, hon," and gently closed the bedroom door behind him.

I lifted the receiver back up. "Did you get all that?" My voice was still shaking a little.

"You've got to get out of that house. I've heard that song and dance before, and he's going to slam you into the wall, Deborah. How can we get you out?"

"Couldn't I talk to Jeanine and tell her what's going on?"

"You think she doesn't know already?" he said. It was more of a statement than a question. "She's sharp."

"Well, why isn't she doing anything, then?"

"Isn't it obvious that she doesn't care?" Then, more softly, he added, "We can do something with you. You can go to college far away."

"How in the world would that work?" My first thought was that I didn't want to be far away from Mark. "Besides, that's a year away."

"I don't know, but there's gotta be a way. You can apply for loans and grants, and your senior year will go by fast with me keeping you busy. You're so smart, you can get into a good school somewhere. You remember what you said about how much it means to you to be a photographer? If you wrote that down in a college application, they'd have to have you. Then one day you can look back at him and say, 'Thanks for nothing,' and live your life on your own terms."

I noticed an edge of deep sadness in his voice. "Mark, what's wrong?"

He didn't reply at first, then said, "Mom called. She's staying in California with her sister for a while, and she told Dad not to visit yet. She says it's too much for her to live with a husband and a kid. That must mean me, the kid who cooks dinner most nights, picks up after her, and keeps the house from falling down."

As he took a breath, I could tell that he was shaking. My arms wanted to hold him so much that it made my whole body ache. "Oh, Mark, you're so good."

"No, something's wrong with me," he said, still gulping for air. "Something's wrong."

"No, not with you."

"Oh, there's more I need to tell you, but I can't do it over the phone. Look, I love you."

Those words lit up a kind of joy inside me that I couldn't remember ever feeling before. I was so amazed that he loved me, so amazed that he would say it right out loud, that I didn't give much thought to whatever it was he still needed to tell me.

A few days later, Mark and I went to the diner. No Fatima anymore (I heard she was back in Greece), but a younger Greek hostess showed us to our booth, smiling distantly. The heat outside was thick and mopey, but inside the cool air was as smooth as Mark's hand.

"So what's this other thing you can't tell me over the phone?"

Mark rolled his eyes. "It's nothing," he said in whisper, "but I can't tell you in here, either. Let's eat, and we'll talk later in the car."

By the time we reached the car, I was crawling with anxiety. Was he in love with someone else? Was he moving to California to be with his mother? Looking across the diner parking lot, I could see the outdoor pool at the swim club. The lights were on, and tiny figures kept falling into the shimmering water.

"So here's the deal," he said. "I was working on the car with Jim, and when we were putting the tools away—Oh, God, how are you going to take this? Hey, promise me you won't freak out, okay?" His cheekbones seemed higher, his lips somehow fuller.

"I won't. Just tell me already."

"Okay, he comes up behind me, and he presses his body against me—you know, from the back— and he kisses my neck."

"He what?"

"I know. I can't believe it. I said, 'What the hell are you doing?'"

This wasn't so bad. "And what did he say?"

"He said he didn't know, that he had never done this before, but he felt like he should."

"Why would he say that? Why would he feel that way?"

"I don't know. Maybe he's a gay. But hey, you're taking this really well. I'm so glad you're not freaking out."

"Why would I freak out? I mean, it's not like you liked it, right?"

Mark paused.

"Did you like it?" Now I could hear the wind in the trees overhead.

"Deborah, I really love you. I mean it. But you know, I've been thinking about it and, well, it was kind of a turn-on." He dropped his head on the steering wheel and sighed. I thought he might start crying. "I'm so sorry, Deborah. I mean, I don't mean I think about doing it with him. It's just that it excited me somehow."

I leaned back. What if Mark was gay?

"I don't know," he continued, as I remained silent. "I think with my mom rejecting me, and you and I talking about making love and stuff, I'm just in a space where I could react to something like this. It doesn't mean I'm gay, just that it happened."

Now he straightened up and turned to face me, trying to smile, his ponytail coming undone. I must have looked sad, because he said, "I'm probably not gay at all. But nothing like this has ever happened, and hey, when can we make love?"

"The sooner the better," I answered.

That night, as I sat down at the kitchen table with a square of leftover brownie on a paper towel, Jeanine walked in from the laundry room. She looked startled. "Sorry," I said.

"It's nothing," she answered. Noticing the brownie in my hand, she went to get herself one. "You want some milk, too?"

"Nah, this is fine."

She sat down next to me with her own brownie, a much bigger piece, and half a glass of milk. "I've gotta tell you, I'm just exhausted lately," she said.

"I know what you mean," I answered, trying to sound friendly. She looked at me doubtfully. "I mean, you have the new business and everything.

"Yeah, everything."

She was actually staying and talking to me, sitting still for once after so many busy weeks of coming and going. It seemed like a good time to test the waters. "You know, I was thinking about college."

"Sure, you're a smart girl. You should go. There's a decent community college close by. If you got a job, you could get a cheap car and you'd be set."

"Well, I was wondering more about a college where I'd live in a dorm."

She stopped eating and looked at me. "Depends on what kind of help you could get, but why not? There's loans and grants. Maybe you could get a scholarship. What would you study?"

"I was thinking about art, mostly photography."

"Not much of a way to make a living," she said, getting up to grab another brownie. "And you know, your dad and me, our new business is going to take a while, so you can't depend on us."

"I know," I said.

"Just to make sure you know," she answered, then took her brownie and headed into the bedroom.

I felt a slight chill. There was my college money, but how much was there? "What do you want from Jeanine, really?" the rabbi had asked me last week. Before I could answer, he said, "Because she's not going to give you much, probably not anything."

"How do you know?"

"I've seen people like her for years, burnt-out social workers. Even if they can retire with good pensions, they tend to be the most apathetic people I've ever met."

"But she has a son, and she helped so many girls."

"Exactly," he answered.

Mark picked me up the next Saturday morning. I left a note on the counter explaining that we were going out for breakfast and then visiting two community colleges. I was wearing a wraparound skirt and a sleeveless blue top. I had on my newest pink silky bra and matching underwear, a pair of sandals, and no makeup, because I knew it could smear. When I sat down in the car next to Mark, I saw that he was smiling. I smiled too, and soon we were laughing and laughing and we couldn't stop smiling.

The driving test was easier than I imagined it would be. I drove Mark's car through a housing development near the testing center with a guy from the motor vehicle department in the front seat, looking bored and distracted. Every so often he would see someone he knew and yell out, "You coming to the game, Bernie?" I filled out some forms and had my picture taken while I grinned at Mark, who was still grinning back. Then I got my license: a shiny, sealed card that I stowed away, like a small secret, in my pocketbook.

Mark's house was tucked away in a development not far from mine, but composed of shorter, slimmer identical ranch houses. He escorted me inside with a flourish. "Now, my lady, would you care to see the kitchen first for a little snack, or the bedroom?"

"You're making me nervous."

"Sorry. I'm nervous, too."

We went into the living room instead and sat down on a yellow floral couch. Mark put his arm around me and leaned over to kiss me on the lips. It was a slow kiss. When he was done, he whispered, "Still nervous?"

"Yes." I couldn't help giggling.

He took my hand and led me to his room. It seemed small and dark, a brown cave with only a bed, a desk, a chest of drawers, and brownish woven curtains. He closed the door and we sat down on his bed. He kissed me again, and this time I felt my body waking up. I wanted to lie down, I wanted him to lie down on top of me, I wanted this kissing to go on forever.

"What do you want? Tell me, Deborah."

I couldn't answer.

"Come on, it's women's lib and all. Talk to me."

I started shaking a little, but I said the words anyway. "I want you to kiss me. I want you to lie down on top of me."

My eyes were filling up with tears, and at the same time my nipples were completely aware of his every move. His eyes, so dark and intent, were watching mine as he leaned into me with even more feeling. He pressed his lips on mine, pushing me back and climbing onto the bed until he was lying on top of me. He held my head in both his hands, which I loved best of all.

It surprised me that he was the same height as me. He had always seemed taller. He unbuttoned my shirt, and the wraparound skirt came off easily, too. I started to unbutton his shirt, but I needed both hands and it took some time. Then a chest appeared. A man's chest: flat, hairless, like a landscape I'd never seen before. He unzipped his pants, turned away from me, and slipped out of his jeans and underwear.

When he came back to the bed and lay down alongside me, he said, "You can touch it. It's okay." I reached my hand down to his penis. It was warm, completely alive on its own terms, as I felt the veins in the sides, the velvety tip and rim at the top. Its length fit perfectly in my hand. I squeezed it a little but he sighed, took my hand away and said, "No, that will be too fast." Then he returned to kissing my shoulders, and soon my breasts.

What was this? A falling away from the world or into the world? I felt his hand move up my leg. I felt his lips on my nipple. A falling backwards, a falling inward maybe. Everything like silk stretching and kissing, something not in this language. What was an orgasm, and was I starting to have one, with his fingers moving back and forth, his mouth all over my breasts? Like something so good that takes you into the cave and warms you in the way only it can. It got hard to breathe. I gasped and pulled his head to mine, kissing him as hard as I could.

Something, something, something.

Then there was a pause and he was sitting up, smiling at me, opening a plastic packet. He took out a tan rubbery thing and tried to unroll it onto his penis, but it kept trying to roll back up like a window shade that wouldn't stay down. I sat up to watch, and he laughed when he finally got it anchored down.

I lay back down and felt him guiding his penis into me, just like the textbook descriptions of intercourse. Everything was so smooth and wet, so ready, that he went in easily. No pain, no breaks. It was like I had done this all my life without ever actually having done it. He pushed in and pulled out, all the time holding my head, kissing my lips so much they felt a little sore. I felt his whole body coming inside me.

Then he sighed, called my name, fell into me, said my name again and collapsed. Suddenly he had weight again, but somehow it didn't crush me. He raised himself up on his elbows, kissed me, and said, "You're incredible." But what did I do that was so incredible? We curled around each other and slept in a tangled circle until his hands woke me up, and we did it all over again.

Sometime in the late morning we got out of bed and took a shower together. We giggled most of the time and even sang "Shalom Rav," a prayer for peace, and some of the other youth group songs. Our voices sounded gloriously intertwined. Afterwards we went out for fried chicken, giggling every time we looked at the marvel of one another.

Chapter Fifteen

I lifted up a stack of jeans at Karmic Clothes and refolded the size fives, right after some kids rummaged through them without buying a thing. Liz had called me after Mark told her about the auction, and said I should come work for her. She could pay me two dollars an hour under the table, so it worked out to more than I ever made at our booth.

"Hey, those look neat enough," Liz said. "Come on back here, I have some pudding cupcakes." These were a new item at the bakery, and Liz and I loved them dearly.

I dropped the stack of jeans and joined Liz in the back room, where she sat at a card table. My job consisted of ringing up the few sales we had each hour, straightening piles of jeans, and rehanging the peasant shirts and T-shirts after reckless mobs of cheerleaders stormed through them. Mostly, I fetched different foods for Liz and me. Liz's main occupation was to sit in the back reading novels and analyzing my life when she got bored, which was often. We talked photography constantly. She was installing a darkroom in the small basement room under the store, and reminded me that I could come use it any time. Hell, she would even give me a key.

"The problem with your father is that he sees relationships as drugs. I know this problem, Deb, because I've done the same thing. You get going with someone and get a lift off all the newness. But soon the newness wears off, and then what? Then there's someone else in the corner that has all the promise of another lift. No new relationships, so he flips out."

"Maybe, but what does that have to do with how he treats me? Does that mean he's going to dump Jeanine eventually?"

"I think," said Liz, pushing her bejeweled tortoiseshell glasses up a bit, "he's in too deep. You said they got engaged after dating for what, two months? He was running to something, running fast before it vanished. Look at what happened: he got the prize, but once it wasn't new anymore he needed something else. He can't divorce Jeanine. He's got no cause, he can't afford it, and he would look like an idiot. Meanwhile, the frustration in him builds up like a volcano."

The cupcake was delicious. "They really know how to make cupcakes, don't you think?"

"Yes, that's why we're eating them. As for you and your dad, my theory is that even though you're his daughter, he doesn't know how to deal with you except as a female. So when the divorce started he was good to you, eh?"

"Yeah."

"And now he treats you like crap?"

"Yeah."

"See? It just goes to prove my theory. Relationship as drug. You were a good calming drug, not a psychedelic one like his sexual relationships. You were more like Valium after a hard day. But you—and this is where it gets ugly—never left. He can't get rid of you. So what else can he do, given that he's a prisoner of his addiction, but treat you like shit and hope you'll get rid of yourself eventually?"

I pondered what Liz had said. Maybe her explanation was right, especially since she seemed to understand so well how people really worked, as if everyone had little motors she could take apart and reassemble. If Dad was addicted to relationships—and according to Liz all of us were addicted to something—then what was my addiction?

"So how could he get out of the addiction? I mean, what would he need to do?"

"That's just it," she said, clapping her hands but not smiling. "He can't unless he wants to. All the more reason for you to leave. You can't change people, babycakes," she said, as Uncle Carl walked in from the back and kissed the top of her head, "even old Carl here."

"Especially old Carl here," he replied. "You want me to go over the orders now and figure out the mess?"

"Absolutely." She explained that something was all screwed up with her Faded Glory order. "Men, they love to fix things," she added, loud enough for Carl to hear. Then, in a lower voice, "Not what I thought the love of my life would look like. I mean, he's an old man! He's almost twenty years older than me, but babe, I gotta tell you, between the sheets it's like there's no age difference at all." She looked unusually quiet, even sad. "This is changing who I thought I was supposed to be."

"What do you mean?"

"I was the fucked-up, seen-it-all broad—and now here I am, settling down in Jersey. Last week I got a recliner for the living room. It's all *very* disturbing." She raised her eyebrows.

The bells over the front door jangled, and Mark appeared. He grinned and tossed his hair back dramatically. "Come on back," I said, laughing. "Liz is figuring out my life."

"Glad someone is." He pulled up a chair and I gave him the last bite of my cupcake. I loved the dimples in his cheeks that showed only when he smiled—and right now he was smiling at me. I smiled back. "So where are we in the story?" he asked.

"I was getting ready to tell Deborah what to do with her life." Liz winked at Mark ("If only I were younger," she often told him) and turned back to me. "Now, given that your father is sick of you, I think your best move is to get the hell out of there. And if something's stopping you, ask yourself this: Are you absolutely sure he never touched Eshe?"

I was stunned. Not even Eshe could have such low taste, not even Dad could sink that low. Besides, when would they have found the time? Eshe only went to the taxi service a few times by herself. As I rattled off my list of reasons, Liz and Mark looked at each other briefly, then turned back to me. Besides, I asked, why were we even talking about Eshe? Mark and Liz exchanged another look that I didn't like.

"So what about just ditching Dad and going to live with Mom? What's wrong with her?"

I sighed. "Everything. I mean, she didn't want me. She made that clear."

"Yeah, so clear that she showed up at the temple for our service," said Mark.

I looked at him incredulously, then back at Liz. "I can't. I made a stand here."

"So what?" said Liz. "You think I haven't broken a million stands I've made? You got too much pride, kid."

"It's not pride. It's just that that part of my life is over. My mom and all her relatives just aren't part of my life anymore." With those words came a rush of memories: Mom holding me from behind and crying, screaming at Dad, driving away fast, tricking me about the therapist, leaving the cookie sheets out for me with the cold knishes. No, I told myself, I can never go back. I want to grow up to be a woman like Liz, technicolor and sharp, maybe sometimes double-exposed, but never just a blur of sadness like my mother. "She's just not my mother anymore."

Liz swiveled around fast on her stool. "Sweets, your mother is always part of your life. You want proof? Look at your belly button—or hey, look at your own face. Family isn't just a phase you get through."

I shook my head, unsure of what to say next. Mark came to my defense. "It's not like that all the time, Liz. There are some things you've got to get away from, if you want half a chance at a life." I knew he was talking about his own mother, but I was grateful for the support.

"Oy," Liz exclaimed. "Well, what about your brother and sister?"

"What about them? We never see them anymore."

"Hmmm," said Liz, nodding.

"What are you getting at?"

"Obviously not a winning number with your stepmother."

"She's Jeanine, not really my stepmother."

Liz rolled her eyes again. "Okay, what about getting an apartment?"

"How am I supposed to rent an apartment on my own? I mean, it's not like I have many options."

"Hey Liz, how come you know so much?" Mark asked, winking at her.

"Because, little Shana Punim," she replied, "I've been in group therapy for years. I've done every drug known to mankind. I've slept with more people than most people even know. So if anyone knows everything, it's *moi*. Now Deborah, here's an idea. Have you thought about graduating early?"

"Like in December?"

"Yeah, exactly. You have good grades. Can't you get out of some of that high school bullshit and go directly to college—pass go, collect $200, and say goodbye to Jersey?"

I thought about it, and a little thrill began rising in me. "I might need a few more classes," I ventured cautiously.

"So leave anyway," Mark said. "Take some classes at Brookdale this fall, get an early start. There's that program where you can earn dual credit—you know, high school and college at once." I'd heard Jeanine mention this program over the phone to one of "her" girls.

"Are you for real?" I asked him. Didn't he realize that my graduating early and going off somewhere would mean leaving him behind? "I mean, where would I go? What would I do for money?"

Liz sat up and smiled. "Student loans. Student grants. Live off the government, baby!"

Mark smiled, too. "It's gotta work. Why not start applying to art schools right now?"

"Or do you think I should do journalism school? Because photojournalism might be a better option."

"But is that really what you want to do?" Liz demanded. I shook my head. "Look, you've got talent behind the camera, easily as much talent as I had at your age. Only I blew it. I went for the bad boys instead of staying with photography."

"But you traveled all over the world," I protested. The idea of adventure grabbed me, but I kept coming back around to the question of why I would ever want to leave Mark.

"Yeah, but with schmucks! Baby doll, you should aim for the best art program in photography you can find. Aim high and aim now, and don't step off the path. You've got something special, and you can do pictures that change how other people see."

Now suddenly Liz looked sad again. "Hey puppies, I need a Tab. Want something cold?" When we waved no, she left us alone at the store.

Mark took my hand, bent over and kissed me. "The beach tonight? Jim's got a girl, and he wants us to go together."

"Okay, but I'm scared about this college thing. I mean, how will it be if we're apart?"

Mark stood up. "Why are you worried? You think distance will screw us up?" He kissed me again. "You think I could forget you?"

"No, it's just that I would miss you. But maybe I don't need to go far. Maybe I could go to some art school in New York or Philly."

Mark sat back down. "You can't go too far. I'm with you, and who knows? Give me some time, and maybe I'll do the same. I mean, what do I have to keep me here?"

"But it's June, and how are we going to get it all together by what, January or so?"

He hummed. "Don't you believe in God?"

"Do you?" I was wondering if I still believed what I did when I was little, that God was in all the trees.

He hesitated. "I don't know. I believe in faith, though. Let's go to the bookstore and look through all the college catalogues we can. Let's just hustle like crazy and see what we can do. And we need to talk to the rabbi. He'll have some ideas."

I felt a little calmer. "So we could go to college together? We could get an apartment together?"

"Sure," he answered, a little too fast. Then he bent down and kissed me on each cheek like the French do. We giggled together, and I felt something foreign warm my bones: I felt beautiful.

Chapter Sixteen

Predictably, my biggest fight with Dad happened when I told him I had acquired a driver's license. I knew I had to tell him eventually, if only in order to show him that I was ready live on my own and go to college early. I told him I wanted to drive for the family, do my part.

"You got your license already?" When I pulled it out and showed it to him, he said, "You don't weigh 119 pounds. You're fatter than that."

I insisted that I did weigh 119, and he insisted I didn't. "Want me to get on a scale?" I demanded.

He changed the subject back to the license. "You may be old enough, but you've never been coordinated enough to drive. I know driving. What have I been telling you for the last year?" He was leaning on the kitchen counter, where he had just finished off a Boston cream pie made by Mrs. P.

"You told me to wait. But I figured if I got my license now, you would see that I was okay."

"I would see that you're okay?" His face turned into an angry puzzle. On this Sunday afternoon Jeanine was at Two Guys with Sal and Mrs. P—and here we were, alone together in the house as if they had never moved in. "You mean that I would see that I'm wrong? You're always trying to defy me, and it's time for this to end." He sounded strangely calm, but he looked exhausted and flushed.

"Dad, I just wanted to get this taken care of so that I could be less of a burden, take on some more responsibility, you know." My hands shook more out of anger than fear.

"Bullshit!" He bit his tongue, a sure sign that he was ready to step off that steep cliff of self-control. I knew what was coming: first the yelling, so loud that his voice seemed to ring in two tones, and then, if I didn't get out of the room fast enough, something thrown. The pie pan wouldn't be much to fend off, but who knew what he would choose.

"I need to study," I said in a calm voice, trying out the psychology that Mark used with his alcoholic mother. ("Just talk quietly about what you need to do and ease out of their space, like backing away from a bear," he had told me.) When I turned around and headed toward the laundry room, planning to exit through the garage and then slip back in the front door and upstairs to my room, Dad exploded.

"Don't you dare leave this room!"

"Don't tell me what to do!" I screamed back. To my surprise, I spun around to face him.

He took a step toward me. "You leave this room and you're dead." Then he rushed at me, kicking his left leg like a fighter in a Kung Fu movie. I moved fast, but not fast enough. He caught the back of my thigh, leaving another bruise. And now here he was, face to face with me, breathing hard.

"Don't you ever touch me again," I said. By now I knew that once I got out of the house I would have to keep going, returning hours later after he had calmed down.

"Don't tell me what to do," he said, and slapped me before I knew it was coming.

That's when it all came apart for me. Later, describing the scene to the rabbi, I said I turned into someone else—someone like him.

I lunged at him, punching him in the shoulder and pushing him backwards. He went down, but not before he'd swung a chair at me, giving me a black eye and making me back away in pain. He might be a bear but I could be a lion. The energy raced through me until I didn't care what happened to either of us.

By the end, Dad was sitting on the floor like a big baby as I leaned against the opposite wall, both of us nursing aches, shooting pains, and the memory of what we had done to each other. We were still breathing hard when Jeanine walked in from the garage. She signaled to Mrs. P, who looked horrified, to take Sal around to the front door. She walked into the middle of the room, a shopping bag on her arm, and looked at Dad, then me. I was trembling against the wall, holding my stomach where the seat of the chair must have struck me. For a moment she almost looked like she might help me, but instead she turned to my father and held a hand out to him. He stood up, dusted off his bottom, and stared at the floor like nothing had happened.

"She got her license behind our backs," Dad finally said, as if this were a reasonable explanation.

"Good," Jeanine answered. "That's one less thing for you to worry about, taking her out driving. You've got a lot to teach her about driving safe. Besides, why not get that used AMC Pacer, so she can help with the shopping, take Mrs. P where she wants to go? If I had more time to work with you, we could get through this mess we're in."

What mess, I wondered? Then I caught a glimpse of Dad's face, and all I could think about was how much I hated him. I looked up at Jeanine and whispered her name. Surely now she would finally step in and help, do something like she used to do, like she was trained to do, for girls like me. But Jeanine simply acted like I didn't exist as she moved forward to put away the groceries.

Shamed and invisible, I backed my way into the laundry room and walked around the house to the front door. When I climbed the stairs to my room, Mrs. P was waiting for me with a wet washcloth in her hand. I let her press it to my eye. The lid was already swollen, but at least I could keep it open. She shook her head but said nothing. Then Dad called up for me to bring my license and meet him in the car. I pressed the washcloth against my cheek as I stood in front of the mirror. Just one red blotch on my face, but my ribs hurt, and my ankle, too.

It was almost sunset as I slid into the old Lincoln Continental, which happened to be the car of the week at our house. My eye stung, but I still felt proud as I backed out of the driveway slowly, looking back and forth behind me several times. I put the car in drive and lightly touched the gas. It was a smooth, big car, easy to guide down the street. The air conditioner didn't work, but we cranked the windows open and the hot day was finally cooling off.

Dad looked bored and a little impatient. "Speed it up," he said. He didn't look hurt, although he occasionally rubbed his forearm.

When we crossed Route 9, he surprised me with an apology. "Sorry, hon," he said quietly. "It's too much lately."

"What's too much?" Suddenly, I was the scared animal in the cave again. Driving already made me nervous since I was always trying to avoid brushing up against a car or a tree.

He stared out through the windshield. "I don't know. Jeanine—I put the house in her name, you know, because of the business. There's this one car I got from the dealer, but I didn't know it was stolen goods and now the whole business is—well, I'm putting that one in Jeanine's name too. That way, everything is safe."

Was he in legal trouble, or something like that? I snuck a sideways glance at him and saw a teenage boy in a man's gawky body. Maybe his troubles, coupled with my driving demonstration, made it an appropriate time to tell him about my plans for college. I waited a few minutes and then said, "Dad, I'm thinking about maybe getting out of your hair this winter, getting an early start on college."

He froze up immediately. "I don't think that's such a good idea. Wait until next fall, or maybe take a few years off. Work, learn something about the world."

I couldn't understand why he didn't leap at the idea of getting me out of the house. "That's just it, I could start working this winter and support myself. There're plenty of grants and loans I could be eligible for, if you sign a letter saying I'm no longer your dependent." He was quiet now, a little more relaxed, so I continued, "And it would be a great thing for me. I could stop wasting my time in high school and really learn something. You guys would have an extra room in the house to use for whatever, and you wouldn't have to feed me."

"How are you gonna feed yourself? That money of yours—I told you that it was yours and all, but not so soon. You need to wait for it a little while." He was talking about my Bat Mitzvah money, my college money. Something in the sharpness of his voice troubled me, but I forged ahead.

"I could work part-time, get an apartment, share it with some people."

"Some people? Is Mark part of this harebrained scheme, too?" The veneer of ordinary conversation between us had vanished, and now he was screaming again.

I wasn't about to crawl away this time. I yelled back, "We could go to college together and share expenses. Two can live at cheaply as one." Where did that expression come from? Suddenly I remembered that my mother used to say it, recalling the time when she and Dad were first married and had so little money. It was the argument she proudly offered to Mimi.

The veins bulged on his neck. "So this is just another lie, another way to get what you want and damn anyone else, just so you can live with your boyfriend? You're seventeen, and you'll damn well live in my house until it's time for you to go!"

"No, no, it's really so I can go to college. I don't have to live with Mark." Or maybe I did, but why did he need to know that?

"Why do you need college? You make art projects. You think college can teach you anything? You think you can get a better job at the Dairy Queen once you have a college degree? Hey, maybe you can be manager if you play your cards right. Or if you're really talented, you can make the peanut buster parfaits."

"Screw you," I said quietly. I was like one of those boxes at the auction that we duct-taped together week after week: eventually the contents seeped out, no matter how hard we tried to hold it together. He didn't hear me, but somehow it was enough that I heard myself. Screw you, screw you, screw you, my mind kept repeating.

"Speed it up," Dad demanded. His voice edged into me, jolting me to push down on the pedal a little more.

I wanted to cry, but I couldn't give him the satisfaction. "Stop telling me what to do with my life. I'm way more mature than most kids my age, and I'm sick of you thinking that I'm always the problem. I don't do drugs or drink, I don't run away or steal. I work hard, get good grades. This is what I want to do with my life. If I take all the responsibility for myself, why is it a problem?"

Just then we heard a loud bump, and I realized I had run up over the curb. The car died and I froze up in fear again. The old dread that I always ruined everything came rushing back.

"Look what you did! You can't even drive a car, and you want to run your own life?"

I turned the key, but nothing happened. Tears came rushing out despite my urging them not to. When I turned the key again there was a grinding sound, and then nothing. I pumped the gas pedal as I turned the key—still nothing. I was trapped with him, both of us furious.

"Let me fix it," he said in disgust.

"No."

"Goddammit, get out and let me fix the fucking thing."

I walked around to the passenger side, but I didn't get back inside the car. I had completely screwed everything up again. The anger that had made me strong was a false front—the real me was back, a wimp who couldn't do anything right. I leaned against a tree, shaking and crying as quietly as possible so Dad wouldn't notice as he peered under the hood. *Screw you* kept echoing in my head, but in tandem with that old refrain: See what you've done now.

Jeanine came to pick us up, but she was too preoccupied with the situation facing their new business to even care about the wreck. She pulled up next to us, signaled for us to get in, and—without even a wave to acknowledge me in the back seat—started talking to Dad. "Look, things are a mess, and we've gotta deal with this today." It was all "a mistake," but they needed to suspend the food delivery business and talk to the city right away, according to Manicotti—something about getting a city license for the business.

"What else did he say?" Dad asked. His voice sounded subdued but also tired.

"That we were going to need a shitload of luck, and even then it might not work."

I wanted to ask if Dad might go to jail, but I knew if I said anything he might turn around and hit me.

"Stop here," Dad told Jeanine. "We can turn onto the highway at the corner, and she can walk home."

I knew he meant me, so I got out of the car. Before they sped off, I asked what I should do to help.

"You? What could you do?" said Dad, shaking his head in disgust and staring through the stained windshield. Jeanine just rolled her eyes.

"Even the guy with the tow truck said it was fluke accident," I told Mark over the phone later that night. "What's so weird is that one little bump could actually break the axle. Now the car is worthless."

"It could happen to anyone. It's okay."

"No, it's not," I said, starting to cry again. "Dad said I was worthless, that I couldn't even make a turn properly. He said there was no way I was going anywhere, let alone college."

Mark was quiet for a while. "You could just go, and he couldn't stop you. What's he gonna do? Go after you and bring you home?"

"But what if my dad is in trouble? Jeanine said even having a lawyer might not be enough."

"Your dad is the kind of guy who can wriggle out of stuff like this. I would guess he does illegal things all the time. I mean, he owns a taxi service in New York City!"

"But what about the paper saying I'm independent? If he won't sign it, then I can't get any of the money I need. Now he says no car. How am I going to get to work?"

"Never mind that. I'll get my hours readjusted and pick you up." I smiled. Mark worked at Two Guys, where his boss appreciated his knack for selling blenders and toasters. He said Mark was better at reaching housewives than any woman.

"Let's just figure out how much we can save, okay?" Mark's voice was like that first cool breeze that surfaces in late August, marking the end of a scorching summer.

The next night we were back on the phone, me in my bed, he in his. The first few pages of the notepad on my lap were scribbled with numbers and budget figures. I explained each item to Mark, asking his advice about the cost of food, schoolbooks, clothes, and other necessities. But he seemed so hesitant and tense that I finally asked, "What's wrong?"

"Look, Deborah, I went over my high school stuff, and I'm not in the shape you're in. I have barely a 2.2 average. All the shit with my mom just screwed up my grades last year. I can't start college early."

"What about a community college? We could both go to Brookdale, right?"

He sighed. "I also feel like I can't leave my dad."

"What do you mean?"

Mark sounded nervous as he talked about how his father really needed him, especially now that Mark's mother had left him. Last week, without even telling me or talking to me about it first, Mark had promised not to leave his father. "I told him I'd stay," he ended weakly. "You know how my dad is."

I did know. Mark's father was the sweetest adult I had ever met, yet he seemed totally helpless at the same time. He could barely make toast, and the only reason he still had a job at the transmission place was because his brother-in-law owned the place.

"But what does this mean for us?"

"It means you have a chance to find to the best program you can get into. Apply to Oklahoma! Apply to Chicago! When you turn eighteen in April, you know I'll already be eighteen, right?"

"What does that have to do with anything?"

He paused, and then in a low voice said, "It means I can marry you."

Both of us stopped, breathless. "Marry?" I repeated. My heart seemed to fill up with light, moving as fast as sound, and my shoulders shook with happiness.

"I'll be right over. Unlock your window."

We had never met at my house before, but how could we not? Mark parked a block away and cut through the back yards to reach our house. Leaning out my window, I could follow his progress by listening to the dogs yipping at the ends of their long chains. Finally, I saw him standing on the ledge outside my window. He pulled himself onto the lower roof and crawled his way up to the little deck of shingles outside my window. In a flash, he leapt over the sill and into my bedroom. It was all we could do to keep from laughing out loud.

All the lights were out as we wrapped ourselves around each other and kissed. I was going to college! I was getting married! I locked the door and we climbed into my bed, but it creaked too much. So we lay down on the bedroom floor instead, in the spot farthest away from the door. He kissed my blackened eye very gently and placed his hand lightly on all the places that were turning purple and blue from bruising.

"What I would do to your father, if it would help you," he said. "I hate that he hurts you." I shushed him. The guest room was directly under mine, but we still needed to be careful. We made love and kissed, slept and woke. Then he slipped out the window, landed in the grass, and ran back to where his car was parked a few blocks away.

I looked at the sky toward a large oak tree, its leaves blowing hard in the wind. Stars were more vivid than I ever remembered before. But there was something about the shape of the sheltering tree and the expanse of dark blue salted with stars that made me feel like I was home in a way I couldn't remember feeling since I was a kid, when I first aimed an Instamatic at the tops of trees. How could I leave this? But wouldn't trees, sky, and stars travel with me wherever I went?

Chapter Seventeen

A few months later I rushed into Karmic Clothes, dashing past the new "Jeans in Memory of the Kings" sale posters on the wall. They displayed images of Elvis and Groucho Marx arm-in-arm, a tribute drawn by Uncle Carl after both celebrities had died in August. Liz met me at the entrance to the back room, looking pleased that I had arrived so quickly after receiving her call. Her message was that not just one, but all three letters from the art schools had arrived at the same time. "Coincidence?" she asked on the phone. "I think not."

We had decided to use the store as the return address on all my college applications. I had applied to three to art schools and two nearby state colleges with good art departments. The rabbi had insisted on financing the application fees out of a fund at the temple for "youth in need," and he had helped me revise my application essay. Liz, Uncle Carl, and Mark had helped me fill out the long forms and make slides of my photography essays. I mailed everything out over three days in July when the temperatures and humidity were both nearing 100 and no one bothered to come into the store for jeans.

Now it was mid-September and the leaves were just starting to yellow and fall. Liz led me to the table, which displayed an open box of cream puffs and a lit patchouli candle. "No matter what," she said, as she handed me the first letter, "a gal's gotta eat."

The Chicago Art Institute rejected me. The Kansas City Art Institute accepted me, but said it couldn't offer me any scholarships. The University of Tulsa Department of Art, however, sent a provisional acceptance. A Dr. Katherine Roomers wrote that she was very impressed with the slides of my work and would be happy to admit me next January as an undergraduate student. She cited my 3.8 GPA, my excellent essay about why I was a photographer, and my "artistic yet accessible" photography. She called my ambition "winning" and "fresh," and said she looked forward to meeting me. An accompanying letter explained that a scholarship would cover half of my tuition, and I was eligible to get financial aid—probably a grant, and surely some loans—to cover the other half plus my room and board.

Liz and I pored over the enclosed brochure showing pale, apartment-style dormitories with too many windows. "It's not like you're going to do much but sleep there," she pointed out. "You'll be in the studio for hours and let me tell you, they have darkrooms like nobody's business at those universities."

Just then Mark ran into the store, grabbed me and lifted me off my feet, even before I could show him the letter. "How did you know?" I asked.

He looked at Liz and raised an eyebrow.

"But the letter was sealed," I said, laughing at the conspiracy.

"Re-sealed," said Uncle Carl, rolling his eyes at Liz as he joined us.

"So it's a felony in some states to open another person's mail," Liz conceded, "but seriously, I couldn't help it. Where can I lose control these days in my life? I tell you, I gotta have some excitement." Uncle Carl cleared his throat, and Liz added, "Besides him," as she pointed to Carl.

"Just wait till we tell the rabbi," said Mark, lifting me again. But when he put me down, all I could think about was that eventually I would have to tell Dad.

That night, Mark and I planned to see the rabbi and tell him we were engaged. But first Liz and Mark (with Uncle Carl minding the store) would come over to the house with me. Dad and Jeanine would be home earlier than usual so that Jeanine could take Mrs. P to the doctor. With the women out of the house, Liz and Mark would help convince my father to let me go to college early.

Liz and I spent the next few hours firming up my many pages of financial scenarios. Then I talked on the phone to the university's financial aid people, all on Liz's dime. ("Don't worry, kid," she assured me, "this is nothing in the great cosmic design of money and energy.") It all seemed easier and more possible than I had expected. First we went over the cost of dorms vs. apartments and settled on the dorm room option. ("Shitty food, but hey, who has time to eat, and what's good in Oklahoma to stuff your face with anyway?") The money I had saved would go for a plane ticket, although I'd never been on a plane before. There was barely enough left over for books and supplies, but Liz said she would throw me a fundraising party.

I was ecstatic, but my ecstasy proved to be short-lived. When I arrived home with Mark and Liz trailing behind me, Mrs. P. informed me that Dad and Jeanine had just called. They had to meet with Manicotti after work, so they would be late again. When I asked her about her doctor's appointment, she just said, "Rescheduled," and pointed casually to a platter of her famous lemon bars.

"Damn!" exclaimed Liz. Mrs. P turned and lifted an eyebrow, but she gestured with her free hand for Liz to take a lemon bar. She even smiled after Liz took a bite and told Mrs. P that these were the best lemon bars on planet earth. Mrs. P bowed slightly and went back into the kitchen.

"Hey kid," Liz said, nibbling on another lemon bar as we walked back to the car, "we *will* do this. Screw the establishment and full speed ahead!"

"We will do this," said Mark, tickling me. "It will happen, it *will* happen!"

The rabbi stared cross-eyed at the two of us. "Let me get this straight. You're telling me that you're one another's first loves, and now you're engaged?" We had spent the first ten minutes laughing together over the college news. But when Mark said that now we could get married, the rabbi stopped short in his exuberance.

"Yes, Rabbi, we hope to marry as soon as Deborah gets back from school next spring. I'll move out there with her next fall." My life was all set—it seemed so clean and easy, like falling asleep after a long day.

The rabbi was still shaking his head. "Look," he said, "I'm not going to lecture you on being too young. God knows, you've both been through enough to gain more maturity than a lot of thirty-year-olds, but promise me one thing."

"Anything," I said.

"That you'll come to me for eight weeks of premarital counseling before Deborah starts school. I always do this with couples. And you need to promise me something else, too."

"Sure," Mark said.

"That you won't tell your families. Parents, especially those as unstable as yours, tend to react strongly to this kind of news. You need time to talk about this just among the three of us."

"Time for what? I mean, we're pretty sure," Mark said.

"I don't doubt that. But trust me on this one. Don't tell the youth group, either." We nodded obediently.

When I got home that night, I was surprised to learn that Dad and Jeanine had never returned. Mrs. P. and Sal had gone to bed already, so I wandered the house looking for clues as to what might have happened. Last week, Dad told me that they were almost squared away on the licensing deal. "It just took greasing the right wheels," he had said.

"You bribed someone?"

"Let's just say I put some fuel into what would move things faster through the system."

I sat down on the landing to the stairs. It was 11:14 PM, although I should have been home by ten, my usual curfew. Mark had insisted that we drive to a small corner of a field to really celebrate. It turned out, though, that he didn't have a rubber. By the time we drove to the drugstore, giggling all way, and then back again, we were so tired that we decided to simply go home. But that's not what concerned me now—all I could think about was that something bad must have happened to Dad and Jeanine.

The sound of a key in the lock released me, and I rushed toward the door. They looked exhausted and worn, somehow older. "What the hell you doing up?" Dad asked.

"Hank, I'll be in the tub," Jeanine said as she disappeared around the corner.

"I was waiting up for you. I wanted to make sure you were okay."

"Oh, my good little daughter wants to make sure I'm okay," he said in a mocking tone.

"Because of the license deal, and all you've had to go through with that."

He headed toward the fridge with me following close behind. "So you want to know what's going on? You want to know?" He bent over, uncovering a pot roast and sniffing it, then shifted through several containers of leftovers laying around. "You want to be sure I'm not going to the big house, so that you'll still have your precious meal ticket."

"That's not what I meant, and you know it," I said. Now an edge had come back into my voice.

He sat down at the counter and spread out his finds. "I'll tell you, then," he said. He sounded almost drunk, although I could tell he was anything but. "We had a little trouble with the local precinct. Let's just say I was a special guest of the City of New York this afternoon."

"You were in jail!"

"Let's just say I had some time to put my feet up for once. Besides, the guys with me were all just like the schmucks I have working for me."

He went on to explain that the cop he'd slipped some money to had bragged to his partner, and word got out. ("You'd think the imbecile would be bright enough to keep his mouth shut, but no. I bribe my first cop, and I get a shithead.") When the captain of the precinct found out, he brought Dad in for questioning, then Manicotti arrived and got him out.

"What did Manicotti tell them?"

"That it wasn't bribe, just a poker debt."

"But you don't play cards."

"I do now," he said, grabbing a hunk of meat with one hand and a bunch of potato chips with the other.

"So it's all over?"

"No, it's not over. This is real life. We've got to go to court, but Manicotti will get it dropped. He's going to have his friend speak to this cop and get him to say it was just poker, that he only said it was a bribe as a joke. That guy is a big joker, so it'll work for him to say this."

"But what if it doesn't?"

He paused, looking past me as if he had never considered that possibility. "It will," was all he said as he went back to his food.

The phone rang, which seemed strange at this hour. I picked up the receiver.

"Oh, I'm so glad it's you. Hey, I only have a minute, but thank fucking Jesus you're the one who answered." I went hot and cold at once at the sound of Eshe's voice.

Dad looked at me curiously, but I waved him away and said, "It's for me." He shrugged and carried his food to the living room so he could eat in front of the TV. I turned my attention back to Eshe, still astonished by the sound of her voice—especially with Dad close by and yet completely in the dark. "Yeah, I'm here."

"I'm in Florida, working as a waitress, living with another girl in this cool house on stilts. I just wanted you to know it's cool. It's all come out cool."

"How did you get there?"

"Babe, you don't have time for that story, but believe me, I've seen enough on the way to getting here to make me an old lady."

My mind raced. "What have you been doing? What happened with—"

She cut me off. "I said"—her voice got edgier—"it's all cool. Things happen. People lose things all the time. I just wanted to let you know," she added, her voice softening, "that if you need to, you can come here. I can set you up away from him."

"My dad? What exactly happened to you?"

"What do you mean, 'what happened?' He was getting ready to testify against me, get me locked in that center until I turned fucking eighteen."

"No, that's wrong. He had just given your mother money to get her out of the picture."

She sighed. "I have to go now, but don't believe things so easy, 'kay? And if you need me, you just call this number and ask for Q. You don't tell another soul any of this, got it?" I nodded and wrote down the number on a scrap of paper, still listening as the phone went dead.

Last summer had been the summer of Eshe and the end of Fatima. But this summer, I thought to myself, as I stored the carefully folded paper in a seldom-used compartment of my wallet, this summer was the summer of Mark. And that made all the difference in the world.

Chapter Eighteen

"Now, tell me why you want to get married," the rabbi began, as we sat in his air-conditioned office gulping down ice water. "Deborah, you go first."

I placed my water carefully on a plastic coaster with a picture of Che Guevara. "I guess it's because I feel like Mark is my other half. He makes me feel complete. He understands me, and I think we're really good together. We can help each other our whole lives."

"So are you saying that without him, you're not complete?"

"Well, maybe not incomplete, but broken. This is a way to glue myself back together."

I could tell that the rabbi had a strong opinion, but he was keeping it under wraps for our sake. "Now Mark, what about you?"

"I just feel ready." He started laughing, "I mean, I love Deborah, she loves me, we work well together. You know, some people find their soul mates early, so why wait?"

"Why not wait?"

We blinked. The rabbi continued, "Why not wait a year or so? Why rush into this?"

"I just feel like we should do this right away," said Mark, more strongly than I expected.

"Why do you feel this way? If it's so good, why can't it wait?" The rabbi sounded a little angry now.

"Why should it wait?"

"Do you have to get married to have sex?" He paused, and we both blushed a little. "I didn't think so. Do you have to get married to be together?"

"No," I said, "but if this is it, why not just get married now? Then we're safe."

"Aha! That's what I was waiting to hear. Marriage makes you safe? Why would you think such a thing, especially given the dangers of your families? Considering your parents, why would *you* rush into this?"

"I don't know!" Mark was almost yelling. "I mean, this is it, and if we don't do it now, we could just lose it. I could blow it, she could find someone else, she could find out that—I don't know—I just need to do this now."

The rabbi and I both turned to Mark. "She could find out what?" asked the rabbi sharply. When Mark started crying instead of answering, the rabbi said, "Complete honesty. That's the only way any of this will work. Complete honesty, if you really love Deborah."

He started crying harder. I was starting to crumble, but I took his hand. Then I started crying too, although I didn't know why. "Find out that…I'm…not good enough."

I was relieved. Of course, he was good enough! But before I could say anything, he continued, "Find out—oh, I'm gonna ruin everything. I'm attracted to guys."

The crying in me stopped short. Mark couldn't bear to look at me.

"Attracted to guys and girls, or just attracted to guys?" asked the rabbi.

"Well, I'm attracted to Deborah, a lot," he said, slowly and clearly.

"Attracted to guys in general, or to one guy in particular?" the rabbi continued.

At this point the center of my body coiled up tightly. I felt like I was going to throw up, like I was going to lose my whole life all over again.

Mark looked at me. "I don't deserve you," he said. "You're too good."

"Answer the question," said the rabbi.

Mark turned back to him. "One guy, okay! I'm attracted to Jim! I still am, and he's still attracted to me, and—"

"And what?" I bravely asked.

"We made out one night. It just felt really good, like it feels with you." He collapsed into his own lap, his back shaking as he sobbed. What did all this mean? Why was the rabbi ruining my life? But when I looked over at him, the rabbi's small eyes were red, too.

A voice came over the speakerphone, reminding the rabbi that services began in ten minutes. "Stay," he said softly. "Stay through the service with each other. We'll talk afterwards." He wiped his eyes, walked over to me, and kissed me on the head. "You'll get through this." He touched Mark's shaking back. "You, too."

Then he left, closing the door behind him. I didn't know what to do. Should I even try to touch Mark? Should I leave? Should I kill myself? Should I tell myself it's okay, maybe it's just a phase?

Mark sat up slowly, then grabbed the trash container and threw up. I touched his back as he was heaving. I still loved him, but love was a hook now, one that twisted and tore as it moved through me. When he was done, he carried the wastebasket to the bathroom, emptied it, and washed his face before he came back to me.

He looked into my eyes. He's so brave, I thought. "I'm sorry," he said, crying a little. "I don't know how you'll ever forgive me. But I'm going to take a walk through the woods, go home that way." He laid his car keys on the desk. "You take the car home. I'll call you tomorrow, see what you want to do."

"What do you mean? Isn't it you who has to decide?"

The look he gave me, full of pain and love, told me he had already decided. He was in love with Jim and in love with me—but immediately I tried to erase that thought. Maybe the walk alone would help him see how much easier it could be with me, how much easier for his whole life.

After Mark left, I considered attending the service, sitting quietly and listening to the prayers, standing when the congregation stood, sitting when the congregation sat. But in order to make it work, I would have to split myself in half—one part of me freaking out that my life was ruined, while the other half publicly prayed like a good girl, almost a woman, who seemed fine on the outside. I had lost my ability to do this trick, a sweet surprise in all the pain.

I opened my pocketbook carefully and took two aspirin with some water from a fountain in the hallway. I didn't have a headache, but this seemed like a time to take something. Then I lay down on the shag carpet and curled up around the chairs where we had been sitting. The carpet had a lot of blue and green in it, which made it feel like an ocean, an ocean made of wool. I closed my eyes, too exhausted to sit up.

I dreamed that I saw Mark's back getting smaller as he disappeared into the distance. But I also saw other people, lots of trees, and a long dark animal moving through the woods and finally coming closer. It was black and sleek—a wild cat of some kind, probably a panther, although I'd never seen a panther before. The closer it got, the less afraid I felt. Soon I was bending and touching its coat, which was coarse and silky all at once, as this miracle of muscle and speed looked right at me with its intense green eyes. I reached for my camera to snap a few pictures, but there was nothing around my neck—and that startled me most of all.

When the rabbi returned, he carefully turned on the lights to avoid stepping on my head. Then he bent down and held me as I sobbed, soaking his robe. "You'll get through this," he said. "You've gotten through much harder stuff. You'll get through, I promise you."

My head still ached, so the rabbi brought me more aspirin and more water, keeping his hand on my back. The warmth helped. When I finally stood up, I was surprised to see how simple and ordinary the office looked—just another space where people sat and talked. The air was surprisingly cool, though, so the rabbi lent me his sweater as we walked outside into the dark night. It was already after ten o'clock.

"The stars are out," he said. "See how bright they are, even with all this smog from the city."

"Are you going to tell me that our lives are okay, but nothing compared to the stars?"

He laughed. "You think too much. But no, I was actually going to say that looking at them makes me realize how long it's been since I ate anything. Want to go to the diner?"

Once we were seated in a booth, food covering the surface of our table, I felt more human again. I was no longer split in two, no longer crumbling, although I couldn't understand why the panther had made me feel safe. I still had college to look forward to, lots of people who cared about me, a way to live, and the rabbi to put it all into perspective.

"You know," said the rabbi, after he finished his Greek salad, "if he's gay, he's gay. There's nothing you can do to fix it or make it go away."

"Couldn't it just be this one guy?"

"Couldn't it just be that you're the one girl?"

I ate my chicken croquettes quickly, and the more I ate, the better I felt. It dawned on me that I hadn't eaten since noon, because Mark and I were planning to eat dinner at his house that night before making love. Would that ever happen again?

"You have a plan. You have a way you can go," the rabbi said.

"How can I do any of this without Mark?"

"Oh, sweetheart," said the rabbi, surprising me because he wasn't one for endearments, "look at what you've survived already. You're so much stronger than you realize right now."

I drove myself home in Mark's car. When I walked in the door, Dad was watching Johnny Carson. Jeanine wasn't around, and on the floor lay empty wrappers from a whole box of Hostess Yodels. I noticed a new hole in the wall behind him, a chair askew. There must have been a scene, a fight with Jeanine.

"Thought you'd finally drop in on us?" he asked sarcastically.

"I'm sorry. It was important." Suddenly, I was near tears again.

"Important? You were out with your boyfriend, or did he finally see who you are and dump you? I know who you really are," he said.

Yet this time his words didn't tear new strips of pain, as he intended. Instead, they gave me an idea. I rushed upstairs, grabbed a paper from my desk, and rushed back down, snatching a pen along the way.

"Sign this," I demanded.

"What is it? Why should I?"

"It's my independence. Sign it, and I can get all the financial aid I need to go to college, and you can keep the money you owe me forever. Just sign it."

"College?"

"Yeah, I got into art school, a really good art school, and I'm leaving in January."

He looked stunned, but at the same time slightly impressed by my chutzpah. It wasn't like the driver's license at all. He took the paper as if it didn't matter and, with a flick of the pen, gave me ownership of myself. Then he stood up from the recliner and walked purposefully over to the grandfather clock. I followed him without knowing why, and watched as he opened the door of the clock and reached deep into the hollow base, below the swinging pendulum. When he pulled out his hand, he was holding a handful of letters, all unopened, all dusty.

He didn't even bother to say, "Here," or "Sorry I kept these from you." He wouldn't look at me, but focused his eyes on the dark dining room and handed me the letters as if they were contraband. Then he disappeared into his room. I stood in the foyer, which was filled with golden light and the loud, steady, tick-tocking of the clock. I knew without looking what I would find, but I looked anyway. In the left-hand corner of each letter, neatly written in small print, was my mother's name.

Chapter Nineteen

Jim called me from the hospital to tell me that Mark was in the emergency room. Mark had come looking for him after our meeting with the rabbi, and they ended up going to bed together. When Mark got home, he tried to swallow a whole bottle of aspirin but collapsed after twenty. His ears were buzzing so hard that he thought he was hallucinating. Jim found him and took him to the hospital. Racing through the emergency room, I had no idea what I would say to him. I arrived at Mark's bedside just after they pumped his stomach, and found Jim awkwardly holding his hand.

The next day, Mark and I went to the beach alone. It was still hot. We sat where the water came in and flooded our feet, then stopped and went back out. "I don't want you to die."

"I'm so, I don't know, terrible. You're so good, and—"

"You're so bad. I know. You've got to stop saying that." The pain was creased across my face, I could tell. I couldn't believe how much everything could change in twenty-four hours. "I need to let you go. I mean, if you're gay, how can this work?"

Mark didn't answer, but simply put his arm around me. We sat there until the incoming tide had soaked us to our waists, yet neither of us laughed with delight nor jumped up to keep dry. Then we walked arm-in-arm back to the car.

"I will always love you with all my heart and all my soul and all my might," he said, quoting from the prayer we always said together in youth group. We stared so hard into each other's eyes that both of us began tearing up.

One late September day, I got up the courage to call my mother from the back of Liz's store. As we talked, Liz read through the pile of Mom's letters, making stars and swirls near her favorite parts.

"Yes, I could do that. That would be nice," I said into the receiver, my voice oddly formal. "Oh, I'm usually a size seven, sometimes a nine, but always a seven on top."

I looked over at Liz, and she beamed at me. As soon as I hung up, she told me how much she enjoyed my mother's description of watching my father bowl during the time when she was most in love with him. She pointed out a passage in another letter where Mom described how she fell down and sprained both elbows while learning to roller skate. Then there was a great story about Mom walking me around the city in a checkered buggy. Whenever anyone complimented her on her handsome son, she would smile as if it were true.

Altogether, my mother had written me eleven letters over the last five months, detailing stories I had never imagined. Revealing a mother I had never known. She wrote that she was sending me these stories because she didn't know what to say to me anymore, and maybe I would understand what she meant by this when I was old enough.

Ever since Mrs. P moved in, she had been putting all our mail into a special slot in the kitchen, one I had never really noticed. These envelopes traveled straight to my father, who reviewed them late at night when he and Jeanine returned from the city.

Now that the letters were mine, they traveled through other people my mother could never have imagined: first the rabbi, who read them slowly with me, careful to reserve comment whenever he asked me what I was thinking, and then Mark, who repeatedly told me that my mother wasn't as screwed up as his mother and that's probably why I knew my own heart so well. And now Liz had been reading them all morning long, so engrossed in their contents that she locked the front door of the store for a spell after too many customers interrupted her.

"Tomorrow I'm going to meet her at the bagel place next door, just for an hour."

Liz nodded and pushed her purple Elton John glasses back up the bridge of her nose. "Yes," she said, with atypical calm. "But the real question is, what will you wear?"

The day I was to meet Mom for the first time in years, it was so warm that the radio announcers said that temperatures were breaking records. I was the first to arrive at the bagel shop, wearing new jeans and a thin sweater that Liz had ferreted out of one of her many piles of clothing. "This," she said of the blue sweater with embroidered hearts near the shoulders and the pair of pale-blue Faded Glory jeans, "would make a mother's heart happy."

I thanked her and tried them on, then thanked her again.

"You know," Liz had said, "if I had a daughter, I would want her to be like you."

"You and Carl could adopt," I suggested. Just last week Liz had told me that she was moving into Carl's split-level house, although the war medals displayed on the mantel still freaked her out.

"No, I think dealing with his St. Bernard will be enough parenting for us, not to mention just getting used to a decent relationship. God knows, I can barely handle the stability."

From my booth in the bagel shop, I watched the fast-moving Hassidic men behind the counter shoving bagels into ovens, then onto cooling trays and into wire bins. The shop smelled like heaven and resonated with loud strains of Billy Joel. Despite the ovens and the hot day, my fingers suddenly got cold for no real reason. I sat on my hands but then my chest got cold, so I crossed my arms. I felt happy but scared. Just as I was about to order something hot, my mother came bustling in. She carried two shopping bags from Bloomingdale's and smiled so hard I couldn't tell if she was going to break or cry. We hugged longer than I expected. I could feel her small back through her thin vinyl jacket and smell the familiar Jean Nate cologne everywhere.

Once we got our bagels and coffee and sat down, she spent the first ten minutes pulling things out of her bag. First came a white fisherman's knit sweater, several pairs of wool socks with each toe a different color, and thick cotton tights. "I don't know if you'll like these, but you can always exchange them. It's cold in Oklahoma," she paused, "I think." Her voice sounded more like her than before. Then came a black wraparound skirt, a matching black-and-white-striped shirt with a built-in bow tie, a red cowl neck sweater, a first-aid kit, an elaborate Mary Kay makeup kit, nail clippers, a set of peach and white sheets, and multiple sets of Tupperware plates, cups, and bowls with matching lids. We both giggled a lot.

I apologized that all I had for her was one small gift. But when she saw it—a photograph of myself, juxtaposed with images of her as a girl and a young woman—she shed enough tears to smear her blue eyeliner.

After the gifts she asked me questions about Oklahoma, while I interjected my own long list of questions about her job, her friends, and the relatives. Both of us were trying so hard to do this right. We were careful to avoid saying anything about Jeanine, Fatima, or the divorce— and most especially about my father. Halfway through my account of how I would share a dorm room with a roommate from Illinois, Mark and Jim casually wandered in. They winked at me, pretending that we had never met—we had decided that our relationship was far too confusing at this point to explain—and ordered some bagels. They watched me talking with Mom for a while, then they winked again and shuffled out.

Mom told me she planned to redo her bedroom in pale peach, to make it feel like a more relaxing place. "A sanctuary, that's all I want," she said. She laughed with me like I was Geraldine, or the other Bev.

I asked about Roger and Missy, and suddenly realized I hadn't seen them in months. It seemed like Dad was always canceling his Sunday visitations now in order to tend to the business.

"They're fine. I think Roger misses you."

"I don't think he even likes me."

Mom shook her head. "He just doesn't show his feelings, but I can tell. A mother knows." I couldn't help wondering, though, how much my mother really knew me after such a long time apart.

When the hour was almost over, Liz galloped into the shop— dropping in, she told me later, because she suddenly realized she was going to die unless she got a salt bagel right away. She acted like finding me and my mother there was a big surprise, but the surprise didn't stop Liz from telling her that I was a super worker who really brought in the business. My mother launched into a long conversation with Liz about where casual clothing was headed.

"Stone-washed jeans. You take my word," Liz said. "It's gonna be denim like you've never seen. It's going to go on for years. A psychic told me. More vests, jackets, jeans, even dresses."

Liz scampered back to Karmic Clothes right before I walked Mom out to her car, a red Buick with a large dent on the passenger side. "Not my fault," Mom said. "An ambulance hit me."

"What happened?"

"Now, Deborah, don't get hysterical," she answered. Her voice seemed so familiar—much more so than Fatima's, Eshe's, Jeanine's, or even Dad's. "It wasn't on duty. Matter of fact, the guys in it were just going out for ice cream, and they ran a red light. Actually, it was one of the best things that could have happened to me." She unlocked her door and smiled sweetly with her eyes half-closed. "One of the guys—he's divorced too—asked me out."

"So you're dating?"

"Since July. He mostly comes over for coffee after his shift is over. You know I'm always awake, three AM is nothing to me, so he comes over. If it's warm, we sit on the little patio in back, and we drink coffee, talk. Sometimes when your dad has the kids, we see a movie. Well, not so much lately, because you know your dad hasn't been taking the kids. But sometimes we still go to a movie. Roger is old enough to watch Missy for a few hours."

"You're really dating?" At first it seemed unreal that my mother would even look at a man. But ever since I'd read her letters, she had been transformed in my imagination from a paper doll into something three-dimensional, almost life-sized.

"Yes, dating's been good for me. Look, take good care, call me. Don't be a stranger." She turned quickly and pressed me against her with more force that I could have imagined. She started crying. "Don't forget to call me. I'm still your mother, kiddo."

Chapter Twenty

By mid-January I was ready to leave for Tulsa. School started in three days and I had enough money saved, thanks to the party that Liz and Uncle Carl threw for me. Everyone had to give me at least ten bucks, or Liz promised to kick their ass. She also threw in the money that Dad had paid her for the photography class that Eshe never attended. Altogether, I made over $600 that night, and everything was set.

Even the rabbi came to the party, gave me a fifty, kissed me on the cheek, and said he would miss me. He didn't look sad, although the congregation hadn't renewed his contract. They opted instead for a radical, woman rabbi from Florida who excited them more because she had a girlfriend.

"Where will you go now?" I asked him.

"Detroit. Got a gig there, assistant rabbi in a huge temple," he winked. "And a friend there, too."

I noticed how much older his face looked in this light. "Will you tell me about your life, too? I mean, it's only fair, since you've listened to me so much."

The rabbi tousled my hair. "One day. But this is your time now."

"But who knows when I'll see you again? Tell me something."

"Okay," he said, leaning against the "big man" jeans Liz kept piled up in the back of the store. "She's someone I met while working for McGovern, and we've kept in touch ever since. The part you're not to tell anyone," he said, his voice rising just a little, "is that she's a Christian."

"What's the difference between a Christian and a Jew these days?" I asked, in a joking tone.

He smiled at me. "Oh, it's a world of trouble, Deborah."

Seemingly right on cue, one of Liz's friends—a man dressed like Dr. Frank N. Furter of the *Rocky Horror Picture Show*, in garter and fishnet stockings, black bikini bottom, and red and black corset—climbed up on the counter and belted out "Oklahoma." Everyone clapped and sang along. I had a feeling that Oklahoma couldn't be more different.

The afternoon before my flight, I stood in the foyer holding Sal's new kitten. She was sleeping against my chest, like she did most nights, as I rocked her a little. Standing on the floor nearby was my old camp chest, plus a few suitcases I bought at the Salvation Army, three carry-on bags, and a box of photo supplies. Mark and Jim would arrive any minute to drive me to Newark airport.

Dad walked in the front door with Jeanine, both home early to say goodbye. "Look who's still here," he said.

As we stood opposite each other, I could see headlights coming up the driveway behind him. He reached into his pocket and handed me something bundled up—money, I supposed. "Just to help you get started," he said, barely making eye contact.

Dad had been unusually quiet ever since enrolling in anger management classes on the advice of Manicotti. The idea was to prove to the courts that Dad was addicted to rage—that's why he'd lost control and yelled at the judge after he was sentenced to a $10,000 fine. Jeanine thought it was a brilliant move on Manicotti's part. The judge had dropped the contempt charge and didn't throw Dad in jail for a weekend as he'd originally planned. But the classes also made him seem smaller, like all the air was let out of him. There was no yelling of late, but no talking, either—just a quiet gap between us in which we would nod and pass by, as if we hardly knew each other.

"So this all you're taking? Just twenty-two pieces of luggage?"

"Seven," I corrected him. Mark and Jim came in without knocking and smiled brilliantly at me. Over the course of the fall, they had both become my dearest friends. Dad helped them carry all the luggage out to the car.

I slipped into the kitchen. Mrs. P. looked much happier ever since she'd found a small group of Jewish Poles to have coffee with at the diner once a week. She turned away from the dishwasher and leaned her shoulder into me, like a sliver of a hug, then reached into her apron's deep pocket to pull out two rolls of quarters. "Here," she said quietly. "For washing machines. You have to pay most places."

I smiled at her. "Can I use these for the dryers, too?"

She actually smiled back as she reached into her other pocket for two rolls of dimes. "This for the dryer."

Even Jeanine gave me a kiss on the cheek. "Don't let anything stop you, not that you will." She paused, looking serious for a moment, then actually put an arm around me and led me into the quiet dining room. "Look, whatever you do, don't get pregnant."

I was startled to see that she was on the verge of tears, and I knew it wasn't because she would miss me. The late night whisper fights in the bedroom always mentioned "the business," like it was some kind of a curse.

"Not really in my plans," I said, trying to turn it into a joke, but she didn't smile. After a moment it dawned on me that she probably had to leave home because she got pregnant. I started to say something, but she cut me off by walking quickly into the kitchen for more coffee. Where was her child now, the one she must have given away?

I walked over to Sal, who was watching TV. He was laughing so much at a cartoon show that he barely noticed me. I bent down and handed him the kitten, then kissed him on the top of the head. I had said goodbye to Roger and Missy on Sunday. Not that they noticed much, but Missy did look up from *The Wonderful World of Disney* and nod at me. Roger actually got up and shook my hand, after placing his new Charles Dickens novel face down on the couch. "Nice knowing you," he said. He had become oddly formal with me since the wedding, and I couldn't help wondering if it was because Dad seldom used his visitation times to bring him and Missy to the house.

"Don't you think you'll see me again sometime?"

He half-smiled. He had grown over four inches that fall, and was actually taller than me now. Somehow, he looked like an elongated version of Mom. "Could be."

"Could be that we become great friends when we get older, and take our families on vacations together in the Catskills."

"But not like Dad and Sheldon," he begged.

"Deal."

He looked down at me solemnly and then started laughing, and I realized that I hadn't heard him laugh for years.

Once in the car, I settled into the front seat next to Mark, who held my hand whenever he didn't need his own for switching gears. At a stoplight he bent over to kiss me on each cheek. "You know," he said.

"Yeah," I answered. He smiled, a wide smile that lifted his cheekbones and made him seem more like the man he had become.

I remembered the bundle from Dad and reached in my pocket. He'd given me $500, all in twenties. I stuffed the bills into my purse and watched the rain falling in patterns on the car. Jim, who had treated me like Mark's best friend ever since he and Mark had started dating, began to sing "Don't give up on us, baby," a David Soul song that I loved even if it was schmaltzy, according to Liz. The moment seemed unreal: was this my life, or a dream of my life? When we arrived at the airport, the rain was light and soft as if it were dawn and not late afternoon.

Mark and Jim carried in my luggage and sent me to stand in line with the ticket I had purchased with Uncle Carl's credit card. The airline steward took my ticket for a moment, then handed it back to me. I checked all the bags, except for the carry-ons, and paid for the extra weight.

Then I was at the gate, hugging Jim first. I wanted to say, "Take care of him," but it seemed stupid. Next I went up to Mark, who was crying a little, "You did it, you found a way out." He held me for a long time, our weight pressing into each other like we had always been this close, like we would always be that way. By the time he finished, I was crying, too.

Now I was walking onto the ramp to the plane. Now I was sitting down in my window seat and putting on my seatbelt. Now I was taking off, just like the plane was taking off. The speed of the plane along the runway threw me back. Soon we rose smoothly into the white-blue haze of night clouds, and then gradually emerged from the haze. Stars everywhere and the airplane floating steadily among them, its wings forcing me away from the place where I grew up, toward a place I had never been.

Amidst the stars, suspended as if we were sailing through them, hung the moon in its old circle of cloud. As a child I had watched this same moon as it hovered steadily, the light around it a ring of pink fading into blue. Maybe I had noticed this very scene all my life, yet this beauty, was what made me pick up my camera again and again. But now, for the first time, I was in the scene. And no matter how far I flew, the moon remained the same distance away, like a god who actually loves us from afar, or like love made visible—a darkness that the light shines on, a darkness ringed with color.

I watched carefully even as the plane pointed its nose downward, to where I could see below the lights of the next life.

Acknowledgements

This is a book I've been writing since at least 1996 on paper, and for years beforehand in my head, so it's no wonder that there are many people to thank:

- ⅄ Chester Sullivan, my fiction teacher at the University of Kansas, taught me the value of story over sentiment, and his writing shows me new ways to see the world.

- ⅄ Phil Brater, the late Ben Burnley, Mark Zeitlin, and a wide array of people from the 1970's Englishtown Auction, Temple Shari Emeth, and other central New Jersey haunts carried me through difficult times and helped me frame a story of healing.

- ⅄ So many friends have been readers of one or another version of this novel: Judy Roitman, Denise Low, Kelley Hunt, Ken Lassman, Sandy Sanders, Katie Towler, and especially Victoria Foth Sherry, who served as final editor (and helped me with everything from Orthodox Church touches to 1970s fashion and car seat laws). Thanks also to the BVDs (Brave Voice Divas & Daredevils) and the Wabi Sabis.

- ⅄ My family of origin supported me in telling a story that overlaps with their own stories. Thanks to Lauren Pacheco, Jen Applequist, Barry Goldberg, Barbara Goldberg, and the late Mel Goldberg. I've been writing this book during most of my children's lives, so thanks also to Daniel, Natalie, and Forest Lassman for putting up with long stretches of their mom vanished in her computer.

- ⅄ Steve Semken and the Ice Cube Press (and special shout-out to Laura and Fenna) are the epitome of the best of publishing. Steve's belief in his writers, his commitment to marketing and distribution, and his art in creating beautiful books lifts up those of us lucky enough to work with him.

⋏ Ken Lassman has supported me in finding a way to tell this story, and in the telling to celebrate the healing that lights up humor, perseverance, and wonder. His love shows the way to heal a fragmented past into a present of wholeness and awe.

Caryn Mirriam-Goldberg is the Poet Laureate of Kansas and the author of 14 books, including a forthcoming non-fiction book, *Needle in the Bone: How a Holocaust Survivor and Polish Resistance Fighter Beat the Odds and Found Each Other* (Potomac Books); *The Sky Begins At Your Feet: A Memoir on Cancer, Community: Coming Home to the Body* (Ice Cube Press) was a Starred Book by Library Journal. Her anthologies include: *An Endless Skyway: Poetry from the State Poets Laureate* (co-editor, Ice Cube Press) and *Begin Again: 150 Kansas Poems* (editor, Woodley Press); and four collections of poetry. Founder of Transformative Language Arts—a master's program in social and personal transformation through the written, spoken, and sung word—at Goddard College where she teaches. Mirriam-Goldberg also leads a number of writing workshops. With singer Kelley Hunt, she co-writes songs, offers collaborative performances, and leads writing and singing Brave Voice retreats. She blogs at www.CarynMirriamGoldberg.com and for several yoga sites.

The Ice Cube Press began publishing in 1993 to focus on how to live with the natural world and to better understand how people can best live together in the communities they share and inhabit. Using the literary arts to explore life and experiences in the heartland of the United States we have been recognized by a number of well-known writers including: Gary Snyder, Gene Logsdon, Wes Jackson, Patricia Hampl, Harriet Lerner, Greg Brown, Jim Harrison, Annie Dillard, Anna Lappé, Ken Burns, Kathleen Norris, Janisse Ray, Alison Deming, Richard Rhodes, Michael Pollan, and Barry Lopez. We've published a number of well-known authors including: Mary Swander, Jim Heynen, Mary Pipher, Bill Holm, Connie Mutel, John T. Price, Carol Bly, Marvin Bell, Debra Marquart, Ted Kooser, Stephanie Mills, Bill McKibben, and Paul Gruchow. We have won several publishing awards over the last nineteen years. Check out our books at our web site, join our facebook group, visit booksellers, museum shops, or any place you can find good books and discover why we continue striving to "hear the other side."

Ice Cube Press, LLC (est. 1993)
205 N. Front Street
North Liberty, Iowa 52317-9302
steve@icecubepress.com
www.icecubepress.com

trips far out
and trips for real
Fenna Marie & Laura Lee